"When evangelicals in the United States, living in the most prosper-
ous global economy, still give less than 3 percent of their income to
Christian causes—something is wrong with our understanding of
God's mandate for generous giving! It's time to repent of our materialism and greed. This dialogue about the core issue of tithing and
its implications for our responsibility to be more generous givers is a
timely word about a pressing issue. Written by experienced stewards
and scholars, their insights and example will motivate you to consider
the biblical, theological, and practical aspects of giving in a fresh way.
More than that, implementing their insights will move you—and the
people you influence—toward God's ideal of generous giving."

Dr. Jeff Iorg
President, Golden Gate Baptist Theological Seminary

"What do you say to someone who has recently become a Christian
and who wants to know what amount he should give to the church?
The Bible and church tradition often refer to the tithe, a tenth of one's
income, as an answer to this question. But many writers have insisted
that the answer is more complicated than that. For one thing, the
tithe is mentioned far more often in the Old Testament than in the
New, so all our questions about the relations of the Testaments enter
in. For another thing, the tithe in the Old Testament is integrated
into a general theological structure involving priesthood, ministry to
the poor, ceremonial feasts, and inheritance of agricultural land. And
there may have been more than one tithe: some scholars estimate that
the total obligation of an Israelite was actually between 20 and 30 percent. And there are questions about the frequency of the tithe, in view
of Israel's system of Sabbatical years. So even if the New Testament
carries on the Old Testament tithe, how do all these details function in
the life of the church? *Perspectives on Tithing* does not shy away from
these difficult questions, and it presents four leading views of these
matters from able representatives of their positions.

   "Given that most evangelicals contribute only around 3 percent
of their income to the church, in a time of great opportunity for the
church's ministry, tithing is an important issue. I commend this book
as a valuable resource."

Dr. John Frame
Professor of Systematic Theology and Philosophy, Reformed Theological Seminary

"David Croteau's work of pooling together the various perspectives regarding the practice of tithing in Christian discipleship is a treasure for the Kingdom. In the sphere of personal stewardship, he's crafted a collection of perspectives that are very much alive in evangelical thought. He demonstrates how the healthy tension of orthodoxy and orthopraxy is vital to the walk of faith. That balance is not easily achieved when each contributor is so passionate about his particular perspective. However, Croteau weaves the mosaic in such a fashion that the pastor/theologian can acquire biblical balance without compromise."

Dr. John L. Yeats
Director of Communications for the Louisiana Baptist Convention
and Recording Secretary of the Southern Baptist Convention

"As a pastor, I prioritize reading that will help me answer my congregation's questions in a way that builds their obedience and closeness to God. This book helped me (us) be more informed about the principle of tithing both as a response to scriptural instruction and as a way to worship Him."

Dr. Joel C. Hunter
Senior Pastor, Northland — A Church Distributed

PERSPECTIVES
ON TITHING
4 VIEWS

DAVID A. CROTEAU · BOBBY EKLUND
KEN HEMPHILL · REGGIE KIDD
GARY NORTH · SCOTT PREISSLER

EDITED BY DAVID A. CROTEAU

NASHVILLE, TENNESSEE

Perspectives on Tithing: 4 Views

Copyright © 2011 by David A. Croteau

All rights reserved.

ISBN: 978-0-8054-4977-8

Published by B&H Publishing Group
Nashville, Tennessee

Dewey Decimal Classification: 248.6
Subject Heading: TITHE\STEWARDSHIP\PERSONAL FINANCE

Printed in the United States of America

3 4 5 6 7 8 9 10 11 12 • 18 17 16 15 14

Contents

Abbreviations

Contributors

David A. Croteau has authored *You Mean I Don't Have to Tithe? A Deconstruction of Tithing and a Reconstruction of Post-Tithe Giving*, and contributed to *What the New Testament Authors Really Cared About: A Survey of Their Writings*. He is also the managing editor for *Learn to Read New Testament Greek Workbook*. He now serves as Associate Professor of Biblical Studies at Liberty University in Lynchburg, Virginia. In addition to receiving his bachelor of arts in counseling from California State University, Fresno, and his master of divinity from Golden Gate Baptist Theological Seminary, David has earned the master of theology and doctor of philosophy from Southeastern Baptist Theological Seminary. David, his wife Ann, and their children Danielle and D.J. reside in Lynchburg, Virginia.

Ken Hemphill has authored many books, including the *The Prayer of Jesus; You Are Gifted: Your Spiritual Gifts and the Kingdom of God; Core Convictions: Foundations of Faith; The Names of God; Revitalizing the Sunday Morning Dinosaur; The Antioch Effect; and Life Answers: Making Sense of Your World*. Ken is currently the National Strategist for Empowering Kingdom Growth, an initiative designed to call individual Southern Baptists to renew their passion for Jesus and the reign of His kingdom. He is also teaching at Southern Baptist Theological Seminary and North Greenville University. He has served as the president of Southwestern Baptist Theological

Seminary in Fort Worth, Texas, and various pastoral positions in Virginia, Kentucky, and North Carolina. He has doctoral degrees from Cambridge University and Southern Baptist Theological Seminary.

Bobby L. Eklund has authored or co-authored several books, including *Spiritual Awakening; Lord Do It Again; Building for Kingdom Growth; and Partners with God: Bible Truths about Giving and Children of Privilege.* Bobby is the Founder and Chief Executive Officer for Eklund Stewardship Ministries. After receiving his bachelor's degree from Howard Payne University and a master's degree from Southwestern Baptist Theological Seminary, Bobby earned his doctoral degree from Luther Rice Seminary. He has pastored churches in Texas for more than 30 years. He is the founding partner of the Eklund Chair of Stewardship at Southwestern Baptist Theological Seminary.

Reggie Kidd, Professor of New Testament at Reformed Theological Seminary (Orlando, Florida) has authored *Wealth and Beneficence in the Pastoral Epistles* and *With One Voice: Discovering Christ's Song in Our Worship.* After Reggie received his bachelor of arts degree from The College of William and Mary, he earned a master of arts in religion and a masters of divinity degree from Westminster Theological Seminary. His doctor of philosophy from Duke University is in Christian Origins. He also currently serves as a faculty member at The Robert E. Webber Institute for Worship Studies in Orange Park, Florida, and as the staff chaplain for WPOZ radio station in Orlando, Florida. Reggie and his wife Shari have three sons: Charlie, Bob, and Randy.

Gary North is the author of a 30-volume study, *An Economic Commentary on the Bible* (1973–2010). In addition, he is the author of 20 other books, including *Marx's Religion of Revolution* (1968), *An Introduction to Christian Economics* (1973), *Unconditional Surrender: God's Program for Victory* (1980), *Dominion and Common Grace* (1987), *Crossed Fingers: How the Liberals Captured the Presbyterian Church* (1996), and *The Covenantal Tithe* (2011). He received his Ph.D. from the

University of California, Riverside, in 1972, with a dissertation, "The Concept of Property in Puritan New England, 1630–1720."

Scott Preissler has contributed to many journals and stewardship-related studies. Scott is Professor of Stewardship, Director of the Center for Biblical Stewardship, and Bobby L. and Janis Eklund Chair of Stewardship at Southwestern Baptist Theological Seminary in Fort Worth, Texas. After receiving his bachelor of arts from Taylor University, he received a master of science and a master of arts from Indiana University. He earned his doctor of philosophy in stewardship studies at Union Institute and University in Cincinnati, Ohio. He also served on the editorial team of the Stewardship Study Bible. Dr. Preissler owns the largest collection of artifacts, art, and library on stewardship studies in the world.

Acknowledgments

Is tithing worth debating about? I've heard many conversations regarding the subject of tithing. Everyone has an opinion about what it means and how, or if, it should be practiced. What better way to continue this conversation then through a Perspectives book where one can read the opinions of well-learned scholars who have studied this issue profusely. If "love of money is the root of all kinds of evil," we want to make sure we allow the Word of God to sift our minds regarding this issue of tithing so that we won't find ourselves fighting the wrong battle. I hope this book edifies you as you seek to know Christ and His ways more.

I want to thank the contributors for their willingness to take part in this project. Discussion of the topic could have produced hostile reactions, but you've all been gracious, and I appreciate your working with me to bring the project to fruition. I am especially grateful to Terry Wilder and Andreas Köstenberger, who greatly encouraged me to pursue publishing this book on this heated topic. I have had many conversation partners through my years of studying this issue.

There are too many to name, but two churches that I especially want to thank for allowing me to present a series to their congregations are Richland Creek Community Church (Raleigh, North Carolina) and Redeeming Grace Baptist Church (Lynchburg, Virginia). I pray it was a fruitful time in which you were challenged and drew closer to our Lord. I also want to thank the staff at Givens Books-Little Dickens (Lynchburg, Virginia), whose facility I used for many, many hours in writing and editing. To my wife, Ann, and my children, Danielle and D. J., who sacrificed time in the summer so I could complete my work in a timely manner: I appreciate all your love and support as you exhort me to continue God's work as He has impressed it upon my heart. And most importantly, to my Lord and Savior, Jesus Christ, who has allowed this publication to come to fulfillment. May the work of the authors in this book produce faithful stewards in churches everywhere. "To Him be glory in the church and in Christ Jesus to all generations, forever and ever. Amen" (Eph 3:21).

David A. Croteau

Introduction
WHY THIS BOOK?

David A. Croteau

When you come across an issue where great Christian leaders such as John MacArthur and Charles Ryrie hold to one view and Billy Graham and John Piper hold to another, while scholars such as D. A. Carson seem to avoid a direct answer,[1] you know you're in for a challenge in deciphering the complexities of the issues at hand. Recent statistics show that giving among evangelicals is now below 3 percent.[2] Whatever one believes about tithing, this is not a God-honoring number. So, what should Christians be taught about how much to give?

The debate over how the tithe in the Old Testament relates to those following Christ today is not new. An example of a church excommunicating a member for failing to tithe has been in the news recently.[3] Are churches in the right when they do this? Is someone's failure to tithe because of financial hardships beyond the person's control enough to revoke membership? These are among the perplexing questions Christians and preachers must face in their understanding of giving and stewardship.

Many pastors become anxious over the thought of preaching on the topic of giving.[4] With the publicity of so many ministers getting

---

1. http://tinyurl.com/yzkqs2s.
2. See www.emptytomb.com for current research on giving statistics.
3. The story, "Wheelchair-Bound Woman Kicked Out of Church," originally appeared on the NBC 4 website; see http://tinyurl.com/loretta-davis.
4. Some would say that tithing and giving are unrelated, concluding that the tithe is "paid" to God because believers owe it to Him.

rich off an unsuspecting public, pastors may feel cautious about preaching on stewardship as it relates to money since they may fear being categorized with those who are greedy. This is an unfortunate situation for the American church. While this nation has experienced unprecedented luxury, preaching on the requirements for steward-ship over money has decreased.

The issue of money and stewardship has been a growing concern in evangelicalism. The *Wall Street Journal* recently had an article dedicated to the tithing debate,[5] and CBS recently did a broadcast about it.[6] Larry Burkett's successful ministry attests to the growing interest about money and stewardship. Dave Ramsey has his own Christian radio talk show where he answers financial questions deal-ing with issues such as debt, buying a home, investing, credit scores, and giving. This last area is the topic of this book.

The Place of the Issue of Tithing in Theology

The debate over tithing properly lies (at least in part) under the issue of the relationship between the Mosaic law and Christians.[7] Jon-athan Edwards, perhaps the greatest theological mind America has produced, said, "There is perhaps no part of divinity attended with so much intricacy, and wherein orthodox divines do so much differ, as stating of the precise agreement and differences between the two dispensations of Moses and Christ."[8] Which Mosaic laws apply directly to Christians?

The Mosaic Law and Christians

Some laws cited by New Testament authors apply to Christians. For example, "Love your neighbor as yourself" (Lev 19:18) is quoted in the New Testament in several texts (Matt 19:19; Mark 12:31; Luke 10:27; Gal 5:14; Jas 2:8). But the New Testament has no comments on verses like, "You must not boil a young goat in its mother's milk"

---

5. S. Sataline, "The Backlash against Tithing," *Wall Street Journal*, November 23, 2007, W1.

6. See http://tinyurl.com/to-tithe.

7. See W. G. Strickland, ed., *Five Views on Law and Gospel* (Grand Rapids: Zonder-van, 1996); and T. R. Schreiner, *40 Questions about Christians and Biblical Law* (Grand Rapids: Kregel, 2010).

8. J. Edwards, *The Works of Jonathan Edwards*, rev. and cor. E. Hickman (Carlisle: Banner of Truth, 1974), 1: 465. Note John Wesley's statement: "Perhaps there are few sub-jects within the whole compass of religion so little understood as this" (quoted in D. A. Dorsey, "The Law of Moses and the Christian: A Compromise," *JETS* 34 [1991], 3: 322).

(Deut 14:21). Nor do we see an explicit teaching in the New Testament on whether Christians are allowed to wear clothes with two different types of material (Lev 19:19), in a verse that comes right on the heels of the command to love your neighbor.

The issue is not over the authority of Scripture. Every author in this volume believes that the Bible was inspired by God and is authoritative for every believer. Paul said, "All Scripture is inspired by God and is profitable for teaching, for rebuking, for correcting, for training in righteousness" (2 Tim 3:16). Therefore, we all hold to a conservative and orthodox view of Scripture, though we interpret and apply many texts differently. And all agree that this issue must not be decided ultimately over pragmatic concerns. For those of us who hold to the authority of the Bible, Scripture itself needs to be the final arbiter. Will your church go bankrupt if the members are not told to tithe? That important pragmatic concern should not be dismissed, but we must try to have a friendly discussion over tithing in Scripture first.

What to Avoid

Over the years, the debate about the relevance of the tithe has been lowered to a level not worthy of Christian scholarship. I have heard friends say that anyone who teaches tithing is distorting the gospel. Actually, tithing and the gospel are not closely connected. One of the most popular books written in support of tithing in the last few decades asks some really good questions about how tithing, as part of the Mosaic law, relates to Christians. The author then concluded, without answering any of the questions, that people asking those questions are probably just trying to figure out how to give less.[9]

That seems to be an unfair conclusion. While it is probably true that some would love for the mandate of the tithe to disappear so they could give any paltry amount they wanted, some have altogether different motivations. This debate needs to move past name calling, *ad hominem* arguments, and unfair accusations (e.g., teaching tithing distorts the gospel; not teaching tithing is antinomian).

A Main Issue in Giving

The main area involved in the debate over how a Christian decides to give is the issue of tithing. First, it (unfortunately) needs to

---

9. R. T. Kendall, *Tithing: A Call to Serious, Biblical Giving* (Grand Rapids: Zondervan, 1982), 58.

be stated that the word "tithe" means 10 percent. I have had conversations with many Christians who have been raised in the church who believed that the word "tithe" only meant giving. There is a legitimate debate over the use of the ancient words for the "tithe" and whether they refer to a literal tenth or just a religious offering.[10] However, the word "tithe" in this volume is understood as a reference to a tenth. That is not to say that the biblical definition of tithing is 10 percent of income. This definition must be decided in the following chapters and argued from Scripture.

Christians are approaching this topic today in several ways. Is the tithe the minimum standard? Is it the goal? Is it a wise or mandated starting point? Is it just a good principle to work from? If so, then why? If not, is there another proportion? If the tithe is mandatory, does it all have to go to the local church, or can it be split up and given (at least partly) to other organizations?

Different Views on Tithing

The complexities over the continuity or discontinuity of tithing are numerous. Some say that the tithe was only for Israel and has no application for Christians. Others say that Christians must pay God His tithe. However, there are several mediating views and other aspects that need to be addressed.

For example, while some are comfortable with referring to the "law of tithing," others try to take as much law out of the tithe as possible. Many Christian leaders today believe that the tithe must go to the local church. This view is called "storehouse tithing." Others believe that tithing is commanded for Christians, but it does not have to go to a local church; it can be given to any Christian organization. Furthermore, are we supposed to tithe on the net or the gross? More than one contentious debate has occurred in churches over that!

Important Concerns

There are many approaches to the question posed by this book. Some lean upon their theological system. Different theological systems typically view giving differently. Some from a Reformed perspective, who typically divide the Mosaic law into three parts (civil, moral, and ceremonial/sacrificial), consider tithing as part of the

---

10. See J. M. Baumgarten, "On the Non-Literal Use of ma'ăśēr/dekatē," *JBL* 103 (1984): 245–51; cf. the comments in Reggie Kidd's chapter.

moral law; thus, they might begin their discussion on the amount of giving by stating that Christians should begin with the tithe. Not all in the Reformed camp say this, but some do. Many from the Dispensational perspective view the Mosaic law as a unity and therefore consider all of it as having been fulfilled and none of it directly applying today. They typically don't include the tithe when considering how much a Christian should give. Those who consider themselves theonomists (dominion theology) view the civil and moral laws as binding and thus the tithe is binding as well. However, they are sharply divided over the issue of *where* the tithe must be given—to the church only or to Christian organizations? Many others do not approach tithing through theological systems, but they try to allow Scripture to lead them to their conclusions regardless of their theological systems.

Several authors have approached this issue through the lens of church history. Throughout the ages, men and women of God have taken different sides on the tithing debate. A brief overview of the different views is provided in an appendix at the end of this book. Needless to say, because there is no defined orthodox view on tithing, other arenas need to be considered.

Hermeneutics, the art and science of biblical interpretation, is critical in this debate. Some hold to the maxim: "If an Old Testament law is not repeated in the New Testament, then it is repealed." Others declare: "If an Old Testament law is not explicitly repealed, then it continues." Are these rules for engaging the biblical text sufficient? Some believe they are, while others say they are overly simplistic. Another popular and relevant principle is, "Description does not equal prescription." In other words, just because something is described as occurring in Scripture, this does not mean that the thing described is a command (a prescription) for a Christian. However, the author may have chosen to include the description to urge his audience to follow the example he is describing. Can something that is only described ever become a command for a Christian? These questions will have to be answered elsewhere, but the way a person understands them has an impact on his view on tithing.

Tithing in the Bible

Before getting into the specific interpretations presented throughout this book, the relevant passages are quoted in full with some questions offered. This functions as an introduction to many of the issues that are addressed.

Tithing in the Patriarchs

What is the biblical definition of a "tithe"? The Hebrew word for "tithe" is *maaser* (מַעֲשֵׂר), which means "a tenth part." Many Christians claim that the tithe always refers to giving back to the Lord 10 percent of all income (or increase). They point to Abram as a pre-Mosaic law example of this: "Then Melchizedek, king of Salem, brought out bread and wine; he was a priest to God Most High. He blessed him and said: 'Abram is blessed by God Most High, Creator of heaven and earth, and I give praise to God Most High who has handed over your enemies to you.' And Abram gave him a tenth of everything" (Gen 14:18–20).

It could be that Abram is the perfect example of giving 10 percent of one's income prior to the Mosaic law. But there are questions that need to be answered. Was this Abram's normal practice or was this a onetime event? Where did Abram learn about tithing? Is there any background information from the ancient Near East that would impact what Abram was doing here? Did he have knowledge of an oral form of the law God would give to Moses? In what way was Melchizedek a priest? Did he have authority over Abram? How these and other questions are answered will impact how one views the direct relevance from Abram's example for Christians.

Another passage in Genesis appears to define the tithe as 10 percent prior to the Mosaic law. Jacob was on his way to Haran when he stopped to rest. Then Jacob had a dream:

> And he dreamed: A stairway was set on the ground with its top reaching heaven, and God's angels were going up and down on it. The LORD was standing there beside him, saying, "I am the LORD, the God of your father Abraham and the God of Isaac. I will give you and your offspring the land that you are now sleeping on. Your offspring will be like the dust of the earth, and you will spread out toward the west, the east, the north, and the south. All the peoples on earth will be blessed through you and your offspring. Look, I am with you and will watch over you wherever you go. I will bring you back to this land, for I will not leave you until I have done what I have promised you."
>
> When Jacob awoke from his sleep, he said, "Surely the LORD is in this place, and I did not know it." He was afraid and said,

"What an awesome place this is! This is none other than the house of God. This is the gate of heaven."

Early in the morning Jacob took the stone that was near his head and set it up as a marker. He poured oil on top of it and named the place Bethel, though previously the city was named Luz. Then Jacob made a vow: "If God will be with me and watch over me on this journey, if He provides me with food to eat and clothing to wear, and if I return safely to my father's house, then the LORD will be my God. This stone that I have set up as a marker will be God's house, and I will give to You a tenth of all that You give me" (Gen 28:12–22).

It appears from this passage that Jacob may have been following in the footsteps of Abram with his promise of a tithe. A difference between these two accounts is that while Abram gave Melchizedek a tenth of the spoils of war, Jacob promised a "tenth of all" that God blessed him with. In other words, he promised a tenth of his increase. Several questions arise from this text as well. Did Jacob tithe regularly? To whom was he going to give this tithe? Did he fulfill his promise? Do the "if-then" statements mean that Jacob would not fulfill his vow if God did not fulfill his promises?

These are the two explicit references to tithing before the giving of the Mosaic law. In both passages, it appears that the word "tithe" means a tenth and that both Abram and Jacob gave from increases. But is the tithe described in the same way in the Mosaic law?

Tithing in the Mosaic Law

There is disagreement among interpreters about the description of the tithes in the Mosaic law, the amount of tithes, and the items liable to tithes. Some believe that all the subsequent passages that mention tithing in the Mosaic law are replacing the former passages; others harmonize all the tithe passages into one tithe; and still others, utilizing the Documentary Hypothesis (i.e., the Source Theory of Pentateuchal authorship or the JEDP Theory), say that Israel disregarded earlier laws and only gave one tithe per year.[11] Furthermore,

---

11. See M. G. Kline, *Treaty of the Great King: The Covenant Structure of Deuteronomy—Studies and Commentary* (Grand Rapids: Eerdmans, 1963), 87; B. K. Morley, "Tithe, Tithing," in *Evangelical Dictionary of Biblical Theology*, ed. W. A. Elwell (Grand Rapids: Baker, 1996), 780; E. H. Merrill, *Deuteronomy*, NAC (Nashville: Broadman, 1994), 240–41; J. Milgrom, *Numbers*, The JPS Torah Commentary (Philadelphia: Jewish Publication Society, 1990), 435; Y. Kaufmann, *The Religion of Israel: From Its Beginnings to the Babylonian Exile*, trans. and abr. M. Greenberg (Chicago: University Press, 1960),

single-tithe proponents wonder how the Israelites were supposed to know that *another* tithe was being described since the passages never refer to the earlier passages. Others believe that there are multiple tithes in the Mosaic law—some holding to two,[12] some three,[13] and some even more! Paying close attention to the details aids in figuring out what the laws are describing and prescribing.

The first reference to tithing in the Mosaic law is Lev 27:30–33:

> Every tenth of the land's produce, grain from the soil or fruit from the trees, belongs to the LORD; it is holy to the LORD. If a man decides to redeem any part of this tenth, he must add one-fifth to its value. Every tenth animal from the herd or flock, which passes under the *shepherd's* rod, will be holy to the LORD. He is not to inspect whether it is good or bad, and he is not to make a substitution for it. But if he does make a substitution, both the animal and its substitute will be holy; they cannot be redeemed.

Some believe that this text is a generic introduction to tithing from surrounding pagan practices into the Mosaic law. Since ancient Near Eastern societies had many forms of tithing, the way in which the Lord wanted the Israelites to practice tithing needed to be clarified. However, others might conclude that this was simply formalizing the practices of Abram and Jacob into the Mosaic law. This text describes

189–91; S. R. Driver, *A Critical and Exegetical Commentary on Deuteronomy*, ICC (New York: Scribner's, 1903), 168–73; G. B. Gray, *A Critical and Exegetical Commentary on Numbers*, ICC (New York: Scribner's, 1903), 234.

12. P. C. Craigie, *The Book of Deuteronomy*, NICOT (Grand Rapids: Eerdmans, 1976), 233; P. Verhoef, *The Books of Haggai and Malachi*, NICOT (Grand Rapids: Eerdmans, 1987), 304; A. V. Babbs, *The Law of the Tithe: As Set Forth in the Old Testament* (New York: Revell, 1912), 27–30. The Mishnah's description also seems to conclude with two tithes (see *m. Ma'as.* 1.1–5.8; *m. Ma'as. S.* 1.1–5.15).

13. H. Lansdell, *The Sacred Tenth or Studies in Tithe-Giving Ancient and Modern*, 2 vols. (orig. New York: Gorham, 1906; reprint, 2 vols. in 1, Grand Rapids: Baker, 1955), 56–66; C. L. Blomberg, *Neither Poverty nor Riches: A Biblical Theology of Possessions* (Downers Grove: InterVarsity, 1999), 89; M. F. Rooker, *Leviticus*, NAC (Nashville: Broadman, 2000), 328; G. A. E. Salstrand, *The Tithe: The Minimum Standard for Christian Giving* (Grand Rapids: Baker, 1952), 25–29; H. H. Ward, *Creative Giving* (New York: MacMillan, 1958), 29–30; E. Towns, *Tithing is Christian* (Ivyland, PA: Neibauer, 1975), B–11; R. Alcorn, *Money, Possessions, and Eternity* (Wheaton: Tyndale, 1989), 207. Two ancient Jewish sources favor three tithes (Josephus, *Ant.* 4.8.22; Tob 1:6–9). Furthermore, some authors conclude that there were multiple tithes without specifically stating how many tithes there were: W. Smith, *A Dictionary of the Bible*, ed. F. N. Peloubet and M. A. Peloubet (Nashville: Nelson, 1986), 703; S. Murray, *Beyond Tithing* (Carlisle, UK: Paternoster, 2000), 74; A Layman [Thomas Kane], *Tithing and Its Results* (Chicago: The Layman Company, 1915), Pamphlet No. 1; W. Speer, *God's Rule for Christian Giving: A Practical Essay on the Science of Christian Economy* (Philadelphia: Presbyterian Board of Publications, 1875), 258–60.

what is liable to tithes: produce from the land, grain, fruit, and every tenth animal from the herd or flock. Furthermore, the way in which the cattle tithe is described makes it appear that one-tenth (מַעֲשֵׂר; maʿśar) is the prescribed amount, not some nonspecific number.

Numbers 18:20–24, which describes the Levitical tithe, provides more clarity on the subject:

> The LORD told Aaron, "You will not have an inheritance in their land; there will be no portion among them for you. I am your portion and your inheritance among the Israelites.
>
> "Look, I have given the Levites every tenth in Israel as an inheritance in return for the work they do, the work of the tent of meeting. The Israelites must never again come near the tent of meeting, or they will incur guilt and die. The Levites will do the work of the tent of meeting, and they will bear the consequences of their sin. The Levites will not receive an inheritance among the Israelites; this is a perpetual statute throughout your generations. For I have given them the tenth that the Israelites present to the LORD as a contribution for their inheritance. That is why I told them that they would not receive an inheritance among the Israelites."

The instructions for this tithe are very specific. The Levites were to receive the tithe from the Israelites because they were not getting an inheritance of land in Canaan. In Num 18:30–32, more details are provided about this tithe:

> "Tell them further: Once you have presented the best part of the tenth, and it is credited to you Levites as the produce of the threshing floor or the winepress, then you and your household may eat it anywhere. It is your wage in return for your work at the tent of meeting. You will not incur guilt because of it once you have presented the best part of it, but you must not defile the Israelites' holy offerings, so that you will not die."

The Levites, once they gave a tithe to the priests, were told that they could eat the remaining tithe that they received from the Israelites anywhere. Moses then instructed the Levites about what they were to do with the tithe they received. This is the priestly tithe, which is described in Num 18:25–29 between the two passages above:

The LORD instructed Moses, "Speak to the Levites and tell them: When you receive from the Israelites the tenth that I have given you as your inheritance, you must present part of it as an offering to the LORD—a tenth of the tenth. Your offering will be credited to you as if it were your grain from the threshing floor or the full harvest from the winepress. You are to present an offering to the LORD from every tenth you receive from the Israelites. Give some of it to Aaron the priest as an offering to the LORD. You must present the entire offering due the LORD from all your gifts. The best part of the tenth is to be consecrated."

Technically speaking, the priestly tithe is not a stand-alone tithe, but a sub-tithe of the Levitical tithe. The Levites were to take a tenth of what they received and present it as an offering to the Lord. Presumably, the priests would then receive this tithe. God specified that this offering must be the best of what the Levites received.

The festival tithe is discussed in two primary places: Deut 12:17–19; 14:22–27. In the first passage, the tithe is unceremoniously mentioned:

Within your gates you may not eat: the tenth of your grain, new wine, or oil; the firstborn of your herd or flock; any of your vow offerings that you pledge; your freewill offerings; or your personal contributions. You must eat them in the presence of the LORD your God at the place the LORD your God chooses—you, your son and daughter, your male and female slave, and the Levite who is within your gates. Rejoice before the LORD your God in everything you do, and be careful not to neglect the Levite, as long as you live in your land.

This passage declares that the tithe must be eaten in the presence of the Lord, at His place of choice (tabernacle/temple). Finally, the Israelites are directed not to neglect the Levite. This phrase brings us to an important discussion: How many tithes are commanded in the Mosaic law?

While absolute certainty will probably not be reached soon, the view that there were multiple tithes has much to support it. First, the details of the descriptions of the tithes appear fairly irreconcilable; the differences are significant enough that the texts do not appear to be referring to the same thing. Second, as will be seen below, two tithes are juxtaposed in Deuteronomy 14. It is difficult to argue that this is one tithe. Third, one of the biggest responses from single-tithe advocates is that there are no references to earlier tithes. However, the directive of not neglecting the Levite is probably best taken as a reminder to continue giving the Levitical tithe and not replace it with the festival tithe then being described. Regardless, several of the scholars mentioned above hold to a single tithe in the Mosaic law.[14]

In Deut 14:22–27, an even more detailed description of the festival tithe is given:

> "Each year you are to set aside a tenth of all the produce grown in your fields. You are to eat a tenth of your grain, new wine, and oil, and the firstborn of your herd and flock, in the presence of Yahweh your God at the place where He chooses to have His name dwell, so that you will always learn to fear the LORD your God. But if the distance is too great for you to carry it, since the place where Yahweh your God chooses to put His name is too far away from you and since the LORD your God has blessed you, then exchange it for money, take the money in your hand, and go to the place the LORD your God chooses. You may spend the money on anything you want: cattle, sheep, wine, beer, or anything you desire. You are to feast there in the presence of the LORD your God and rejoice with your family. Do not neglect the Levite within your gates, since he has no portion or inheritance among you."

This passage appears to command the Israelites to use another tenth of the produce of grain, wine, oil, and flocks to worship God in the tabernacle/temple and during the festivals they would celebrate each year. The three main festivals were Passover, Weeks, and Tabernacles. This passage, unlike Lev 27:30–33, allows for the exchange of the increase of crops and flocks for money without adding one-fifth to the total value. The festival tithe is to be eaten in the tabernacle/temple, not in their towns. In the case of an Israelite who exchanged his festival tithe for money, a short shopping list is provided to clarify what can be purchased for the celebration. The passage concludes with a reminder for the Israelites to remember the Levites, probably a reference to the Levitical tithe.

The charity tithe is found in Deut 14:28–29; 26:10–16. This tithe has other names among interpreters: charity, welfare, poor. Some believe that this tithe is not about charity or helping the poor at all. They believe that it is another celebratory tithe because Levites are included, and they would not be considered poor. Others argue that

---

14. See footnote 11.

some of those listed as recipients were poor, especially the orphans (fatherless) and widows. Deuteronomy 14:28–29 states:

> "At the end of every three years, bring a tenth of all your produce for that year and store it within your gates. Then the Levite, who has no portion or inheritance among you, the foreigner, the fatherless, and the widow within your gates may come, eat, and be satisfied. And the Lord your God will bless you in all the work of your hands that you do."

This tithe appears to be distinct from the festival tithe because the Israelites were directed to keep it within their gates, not to bring it to the tabernacle/temple. This tithe was to be given once every three years, not every year. Deuteronomy 26:10–16 provides more information on both the festival and charity tithes:

> "I have now brought the first of the land's produce that You, Lord, have given me. You will then place the container before the Lord your God and bow down to Him. You, the Levite, and the foreign resident among you will rejoice in all the good things the Lord your God has given you and your household. When you have finished paying all the tenth of your produce in the third year, the year of the tenth, you are to give it to the Levite, the foreigner, the fatherless, and the widow, so that they may eat in your towns and be satisfied. Then you will say in the presence of the Lord your God: I have taken the consecrated portion out of my house; I have also given it to the Levite, the foreigner, the fatherless, and the widow, according to all the commands You gave me. I have not violated or forgotten Your commands. I have not eaten any of it while in mourning, or removed any of it while unclean, or offered any of it for the dead. I have obeyed the Lord my God; I have done all You commanded me. Look down from Your holy dwelling, from heaven, and bless Your people Israel and the land You have given us as You swore to our fathers, a land flowing with milk and honey. The Lord your God is commanding you this day to follow these statutes and ordinances. You must be careful to follow them with all your heart and all your soul."

This text describes what should take place during the ceremony when certain commandments are being fulfilled, including the giving of the festival tithe and the charity tithe. The festival tithe is referred to in v. 11, but v. 12 switches to the charity tithe. This verse has the reference to the "year of the tenth," and some believe that the third year is referred to in this way because it was the year when three tithes were offered by the Israelites: the Levitical tithe, the festival tithe, and the charity tithe.

The two most prominent views on the number of tithes in the Mosaic law are the ones with two tithes or three tithes. The chart below demonstrates what those who hold these two views believe. The main difference is that in the two-tithe view, the charity tithe replaces the festival tithe in years three and six, while in the three-tithe view, the charity tithe is a third tithe in years three and six. In favor of the two-tithe view is that 30 percent seems extremely high. Advocates of the three-tithe view respond that if the charity tithe replaced the festival tithe, then the Israelites had no provision for celebrating the festivals in years three and six.[15]

	Two-Tithe View	Total for Year	Three-Tithe View	Total for Year
Year 1	Levitical Tithe Festival Tithe	20%	Levitical Tithe Festival Tithe	20%
Year 2	Levitical Tithe Festival Tithe	20%	Levitical Tithe Festival Tithe	20%
Year 3	Levitical Tithe Charity Tithe	20%	Levitical Tithe Festival Tithe Charity Tithe	30%
Year 4	Levitical Tithe Festival Tithe	20%	Levitical Tithe Festival Tithe	20%
Year 5	Levitical Tithe Festival Tithe	20%	Levitical Tithe Festival Tithe	20%
Year 6	Levitical Tithe Charity Tithe	20%	Levitical Tithe Festival Tithe Charity Tithe	30%

Tithing in the Rest of the Old Testament

Several passages outside the Pentateuch mention the tithe. The first is 2 Chron 31:5–6. This text is important because of a certain historical reference:

> When the word spread, the Israelites gave liberally of the best of the grain, wine, oil, honey, and of all the produce of the field, and they brought an abundance, a tenth of everything. As for the

_____

15. Note that the implication of Ex 23:10–11 and Lev 25:20–21 is that no tithe was paid in year 7 of the cycle.

Israelites and Judahites who lived in the cities of Judah, they also brought a tenth of the cattle and sheep, and a tenth of the dedicated things that were consecrated to the LORD their God. They gathered them into large piles.

This passage describes the Israelites living in obedience to the Mosaic law regarding tithing. This demonstrates that the laws about tithing were kept (at least from time to time) and that God blessed the Israelites for their obedience (see vv. 7–10). They were so blessed and gave so much that there were piles of leftover tithes that the Levites and priests couldn't eat. Hezekiah then offered a solution to this problem: "Hezekiah told them to prepare chambers in the LORD's temple, and they prepared them" (v. 11). Specific chambers or rooms (Hb. *lishkah*) were "prepared" for the leftover tithes.

The next passage that mentions the tithe is Neh 10:37–38. Nehemiah explained that the Israelites were giving 10 percent of the produce of the land to the Levites. He then provided some safeguard for the collection: a priest was to go with the Levite when collecting the tithe. Finally, the Levites are directed to give 10 percent of what they receive to the priests.

> We will bring a loaf from our first batch of dough to the priests at the storerooms of the house of our God. We will also bring the firstfruits of our grain offerings, of every fruit tree, and of the new wine and oil. A tenth of our land's produce belongs to the Levites, for the Levites are to collect the one-tenth offering in all our agricultural towns. A priest of Aaronic descent must accompany the Levites when they collect the tenth, and the Levites must take a tenth of this offering to the storerooms of the treasury in the house of our God.

Nehemiah said that the tithes are to be placed in the "storerooms of the treasury." The Hebrew word for storerooms is the same used in 2 Chron 31:11 (*lishkah*). Nehemiah may have been referring to the rooms that were first prepared for the tithes in 2 Chron 31:11. The Hebrew word for treasury is *otsar*. So in the treasury (*otsar*) of the temple there were storerooms (*lishkah*) for the leftover tithes. In Neh 12:44, Nehemiah reported that men were put in charge of the rooms that kept the firstfruits, tithes, and contributions.

The last passage in Nehemiah that mentions the tithe is 13:4–12. Nehemiah, after returning from Persia, explained that while he was gone, Eliashib was in charge of the "storerooms of the house of our God" (v. 4). Eliashib was related to Tobiah, Nehemiah's enemy. He prepared a room for Tobiah where the tithes (and other items) were supposed to be stored. Nehemiah threw Tobiah's furniture out of the chamber. He also discovered that the Levites had been neglected (see Deut 14:27) and were working in the fields. He reinstituted tithing and had all the tithes brought into the storehouse.

Probably the most famous passage on tithing is Mal 3:8–12. The prophet Malachi received an oracle (1:1) from God. God told the Israelites that they were robbing Him by not paying their tithes:

> "Will a man rob God? Yet you are robbing Me!"
>
> You ask: "How do we rob You?"
>
> "By not making the payments of the tenth and the contributions. You are suffering under a curse, yet you—the whole nation—are still robbing Me. Bring the full tenth into the storehouse so that there may be food in My house. Test Me in this way," says the LORD of Hosts. "See if I will not open the floodgates of heaven and pour out a blessing for you without measure. I will rebuke the devourer for you, so that it will not ruin the produce of your land, and your vine in your field will not fail to produce fruit," says the LORD of Hosts. "Then all the nations will consider you fortunate, for you will be a delightful land," says the LORD of Hosts.

God told the Israelites that by not giving their tithes and offerings they were robbing Him. Then God commanded them to bring the full tithe into the storehouse. This is the main text that supports the doctrine of "storehouse tithing." This doctrine teaches that Christians must give at least 10 percent of their income to the local church. If they decide to give it anywhere else, they are robbing God of His tithes, according to Malachi 3. What was the storehouse?

Some scholars believe that the storehouse was the temple. The sentence says to bring the tithe into the storehouse "so that there may be food in My house" (v. 10). The reference to the Lord's "house" would be the temple. So by bringing the tithe to the storehouse, the temple is provided with food. The local church today would be the equivalent of the temple.

Other scholars believe that the storehouse in Mal 3:10 is a reference to the treasury area referenced in 2 Chron 31:11. The Hebrew word for storehouse in Mal 3:10 is *otsar*. These scholars do not find any parallel between the temple treasury/storehouse and the local church. Some deny that tithes are required of Christians. Others say that Christians must tithe but they have control over where the tithe is given—whether the local church, a missions organization, a parachurch group, or any charity (religious or nonreligious).

There are other aspects of controversy in this text. Does the phrase "Test Me in this way" refer to the method of testing (the paying of tithes) or to a test for these specific Israelites in that specific situation? (See the NASB: "test Me now in this.") What is the nature of the blessing that God will pour out today on the obedient? Does the text guarantee financial blessings for those who tithe? Can the references to agricultural blessings be accurately translated into money in bank accounts? Finally, does the failure to tithe still result in a curse or was that a covenant-specific aspect of this text—i.e., was it only for those under the old covenant?

A final passage makes a curious reference to tithes. Amos 4:4 says, "Come to Bethel and rebel; rebel even more at Gilgal! Bring your sacrifices every morning, your tenths every three days." The reference to tithing every three days has puzzled many scholars and commentators. Its significance for the current study is not great.

These are all the Old Testament passages that directly discuss the tithe. Before the Mosaic law, Abram gave 10 percent of the spoils of war to Melchizedek, and Jacob promised to give 10 percent of his increase if he was safely returned to the land of his father Isaac. Several tithes occur in the Mosaic law: the cattle tithe, the Levitical tithe, the priestly tithe, the festival tithe, and the charity tithe.[16] In 2 Chron 31:5–11 the Israelites are told to bring tithes to the temple and the chambers that were prepared in the temple treasury (storehouse) to hold the leftovers. Nehemiah 10:35–39; 13:9–13 detail Nehemiah's reinstitution of the tithe. Malachi 3 contains an oracle against the Israelites for robbing God of His tithes.

Tithes in the Mosaic Law	Passage(s)
Cattle Tithe	Lev 27:30–33
Levitical Tithe	Num 18:20–24,30–32
Priestly Tithe	Num 18:25–29
Festival Tithe	Deut 12:17–19; 14:22–27; 26:10–16
Charity Tithe	Deut 14:28–29; 26:10–16

---

16. Some would say that Abram's tithe was distinct from these listed and that Amos's tithe was distinct from those mentioned in the Mosaic law since it was at a different location with different stipulations given.

Tithing in the New Testament

The Greek word for "tithe" is *apodekatoō* (ἀποδεκατόω) and means "to pay a tenth." Four passages in the New Testament directly mention tithing. The first is Matt 23:23: "Woe to you, scribes and Pharisees, hypocrites! You pay a tenth of mint, dill, and cumin, yet you have neglected the more important matters of the law—justice, mercy, and faith. These things should have been done without neglecting the others." The parallel is in Luke 11:42: "But woe to you Pharisees! You give a tenth of mint, rue, and every kind of herb, and you bypass justice and love for God. These things you should have done without neglecting the others."

In these texts, Jesus explains that the scribes and Pharisees are hypocrites because they pay such close attention to their tithing of herbs, yet they neglect more important matters like justice, mercy, faith, and love for others. The final phrase contains the controversial aspect. When Jesus says, "These things should have been done," was He referring to tithing or the more important matters? Regardless, the next phrase, "without neglecting the others," refers to the phrase that the first part does not. So Jesus said that the scribes and Pharisees should be tithing *and* keeping the more important matters of the law.

Some believe that Jesus was talking to His disciples and the crowds (see v. 1), while others believe that Jesus' primary audience switched to the scribes and Pharisees (see v. 13). Either way, what is the significance of Jesus telling some people (whether His disciples, the crowds, scribes and/or Pharisees) who were under the old covenant that they must tithe? Does this command automatically apply to Christians? Some scholars believe that since Christians are under the new covenant, this text is irrelevant for the debate over the necessity of the tithe. Others believe that Matthew's (and Luke's) inclusion of this account for his audience, a group living under the new covenant decades after Jesus' ministry, is intended to communicate that tithing continues into the new covenant paradigm. It doesn't appear that there is anything in this text that calls for discontinuation of tithing.

The third passage that directly mentions tithing occurs in one of Jesus' parables: "I fast twice a week; I give a tenth of everything I get" (Luke 18:12). The statement is made by a Pharisee as he contrasted himself with a tax collector. There is nothing in this text that would argue for the cessation of tithing, but there also is not much to argue that it should continue.

The final passage that directly mentions tithing is Heb 7:1–10. For some, this is the ultimate New Testament passage for the proof that Christians are required to tithe since it connects a pre-Mosaic law event, Abram's tithing to Melchizedek, with Christians in the new covenant:

> For this Melchizedek—
> King of Salem, priest of the Most High God, who met Abraham and blessed him as he returned from defeating the kings, and Abraham gave him a tenth of everything; first, his name means king of righteousness, then also, king of Salem, meaning king of peace; without father, mother, or genealogy, having neither beginning of days nor end of life, but resembling the Son of God—
> remains a priest forever.
> Now consider how great this man was—even Abraham the patriarch gave a tenth of the plunder to him! The sons of Levi who receive the priestly office have a commandment according to the law to collect a tenth from the people—that is, from their brothers—though they have also descended from Abraham. But one without this lineage collected tithes from Abraham and blessed the one who had the promises. Without a doubt, the inferior is blessed by the superior. In the one case, men who will die receive tenths, but in the other case, Scripture testifies that he lives. And in a sense Levi himself, who receives tenths, has paid tenths through Abraham, for he was still within his ancestor when Melchizedek met him.

This passage must be given serious consideration in the tithing debate. Who was Melchizedek? Was he the preincarnate Jesus? If so, how would that impact Christians and tithing? Once the person of Melchizedek is established, those who believe this passage should not be used to advocate the necessity of the tithe point to the overall argument of Hebrews. They would say that this passage is about the superiority of the Melchizedekian priesthood over the Levitical/Aaronic priesthood, not about whether tithing continues or not. Those who utilize this passage for tithing typically focus on v. 8: "In this case mortal men receive tithes, but in that case one receives them, of whom it is witnessed that he lives on" (NASB). The middle phrase says that "one receives them" and that this person "lives on." Who is it that "lives on"? If it is Melchizedek, then this does not necessarily support pro-tithing advocates. Some believe it is Jesus and thus use this text to argue for the continuation of tithing.

Conclusion

Every text that explicitly mentions tithing has now been examined. Texts that may allude to tithing, without directly referencing it, could also be important in this debate. For example, 1 Corinthians 9 or chap. 16 could be discussing the concept of tithing, even though Paul did not mention the word directly. Regardless, this debate needs to center on Scripture; the Word of God is our center, our standard, and the final arbiter of all truth. Therefore, we should all allow the text of Scripture to determine our conclusion on tithing, not history, not tradition, and not pragmatics.

PART I

CHAPTER 2

The Foundations of Giving
Ken Hemphill and Bobby Eklund

Position Statement

We assert that tithing is the foundational base from which believers can and must be challenged to become grace-givers. We further assert that Adam received instruction about giving from God the Father, that the tithe was established prior to the giving of the Mosaic law, and that He continued to teach mankind about giving through His servant Moses.

We believe that Jesus assumed the tithe would be practiced by His followers, not as a legalistic minimum, but as a base for beginning a new journey in the giving of oneself. We believe that Paul taught and practiced biblical giving,[1] which is both gracious and cheerful. These challenges to give beyond the tithe are based on the assumption that a believer under grace would never do less than those who had lived under the Mosaic law.

---

1. In defending himself before the Sanhedrin, Paul declared himself to be "a Pharisee, a son of Pharisees!" (Acts 23:6). He could hardly have made such a bold claim in front of this body if he were not a tither, a requirement of the Pharisees. Some who oppose tithing note that Paul did not teach on tithing, thus by his silence we can deduce that he did not think it necessary for NT believers. But Paul did not mention hell either, so by his silence are we to deduce that hell is not a reality?

Stewards from the Beginning

The God of Scripture is a God of order. He does not leave us to wander and wonder about what pleases Him or about His requirements for His children. Rather, He provides loving guidance for every area of life—our relationship to Him and to His church, our relationships with one another, our work, marriage, homes, and families, His plans for us in the next life and for sharing the gospel. In the earliest days in the garden of Eden, He appointed men and women as stewards over everything He had created and provided careful instructions on how to carry out this assignment in ways that please, honor, and glorify Him.

There are more verses in Scripture that relate to money and the handling of money than any other single topic save those of love and God's wrath. One-third of the New Testament parables refer to money or financial matters. Why would this be true? Because God knew that possessions (to include all resources, but specifically money) would present spiritual challenges for mankind. This truth was first demonstrated in Cain. It was true for Achan, Judas Iscariot, and Ananias and Sapphira. In each instance, human failures pointed to the real issue–a disobedient heart. The regular, intentional giving of tithes and offerings affirms God as Creator/Owner and confirms one's role as a steward. "Each week as we compute our tithe, we have a concrete example of the goodness of God. The very fact that we have a tithe to bring indicates that God has given material blessings. As we calculate our tithe, we better understand God's provisions."[2]

The practice of giving encourages the steward to (1) give himself, (2) align his priorities with God's, (3) keep the needs of others on his heart and mind, and (4) acknowledge that his stewardship encompasses not only the tithe but the remaining 90 percent. Perhaps Jesus summed it up best when He said, "No one can be a slave of two masters, since either he will hate one and love the other, or be devoted to one and despise the other. You cannot be slaves of God and of money" (Matt 6:24). In his commentary on Matt 6:24, Craig Blomberg stated:

> Against those who might protest that they can accumulate both spiritual and earthly treasure, Jesus replies that they have only two options. They must choose between competing loyalties. "Master" suggests a slaveowner who required total allegiance.

---

2. B. Eklund and T. Austin, *Partners with God* (Nashville: Convention Press, 1994), 78.

People could not serve two masters in the way in which people today often work two jobs. "Money" is more literally *mammon*, referring to all of a person's material resources. Of course many people do try to cherish both God and mammon, but ultimately only one will be chosen. The other will be "hated," even if only by neglect. "Love" and "hate" in Semitic thought are often roughly equivalent to choose and not choose.

. . . Jesus proclaims that unless we are willing to serve him wholeheartedly in every area of life, but particularly with our material resources, we cannot claim to be serving him at all.[3]

The Foundations of Giving: Before the Mosaic Law

"In the beginning God created the heavens and the earth" (Gen 1:1). The Genesis account declares God to be the Creator of everything that exists on earth and in the heavens. In the unfolding of human history, God asserted that not only has He created everything that exists, but that it is all His by right of creation. "The earth and everything in it, the world and its inhabitants, belong to the LORD" (Ps 24:1). This same thought occurs throughout Scripture.[4] Humans acknowledge and express God's ownership in a variety of ways, but for our purposes we have focused on obedience in giving and worship since they are inextricably bound together.

Giving is a Normal, Worshipful Response of the Created to the Creator

In Genesis 1–4, God, through His servant Moses, introduced at least three principles related to giving (offerings) that are repeated throughout Scripture. "Now Abel kept flocks, but Cain worked the soil. In the course of time Cain brought some of the fruits of the soil as an offering to the Lord. But Abel brought fat portions from some of the firstborn of his flock. The Lord looked with favor on Abel and his offering but on Cain and his offering He did not look with favor. So Cain was very angry, and his face was downcast" (Gen 4:2–5, NIV).

Both Cain and Abel likely learned from their parents that giving back to the Creator is a natural and normal response of those created. Appearing this early in human history, the instruction regarding giv-

---

3. C. L. Blomberg, *Matthew*, NAC (Nashville: Broadman Press, 1992), 124.
4. Lev 25:23; Job 41:11; Ps 33:6,9; Hag 2:8; John 1:3; Acts 17:24; Heb 11:3.

ing could only have come directly from God as He guided Adam in his God-directed role as steward. Cain and Abel, though with different hearts, were responding to God the Creator in worship through giving. By the time Abram appears in Genesis, the concept of giving a portion back to God as an offering of gratitude is understood and defined as 10 percent.[5]

Language describing giving as "legalistic" or an "obligation" is not the principal theme of any biblical discussion of giving. Perhaps some would cite the Malachi passage, which occurs long after the practice of giving a tenth[6] was well established. But the picture in Malachi is that of a loving Father who demonstrates extraordinary patience in explaining to His children how and why they have offended Him and provides a way to restore fellowship and blessing.

Even as God charged His people with unfaithfulness, He graciously identified two ways their unfaithfulness to Him was expressed: disobedience in their marriage relationships (2:10–16) and disobedience in their giving. He recounted why they were suffering various consequences of this pattern of disobedience and challenged them to see the difference that obedience can make in the life of His followers (3:8–12). In the preceding verses, God outlined a pattern of disobedience that spanned the centuries: "Since the days of your fathers, you have turned from My statutes; you have not kept them. Return to Me, and I will return to you," says the LORD of Hosts. But you ask, 'How can we return?'" (v. 7).

Nowhere else in Scripture does God encourage His children to put Him to a test (see v. 10). Far from taking a punishing stance that appears richly deserved, He said in essence, "Here's why you're in the mess you're in. You've deeply offended Me by your disobedience, but here's a better plan—one that leads to blessing!" The very fact that God addressed their disobedience in not tithing highlights the importance He placed on it. This was certainly not for His benefit since He already owns everything! No, it is to man's benefit to be obedient in the tithe—it is a pathway to spiritual, and sometimes economic blessing. Malachi cited the blessings resulting from bringing "the full tenth into the storehouse": (1) God would "open the floodgates of heaven and pour out a blessing for you without measure"; (2) He would "rebuke the devourer for you, so that it will not ruin

---

5. Gen 14:20.
6. The tithe in Scripture means 10 percent, literally "the tenth part," from the word *maaser*.

the produce of your land"; (3) "your vine in your field will not fail to produce fruit"; and (4) "all the nations will consider you fortunate, for you will be a delightful land" (vv. 10–12).

We cannot overlook the importance of the reference to the "whole tithe (ten percent) which settles the issue of what constitutes the tithe—anything less (or more) than ten percent is not a tithe. Too, it is important to note also that the place or designated repository for the tithe was to be the 'storehouse,' (v. 10)."[7] Moses had instructed Israel that "Every tenth of the land's produce, grain from the soil or fruit from the trees, belongs to the Lord; it is holy to the Lord." Also, "Every tenth animal from the herd or flock, which passes under the shepherd's rod, will be holy to the Lord (Lev 27:30,32). After Israel settled in the land, they were to bring the tithe annually to the sanctuary and consume a portion of it "before the Lord," leaving the remainder with the Levites, who were in turn to share a tithe with the priests.

The storehouse clearly refers to God's house (Deut 12:5–7; 26:2), the place of worship for His children, and for present-day believers that would be the meeting place of a local congregation. There is no provision made for another place or storehouse in which tithes would be deposited. Even in the matter of a tithe being dedicated to aliens, the fatherless, and widows every third year, the giving was done through the priests serving in the temple.[8] While believers can and should make contributions to causes dear to God's heart—the poor, imprisoned, fatherless, widows—tithes and offerings are to be brought to His storehouse. "The place where God's name dwelt would have been the tabernacle or the temple. They were not to take the tithes to a place of their own choosing but to the place designated by the Lord. This is probably what Malachi meant when he declared, 'Bring the full tenth into the storehouse so that there may be food in my house' (3:10a)."[9] He had already spoken on the tithe through Moses in Lev 27:30 where He said, "Every tenth . . . belongs to the Lord; it is holy to the Lord."[10]

Are we to seriously believe that God, who by this time had personally instructed His followers in all matters related to giving and

---

7. R. A. Taylor and E. R. Clendenen, *Haggai, Malachi*, NAC (Nashville: Broadman Press, 2004), 415.

8. For a more complete discussion regarding OT practices, see Eklund and Austin, *Partners with God*, 64–66.

9. K. Hemphill, *Making Change* (Nashville: B&H, 2006), 100.

10. God also spoke of the tithe in Lev 27:32; Num 18:21–32; Deut 12:5–19; 14:22–27.

to the tithe, suddenly declares the tithe is no longer important, no longer considered holy? There is no such statement in Scripture and no basis for teaching that such a declaration was uttered or intended.

The Gift Cannot Be Separated from the Giver (specifically, his/her heart condition)

Even more importantly, the first recorded acts of giving in Genesis provide insight about the hearts, dare we say, heart *condition*, of the givers and God's expectation or design for giving. Many examples in both the Old and New Testaments depict worshipful, joyful, or cheerful giving positively, and portray grudging or cheerless givers negatively. This contrast is vividly portrayed in the account of Cain and Abel.[11]

Cain's heart condition is apparent since he did not give the first-fruits but "some of the land's produce." Then he responded to God's lack of regard for his offering with an outburst of festering anger against God and jealousy against Abel since God accepted his offering. Cain then murdered his brother. Genesis 14 recounts how Abram gave a tithe freely, willingly, and worshipfully to Melchizedek, recognizing God's hand in his victory over King Chedorlaomer and the kings who were with him. The Macedonians begged to participate in the offering Paul was gathering for the impoverished saints in Jerusalem, even though they themselves were impoverished, having "first given themselves" to the Lord. When Jesus observed the love of the poor widow as she sacrificed two copper pennies, He made a clear distinction between her gift from a heart of love and those of people whose gifts had cost them nothing. The giving of tithes and offerings in Scripture cannot be separated from the heart condition of the giver. Larry Burkett—author of many books on stewardship, money management, and financial topics, and founder of Christian Financial Concepts—was fond of saying that a person's giving is an "outward indicator of his inward spiritual condition."[12]

There Are Prescribed Requirements for Giving

Adam's sons, in obedience, thus gave back "some" or "portions," as they likely had seen their father do. The words "firstborn" and "fat portions" appear again later,[13] but they point to the principles

---

11. This same contrast is apparent in later discussions related to Abram and the king of Sodom (Gen 14:21) and the two men praying in the NT account (Luke 18:9–14).

12. L. Burkett, *How Much Is Enough* (Nashville: LifeWay, 1999), video.

13. At the time of the flood, the practices surrounding animal offerings were well defined, i.e., Noah offered "clean animals" and "clean" birds which were both acceptable

of firstfruits (the best of the early harvest), the choice portions (fat) of unblemished animals, and the prescribed way of giving that God required in the case of animal sacrifices.[14]

We learn much later in Scripture[15] how God has a special regard for the firstfruits of the harvest, the firstborn in families, the firstborn of flocks,[16] and the choice parts of animals to be given as a sacrifice. Sinful people know what pleases those they love in human relationships and they give gifts to them accordingly. How amazing that the Creator of the universe would so carefully describe for us what is "a pleasing aroma" (see Lev 1:9,13; 2:2; 3:5) in His nostrils! There can be no confusion or misunderstanding of the fact that God places great weight on an individual's handling of all the resources entrusted to him and specifically his obedience in returning the portion that belongs solely to God.

Beyond the teaching of the latter principle and the blessing to the obedient giver, God's purposes extend to the watching world (now, as then). In our studies we have found it fascinating that the tithe of agriculture was used in a family feast celebrating God's provision and presence: "You are to feast there in the presence of the LORD your God and rejoice with your family" (Deut 14:26). Many view the presentation of tithes and offerings as an issue of strict adherence to the law, but for Israel it was a celebration of their abundance in the presence of the Lord. Can you imagine the impact these joyful celebrations must have had on Israel's pagan neighbors?[17]

It can hardly be overstated that the tithe was considered an important aspect of worship. Malachi wrote in a period when conditions in Israel were turbulent and despair was spreading. He pointedly asked and answered a question that he believed to be at the heart of the problem. "Will a man rob God? Yet you are robbing me!' You ask: 'How do we rob you?' By not making the payments of the tenth and the contributions" (3:8). The result was that they were suffering under a curse. In other words, they had forfeited God's presence, provision, and protection.[18]

---

and well pleasing to God (Gen 8:21–22).

14. See Lev 1–7 for a full description of sacrificial offerings—burnt offerings, grain offerings, fellowship offerings, sin offerings, the cases requiring sin offerings and the types of sin offerings, with attendant rules for making such offerings.

15. Exod 13:11–15; Deut 12:10–22; 26:9–11; Prov 3:9–10.

16. The firstborn of man and animal belong to God (see Exod 13:2).

17. See Hemphill, *Making Change*, 101.

18. Ibid.

God assures His blessings on the tither. Again, a word of caution is needed. A doctrine of material prosperity is not found in this promise. The floodgates of heaven are not filled with money. They are packed with the things of God, heavenly treasures. God is offering an amazing investment program. If we bring a tenth to Him, in return He will open the floodgates of heaven and fill our lives with spiritual blessings. What price tag can we put on the things of God? Some might say that we cannot buy the blessings of God for any price. But God says we can have them for a tenth.[19]

We have nothing to give to the Creator/Owner of the universe, yet He allows us to bring some small token of our recognition of who He is, how He provides, and how we are completely dependent on Him. Thus, should we not delight, rejoice, and be thankful that He names something that will be holy to Him, a pleasing offering, and a sweet sacrifice? One would think that the simple offering He requires, given in obedience, is so slight a request in light of His manifold blessings!

Abram Tithed before the Law

There is a curious story in Genesis that contains the first mention of the tithe in the Bible. This occurs prior to the giving of the Mosaic law. This has become a key verse in the debate on the matter of tithing and whether it remains normative for the New Testament believer. If Abram tithed as a spontaneous response to the goodness of God, then the later codification of the tithe in the Mosaic law would reflect Abram's response to the gracious activity of God who had given him victory over Chedorlaomer.

In Genesis 12–13 Abram left Ur of the Chaldeans on a pilgrimage of faith. God promised him blessings in order that he and his descendants would, in turn, bless the peoples of the earth. Abram and his nephew Lot, along with their families and numerous belongings, began their journey traveling together until Lot decided to head for Sodom and Gomorrah.

This region was in political turmoil, and as a consequence Chedorlaomer took Lot and all his possessions captive. In a brave rescue mission Abram and his 300 men were able to save Lot along with the other citizens of Sodom. Abram returned a victorious deliverer, having recovered the goods and people of an entire city. As he returned from this successful venture, Abram and his forces were met by two

---

19. See Eklund and Austin, *Partners with God*, 74.

kings in the valley of Shaveh. The first was the king of Sodom and the second was Melchizedek, king of Salem.

Melchizedek met Abram's immediate need by offering him bread and wine. This mysterious king is described as a "priest of God Most High" (14:18). This is the blessing of this king/priest on Abram:

> Abram is blessed by God Most High,
> Creator of heaven and earth,
> and I give praise to God Most High
> who has handed over your enemies to you.

Abram's response was both spontaneous and immediate: "He gave him a tenth of all" (v. 19–20).

Then the king of Sodom reenters the picture. He is mentioned first as one of the two kings who greeted Abram upon his return, but we are not told that he brought anything to Abram, like the bread and wine offered by Melchizedek. Instead, the king of Sodom wanted to negotiate. He offered Abram the spoils of war if Abram would simply return his people. The spoils[20] that he offered to give are precisely what Abram would have anticipated for his heroic efforts. As a defeated king, the king of Sodom had nothing to offer Abram.

The contrast couldn't be more obvious. Abram refused to take anything from the king of Sodom since he might have claimed, "I have made Abram rich." This refusal is based on Abram's oath. "I have raised my hand in an oath to Yahweh, God Most High, Creator of heaven and earth, that I will not take a thread or a sandal strap or anything that belongs to you" (vv. 22–23). The story seems straightforward. Abram "tithed" to God Most High as an act of gratitude and worship, acknowledging God alone as the possessor of heaven and earth.[21]

While it may seem straightforward on the surface, the obvious implications of the verse have been challenged by writers who argue that the tithe is not normative for Christians. They understand that if the traditional interpretation is accepted, the tithe was an act of worship that preceded the Mosaic law and thus has serious ramifications for the teaching of stewardship today.

---

20. Greek *akrothinion*, literally, "the best of the best," "top of the heap," or "choicest" as in Heb 7:4.

21. The teaching or modeling aspect of the tithe is later described in Deut 14:22–23, where Moses, under the leadership of the Spirit, said, "You are to set aside a tenth of all . . . so that you will always learn to fear the LORD your God."

The arguments vary, but they basically center on the suggestion that Melchizedek is not to be identified with the God of Israel but with a pagan deity, El Elyon. Therefore, Abram is offering a portion of the spoils of war to this priest of a pagan territorial god. There is also significant debate about whether Abram offered a tithe of all his possessions at this point or simply a tithe of the spoils of war. For our purposes, that issue is insignificant.

If it can be established that Abram offered a tithe to the one true God prior to the Mosaic law, it would certainly blunt the argument that tithing is a legalism that has no significance under grace. Stuart Briscoe, in his commentary on this passage, has made this very point with great clarity. "It is important to note that tithing is not something that appeared on the scene in the Law of Moses but was commonly practiced long before Moses was born. It is difficult, therefore, to understand where some modern Christians have gotten the idea that tithing is 'legalistic'."[22]

Walter Brueggemann, who held a significantly different view on the composition and unity of this text than most conservative scholars, sees this text as demonstrating the strange powers of syncretism: "While syncretism is indeed problematic, it is also a way in which alien functions are taken from other gods and reassigned to the God of Israel as an enhancement of his glory."[23] Is this text an example of syncretism where Israel adopted for their God the functions of other pagan deities? Are we to explain this text as Abram offering a gift to a pagan deity as payment for his deliverance?

When one has a high view of Scripture and thus maintains the unity and integrity of the biblical accounts, a much different picture emerges. It is clear that the passage contains a strong element of contrast. The attitudes of the two kings are deliberately contrasted. One gave and blessed; the other demanded. This illustrates the two attitudes predicted in Gen 12:3:

> I will bless those who bless you,
> I will curse those who treat you with contempt,
> and all the peoples on earth
> will be blessed through you.

---

22. D. S. Briscoe, *Genesis*, The Communicator's Commentary (Waco: Word Books 1987), 139.

23. W. Brueggemann, *Genesis*, Interpretation, a Bible Commentary for Teaching and Preaching (Atlanta: John Knox Press, 1982), 136.

While Phoenicians and Canaanites used the title "El Elyon" as a term for their god, Abram was affirming that the God who established a covenant with him is the one true God, the possessor of the heaven and the earth. Thus, rather than demonstrating the borrowing of functions of other gods, this passage demonstrates that the God of Israel alone is God.

It would be exceedingly strange to think that Moses, writing under the guidance of the Holy Spirit, would include a story that suggests Abram offered a sacrifice to a pagan deity. It is much more likely that the text shows that the power and the faithfulness of Israel's God are not limited by any earthly parameters. Likewise, the author of Hebrews confirmed Melchizedek as one "resembling the Son of God [who] remains a priest forever" (Heb 7:3). Again, writing under the leadership of the Holy Spirit, the writer could not have conferred such descriptions on a pagan deity.

The key point of the text is not found in the international events described, but in the growing faith of Abram. The key actor is the one true God and the key responder is Abram. It is the recognition that God is the possessor of heaven and earth that prompts the actions of the story. This truth allows Abram to refuse any help from the king of Sodom (Gen 14:22–24) and prompts him to give Melchizedek "a tenth of everything" (v. 20). Melchizedek would be the one local king who recognized the sovereignty of the God of Israel.

The impact of this event on later Israelite history is not to be overlooked. The union of priest and king in Jerusalem would move David, the first Israelite to sit on Melchizedek's throne, to sing of a greater Melchizedek to come in Psalm 110:4:

> The Lord has sworn an oath and will not take it back:
> "Forever, You are a priest like Melchizedek."

Hebrews 7 as a Commentary on Genesis 14

The Genesis 14 passage is complicated and should not be used as the sole text for one's understanding of the tithe and the law, but it is a key text for those who write on the subject. If one can demonstrate that Abram's tithe to Melchizedek was a voluntary act prior to the Mosaic law, it does establish that tithing was not simply an issue of legalistic obedience even in the Old Testament. Rather, it was a spontaneous act of celebration and gratitude. It is for this reason that some writers have argued that Abram made his gift to a representative of a pagan deity, a suggestion which we find totally unacceptable to the intent of the context and the integrity of divine revelation. Therefore, it is worthwhile to briefly consider the reference to Abram and Melchizedek in Hebrews 7. Once again we must confess that the text is complex and there are several difficult exegetical matters, most of which are not germane to the discussion at hand. It is important to ask whether this New Testament author would agree that Abram's tithe of the spoils of conflict were intended as an act of gratitude and worship to the one true God.

It is not insignificant that the intention of the author of Hebrews was to demonstrate the superiority of the priestly ministry of Jesus to that of any other earthly priest. The author introduced Melchizedek in Heb 5:6 where he quoted Ps 110:4. In order to emphasize that Jesus is a perpetual high priest (7:3), the author turned to the only other reference to Melchizedek in the Old Testament, Genesis 14.

After Abram had returned to the Kings' Valley from his rout of the four invading kings, he was met by the defeated but grateful king of Sodom who attempted to strike a deal with Abram. Abram refused to take anything from the king of Sodom based on the oath he had just made to "God Most High, Creator of heaven and earth." That oath clearly reflected the recent encounter with Melchizedek and the blessing he had received from him (Gen 14:18–20).

The author drew attention to the titles "king of righteousness" and "king of Salem" as well as Melchizedek's lack of specified lineage (Heb 7:2–3). Unquestionably, the author was using typological exegesis. Although some older commentators argued that Melchizedek was a preincarnate visit of the Second Person of the Trinity, it is more likely that he was using a typological argument from silence in this setting.[24]

The author said nothing about Melchizedek's parentage, his birth, or his death, so he was a fitting type of Christ. But his focus was not on Melchizedek but on Christ who remains a priest perpetually without qualification. It is precisely at this point that the author commented on the offering of the tithe by Abram (Heb 7:4–10). The author seized on the story of Abram's giving the tithe to Melchizedek to demonstrate the greatness of Melchizedek and thus the surpassing greatness of Christ the high priest. The argument goes thus: Abram

---

24. F. F. Bruce, *The Epistle to the Hebrews*, The New London Commentary on the New Testament (London: Marshall, Morgan & Scott, 1964), 136.

was indeed great but he acknowledged the higher status of Melchizedek as demonstrated by presenting to him a tithe of the spoils of war. Melchizedek's greater status is demonstrated both by his accepting the tithe from Abram (v. 4) and his power to bless Abram (v. 7).

In verse 5, the author spoke of the authority of the Levites to collect a tithe of the agricultural produce from the people (see Lev 18:21). The Levites collected these tithes from their brethren who are descended from Abram. The fact that Abram tithed to one whose genealogy was not traced to the Levites demonstrates that Abram recognized the superiority of Melchizedek.

Verse 8 compared the giving of tithes to mortal men (Levites) with the giving of tithes to one who lives on (Melchizedek). Further, the author argued that Levi, who received tithes, paid tithes to one who was greater. Levi, the great-grandson of Abram, was not yet born when Abram tithed to Melchizedek. In biblical thought an ancestor is regarded as containing within himself all his descendants.[25] Thus when Abram tithed to Melchizedek, in a sense all his descendants— including the Levites—tithed to him.

Two things are worthy of note. It is apparent that the inspired writer of Hebrews treated the narrative of Genesis 14 as a historically inaccurate picture of Abram's tithing to one greater than himself, namely, Melchizedek, who was thus the representative of the one true God. Second, the typological argument throughout indicates that what was true of Melchizedek in a limited and typological way is true in an absolute way of one who serves as high priest perpetually before God. If Abram tithed to Melchizedek, would it not follow that the Christian would offer tithes to the great high priest who is greater than Melchizedek?

Jacob's Commitment to Tithe

Genesis 27 records Jacob's theft of the birthright and blessing from Esau. Jacob was sent away until his brother's anger subsided (27:45). Isaac blessed his son, sought the blessing of "God Almighty," and requested that God would give to him the blessing of Abram (28:1–4). Jacob spent the night in a solitary place on his way from Beersheba to Haran. As he lay sleeping, he had a dream in which he saw angels ascending and descending a ladder. The Lord, who stood above it, identified Himself: "I am the Lord, the God of your father

---

25. Bruce, *Hebrews*, 142.

Abram and the God of Isaac" (v. 13). Further, God confirmed that He would fulfill His covenant to Abram through Isaac and his descendants (vv. 13–14).

Jacob awakened with the firm assurance that the place where he had slept was none other than the house of God and the gate of heaven. Not only was the place awe-inspiring, but his meeting with the holy God was profoundly transforming. To memorialize this event he upended the stone that had been his pillow and poured oil on it. This was a simple but memorable testimony to his encounter with God. Second, he renamed the place "Bethel," Hebrew for "house of God." The third act was a vow and a promise to give a tenth of all that God gave him (v. 22).

Some argue that Jacob was still bargaining with God as he had with Esau since his vow began with the words, "If God will be with me." But the entire context describes a subdued man who was overwhelmed with the promises of God to provide the Abramic blessing through him and his descendants. In response to the authentic self-disclosure of God and in recognition of His greatness, Jacob responded with a promise to give a tenth of all that God gives him.

The promise here of a tithe is again significant because it predates the giving of the Mosaic law and thus indicates a voluntary act of submission and worship. It was Jacob's recognition that God was the source of all that he had, which led him to promise to return a tenth to God. One must wonder if Jacob had heard the story of his grandfather Abram's tithe to Melchizedek and thus responded to God's generous offer in a manner similar to that of his ancestor. Whatever the source of his commitment to tithe, no one can doubt that Jacob intended to return the tithe to the one true God, the God of Abram and Isaac.

Jesus and Tithing

It is certainly important for us to establish that the tithe was mentioned twice before the giving of the Mosaic law, but it is more important for us to look at the teaching of Jesus as it relates to the Mosaic law and specifically to the tithe. We have not dealt with the tithe extensively in the Old Testament since there is little disagreement that the principle of tithing is taught there. There is not total agreement on how many tithes were required, but that is not pertinent to the question of whether we should be teaching tithing as a biblical principle for the Christian.

We grew up in homes where tithing was taught as normative for believers. It was not, however, seen as an issue of legalistic obedience to an external standard but rather as a loving and worshipful response to the Creator who owns and provides everything we need and have. Tithing is one aspect of the stewardship of one's total being.

Thus we found it both surprising and disappointing to encounter believers who wanted to argue that tithing was a reversion to legalism and thus inappropriate for the person who has experienced grace. Most of those persons employed this argument as an excuse for why they gave less than a tithe. We found it perplexing that someone who had experienced grace made available through the cross would desire to do less than someone under the Mosaic law. Such, to us, was a disgrace to grace!

Jesus and the Mosaic Law

Most Bible teachers agree that the Sermon on the Mount serves as a frontispiece to Jesus' life and ministry. It functions as a "kingdom manifesto." Jesus begins with the "blessed" statements known as the Beatitudes. The emphasis is on inheriting the kingdom (Matt 5:3,10) and focuses on those who are "sons of God" (v. 8). Kingdom citizenship has now become kingdom sonship. Inheriting the kingdom is not a matter of one's citizenship in Israel but a matter of one's relationship with the King. Further, Jesus indicated that kingdom citizens would be salt and light in a world devoid of both. In this inaugural address, Jesus articulated His relationship to the Law and the Prophets:

> Don't assume that I came to destroy the Law or the Prophets. I did not come to destroy but to fulfill. For I assure you: Until heaven and earth pass away, not the smallest letter or one stroke of a letter will pass from the law until all things are accomplished. Therefore, whoever breaks one of the least of these commandments and teaches people to do so will be called least in the kingdom of heaven. But whoever practices and teaches these commands will be called great in the kingdom of heaven (Matt 5:17–19).

As we read the Gospels, we discover that the legalistically inclined Jews, such as the scribes and the Pharisees, were scandalized by Jesus' attitude toward the laws regarding the Sabbath and ritual cleanliness. They feared that this popular rabbi had set out to destroy the Law and the Prophets, which is a shorthand way of referring to the entire Old Testament, and they feared He was encroaching on territory they considered their own.

What did Jesus mean when He declared that His intention was to "fulfill" and not "abolish"? Jesus' focus was on the positive and not the negative—He came to fulfill. Scholars have suggested that "fulfill" means "accomplish" or "obey," that is, "to bring out the full meaning" or "to bring to its purposeful end." The mention of the prophets along with the law can help us determine the meaning in this context. The teachings of the prophets were "fulfilled" when what they predicted actually happened. Thus the entire Old Testament (Law and Prophets) pointed forward to what Jesus has now brought into being through His life and teaching.[26] His life brings them to full measure by supplying the final revelation of the will of God. Thus, while Jesus' teaching transcends Old Testament revelation rather than abolishes it, it is also its intended culmination.[27] The author of Hebrews made a similar point with reference to Jesus and the Law and the Prophets: "Long ago God spoke to the fathers by the prophets at different times

---

26. C. L. Blomberg, *Matthew*, NAC (Nashville: Broadman Press, 1992), 103–4, said, "Now Christ makes it clear that he is not contradicting the law, but neither is he preserving it unchanged. He comes to 'fulfill' it, i. e., he will bring the law to its intended goal. This is what the Pharisees and scribes have missed, who therefore need a greater conformity to God's standards (v. 20). Both the Law and the Prophets together (v. 17) and the Law by itself (v. 18) were standard Jewish ways of referring to the entire Hebrew Scriptures (our Old Testament). Fulfillment of Scripture, as throughout chaps. 1–4, refers to the bringing to fruition of its complete meaning. Here Jesus views his role as that of fulfilling all of the Old Testament. This claim has massive hermeneutical implications and challenges both classic Reformed and Dispensationalist perspectives. It is inadequate to say either that none of the Old Testament applies unless it is explicitly reaffirmed in the New or that all of the Old Testament applies unless it is explicitly revoked in the New. Rather, all of the Old Testament remains normative and relevant for Jesus' followers (2 Tim 3:16), but none of it can be rightly interpreted until one understands how it has been fulfilled in Christ. Every Old Testament Text must be viewed in light of Jesus' person and ministry and the changes He introduced by the new covenant He inaugurated. Nor is there any evidence here for the common Christian division of the law into moral, civil, and ceremonial categories or for elevating the Ten Commandments above others. This is not to say that the law cannot or should not be subdivided, but valid divisions will probably require greater thematic nuance and sophistication."

27. R. T. France, *The Gospel According to Matthew*, TNTC (Eerdmans: Grand Rapids, 1985), 114.

and in different ways. In these last days, He has spoken to us by His Son" (1:1–2).

Jesus established a new standard for kingdom citizens that far exceeds the righteousness of the scribes and Pharisees (cf. Luke 18:11–12). The person under grace should go beyond lip service and any legalistic observance of the law. Rather than doing the minimum requirements of the Mosaic law, he should internalize the law so that his entire life is molded by God's Word and the desire to prioritize the kingdom.

In Matt 5:21–48 Jesus illustrated this new kingdom ethic built on the fulfillment of the Old Testament with six units of teaching, each introduced by the phrase, "You have heard that it was said," and "But I tell you." These six teachings were not intended to be a complete statement of Jesus' ethical teaching but rather a series of varied examples that show how the teaching of vv. 17–20 should be applied in practice.

Without attempting to look at each one, we can understand the pattern from the first. Jesus quoted the Old Testament prohibition on murder: "You have heard that it was said to our ancestors, 'Do not murder'" (v. 21). He then went beyond the act of murder to condemn the anger in one's heart as the passion that leads to murder. Seething anger is as worthy of guilt as is the act of murder. The attitude of the heart is so vital that when a worshipper recalls that his brother has something against him, he must leave his gift at the altar and seek reconciliation (vv. 23–24).

In each instance cited, Jesus' ethical teaching was more demanding than the Old Testament law. Kingdom ethics are not weakened but intensified and internalized. Jesus demanded obedience that came from the heart, an obedience that truly impacted one's motives and attitudes. It is readily apparent that such intensified standards are impossible for us to obey and thus must be produced by the Holy Spirit whom Christ sent to indwell His followers. Ezekiel the prophet longed for the day when a person would have a heart of flesh and God's Spirit within him to enable him to obey the ordinances of God (Ezek 36:26). That day has arrived for kingdom citizens!

Since our specific goal is to understand how the Old Testament principle of the tithes and offerings should be applied for the New Testament believer, we should look at the several instances where Jesus mentions giving. We must in each context bear in mind Jesus' stated intention of fulfilling rather than abrogating.

A Kingdom Lifestyle

The central issue of Matthew 6 is how one practices righteousness (see v. 1). In 5:20 Jesus indicated that unless one's righteousness exceeds that of the Pharisees, he cannot enter the kingdom of heaven. The contrast is between external righteousness practiced for the *reward* of men and righteousness from the heart practiced for the *reward* of God alone. Jesus selected giving to the poor, prayer, and fasting since they were important elements of Jewish piety.

The first statement, "So whenever you give to the poor" (6:2), makes it clear that Jesus expected His followers to give generously from the heart with the goal of pleasing the Father. They have neither reason nor desire to "sound a trumpet" since their motivation flows from the heart and not the law and their audience was the King and not man. Here we can see the internalization of the law and the joyous response of the disciple who desires to please the King. It is not an issue of whether or not a disciple gives. That is assumed! The attitude and motive have been transformed. Giving comes from a grateful heart and is practiced for the honor of the King, who will reward the giver (v. 4).

Shortly after His teaching on giving to the poor, Jesus addressed the issues of forgiveness (6:19–21) and giving again (vv. 19–24). When we forgive and when we give, we are expressing the character of our Father. When we forgive others, we are responding to the forgiveness provided to us in Christ. When we give, we use the earthly resources provided by the Father to lay up treasure in heaven, and in so doing we honor the King. Jesus began His teachings on giving here with a warning about laying up treasure on earth (vv. 19–21). Such earthly hoarding has two detrimental impacts: (1) it creates anxiety, and (2) it focuses one's heart on the earthly kingdom and not the heavenly one. The miracle of kingdom living and giving is that it enables us to lay up treasure in heaven. Giving and serving in our earthly context allows us to invest our earthly treasure so that we can enjoy it in the service of the King for all eternity.

Render to Caesar and Render to God

The Pharisees were continually plotting ways to trap Jesus into saying something that would render Him less popular with the crowds or cause Him to utter a statement that might be considered blasphemous. In Matthew 22, the Pharisees sent their disciples along with the Herodians to Jesus with a question designed to entrap Jesus.

They feigned respect for His truthfulness and then asked Him about paying taxes to Caesar. The Herodians only appear here in Matthew. They were apparently supporters of the Herodian family and therefore of Antipas. Their collaboration with the Pharisees here represents the two sides of Jesus' dilemma.

The tax in consideration was the poll tax that was levied on all Jews and paid directly to Rome. This tax was a primary reminder of their political subjection to a foreign power. The Pharisees did not approve of Gentile rule over the people of God. They asked whether it was "lawful" (v. 17) for the people of God to express allegiance to a pagan emperor.

Jesus asked them to show Him the coin used for the poll tax. The coin used for the tax was the Roman denarius, a coin that bore a portrait of the emperor and an inscription describing him as "son of God." For everyday commerce, special copper coins were minted without these features out of respect for Jewish sensitivities. No Jew had to handle the offensive denarius coins except to pay the obligatory tax. The fact that they readily produced the coin provided the platform for a simple response. Since they were using Caesar's money they should pay Caesar's taxes. The verb translated "render" means "to give back," and the verb they used was the simple "give" as if they were making a donation. They were to give back what they owed to Caesar.

This passage is most often used to discuss issues regarding church and state, and questions such as, "Is it appropriate for the Christian to give political allegiance to a state, even if it is corrupt?" Jesus placed this political allegiance within the broader context of the demands of loyalty to God. But we often miss the plain teaching of the statement "give back . . . to God the things that are God's." His first century audience would have clearly understood the "things that are God's" as a reference to the tithe. Jesus fully expected that they would render to God that which was rightfully His.

A Reply to the Pharisees

The Pharisees were the largest and most influential religious political party during New Testament times. They were the legalists who fancied themselves as the guardians of the law. As the leaders of the synagogue, they had great influence and thus exercised significant control over the general population. Under the guise of protecting the law, they had developed an oral tradition that often added to the law. They often opposed Jesus because He disregarded much of the oral law.

In Matthew 23, Jesus exposed the legalistic hypocrisy of the scribes and Pharisees. There are seven specific charges, each of them beginning with the phrase, "Woe to you, scribes and Pharisees, hypocrites." Following the introduction, there is a brief cameo illustrating their failure to live up to their claims to be guardians of the law.

The fourth "woe" relates to the practice of tithing as taught in the Mosaic law: "Woe to you, scribes and Pharisees, hypocrites! You pay a tenth of mint, dill, and cumin, yet you have neglected the more important matters of the law—justice, mercy, and faith. These things should have been done without neglecting the others" (23:23). As one might expect, the legalistic Pharisees had tithed everything, including the herbs in their gardens. Let your mind's eye picture one of the haughty Pharisees on his knees counting out his herbs!

In spite of their fastidious observance of the tithe, they had neglected weightier issues, such as "justice, mercy, and faith." This trio of character qualities recalls the summary of true religion in Micah 6:8. Jesus was going back to the prophets to remind them that inner righteousness is that which gives substance to outward ritual. They had been guilty of picking and choosing and thus ignoring these greater issues of inner truth.

We must, however, be careful to note that Jesus did not condemn them for the "legalism" of tithing. On the contrary, He indicated that, "These things should have been done without neglecting the others" (v. 23). Jesus did not suggest that the Old Testament principle of the tithe should be neglected but rather that it should issue from the heart from whence also should flow justice, mercy, and faith. The law has now been written on the heart and thus obedience springs from the very character of man whose righteousness is internal and not an external show.

We can't ignore the obvious implication. Jesus believed that they should have understood and practiced tithing. That practice now should issue from the heart transformed by the grace of God. Further, they should have understood that to practice the detail of the law while ignoring its spiritual value made them like the blind guide who stooped to drink, pushing aside a tiny gnat and carelessly swallowing a camel.

There is one other reference to tithing in the teachings of Jesus, the parable of the Pharisee and the tax collector (Luke 18:9–14). Jesus told a parable of two men who went up to the temple to pray. One was a tax collector who was so overwhelmed by the enormity of his sin that he couldn't even look up to heaven. The other, a Pharisee, who in his arrogance thanked God that he was not like other people—not greedy, not unrighteous, not an adulterer, and especially not like this tax collector! To back up his boast, he declared, "I fast twice a week; I give a tenth of everything I get" (18:12). What we learn from this text is that fasting and tithing were still practiced in the days of Jesus and further that they, like all good works, cannot justify a man before God.

To place tithing into a similar category with dietary regulations and animal sacrifices, which were clearly superseded through the life and teaching of Jesus, is to directly contradict the teachings of Jesus. The tithe was and is an act of worship through which a person gratefully acknowledges God as the owner and giver of everything. Jesus acknowledged that while it should not be neglected, it should issue from a heart of gratitude and not from a proud legalism that attempts to earn God's favor and prove one's spirituality.

Tithing: A Good Starting Point

While tithing is a good place for us to begin the teaching of stewardship, it is inadequate in light of the gift of God's grace in His Son and His passion that the nations are told about His great love for all men. Why would anyone think that living under grace should grant us permission to do less than man was required to do under the Mosaic law? Grace allows us to become cheerful givers, responding from the heart and going beyond the minimal requirements of the Mosaic law.

Paul provided excellent teaching that leads us beyond the tithe. He has three passages that speak to the issue of generous giving—1 Cor 16:1–4; 2 Corinthians 8; and 2 Corinthians 9. Each of these passages deals with giving that was intended for the saints in Jerusalem. He was mobilizing and motivating the churches in Macedonia and Achaia to join in a cooperative offering for believers in Jerusalem who had been impacted by a famine.

First Corinthians 16

In 1 Cor 16:2, Paul stated, "On the first day of the week, each of you is to set something aside and save in keeping with how he prospers, so that no collections will need to be made when I come." It is not insignificant that this teaching follows immediately on the teaching of the resurrection. Paul ends his detailed instruction about the resurrection with a declaration that should encourage every believer—"your labor in the Lord is not in vain" (15:58).

What does this passage add to our understanding of the tithe as a place of beginning rather than a place of culmination? Here we find three important principles that allow us to build on the foundation of tithing.

1. *The principle of consistency and priority.* "On the first day of the week" not only provides evidence that first-century Christians worshipped on the first day of the week as a celebration of the resurrection of the Lord, it further indicates that giving was a critical aspect of their worship experience. Our giving should flow from theological convictions that enable us to give as an act of worship. Consistency requires thought, planning, and preparation that allow us to have a greater sense of worship as we give.

2. *The principle of personal responsibility.* The phrase "each of you" means exactly what it says. No one is to be excluded. Rich and poor, old and young, male and female—each one is given the privilege and responsibility to participate. No one should ever be excluded from worshipping God through tithes and offerings.

3. *The principle of proportionate giving.* Paul does not specify any certain percentage in this text. Having been nurtured in Judaism, Paul would have practiced tithing according to Old Testament prescription. Paul challenges givers to go beyond the tithe, exhorting them to give "in keeping with how he prospers." Some in Corinth could afford to give larger gifts than others and thus proportionate giving would ensure that the collection would be sufficient to meet the needs of the saints in Jerusalem. Proportionate giving requires us to consider the extent of our blessing. It flows from the overflow of the heart that recognizes God as the source of life and the owner of everything.

First Corinthians 8

The letter we call 2 Corinthians was written about a year after the instructions recorded in 1 Corinthians 16. Prior to the writing of 2 Corinthians, Paul had been forced to write a painful letter (see 2 Cor 7:8) that had grieved the Corinthians. Nonetheless, it produced positive results (v. 9). With the church in a more positive mood, Paul devoted nearly two chapters to the motive for and results of grace-empowered giving.

It is apparent that the churches in Macedonia were further along in their participation in the offering than was the church in Corinth. Paul used the generosity of the Macedonians to stimulate the Corinthians to complete their offering (8:1). The generous response by the churches in Macedonia is made even more exemplary because "their abundance of joy and their deep poverty overflowed into the wealth of their generosity" (v. 2).

Joy and generosity are the twin foundations for worshipful giving. It is joy that leads one to generosity, and generosity, in turn, gives one great joy. Generosity indicates giving that is uncalculating and unpretentious.

Paul indicated that the generosity of the Macedonians was a visible expression of divine grace. The use of "grace" here doesn't simply mean that their offering was *motivated* by grace. It goes beyond that to suggest that it was an *act* of grace. In other words, their giving was made possible by the empowering of the Holy Spirit.

Even a cursory reading of 1 Corinthians will make you aware that some in Corinth were zealous for "matters of the Spirit," and in particular spectacular gifts that provided visible or audible proof of advanced spirituality.[28] Paul attempted to redirect their zeal for gifts by encouraging them to seek to abound for the edifying of the church (1 Cor 14:12).

In our present context, Paul mentioned the "claimed" abundance of gifts to further encourage them to give with Spirit-empowered abandon. Now "as you excel in everything—faith, speech, knowledge, and in all diligence, and in your love for us—excel also in this grace" (2 Cor 8:7). Generous giving is as much a demonstration of the Spirit as prophecy or miracle-working faith. The Spirit had both prompted and enabled the Macedonians to give more than their means appeared to warrant.

Thus the concept of the tithe is still normative for New Testament believers, but it should not be practiced grudgingly as an act of legalism. It should serve as a normative starting point from which believers can move to Spirit-empowered giving or grace giving. Grace giving is marked by three characteristics: (1) it is spontaneous (8:3),

---

28. For more detail see K. Hemphill, *You Are Gifted: Your Spiritual Gifts and the Kingdom of God* (Nashville: B&H, 2009).

(2) it is giving beyond one's ability, and (3) it sees giving as a privilege that allows one to share in ministry.

Second Corinthians 9

While a discussion of 2 Corinthians 9 probably exceeds the limits of our assignment, we believe it is important to look at the results of grace giving. When God's people give offerings as a result of His grace at work in their lives, rejoicing will follow. Note two biblical examples: First, the building of Solomon's temple. When the people in David's day heard that the national leadership had committed to the building of this special building for God, they responded by rejoicing. "Then the people rejoiced because of their leaders' willingness to give, for they had given to the LORD with a whole heart. King David also rejoiced greatly" (1 Chron 29:9).

The rebuilding of the temple is a second example of rejoicing when God's grace is at work in the lives of His people. The following scene took place after the Jews returned from captivity: 'But many of the older priests, Levites, and family leaders, who had seen the first temple, wept loudly when they saw the foundation of this house, but many others shouted joyfully. The people could not distinguish the sound of the joyful shouting from that of the weeping, because the people were shouting so loudly. And the sound was heard far away' (Ezra 3:12–13). The people had given freewill offerings to make this occasion possible. True giving will always be cheerful giving.[29]

Conclusion

Just meditate on the powerful results of grace giving:

(1) *Giving enriches the giver.* Isn't it just like God to allow our giving to become a reciprocal blessing? Thus in 2 Cor. 9:10, Paul mentioned a harvest of righteousness. As we grow beyond the tithe, God gives us both additional opportunities and resources for giving.

(2) *Giving meets needs and expresses worship.* Paul rejoiced that the generous offering of the Corinthians would supply the needs of the saints in Jerusalem (2 Cor 9:12). The phrase "for the ministry of this service" brings together two theologically charged words—*diakonia* and *leitergeō*. The first means "service" and the second "ritual, cultic

---

29. B. L. Eklund, *Children of Privilege* (Grapevine, TX: Southern Baptists of Texas Convention, 2005), 41.

service." In other words this offering was an act of worship that also met the needs of the saints.

(3) *Giving expresses gratitude.* "Thanksgiving to God" dominates the thoughts of this chapter (see vv. 11,12,15). You could say there is a double dose of thanksgiving when we give. First, the giving of the Corinthians was an act of thanksgiving. Second, the recipients of that gift thanked God, producing an overflow of thanksgiving.

(4) *Giving glorifies God.* The sole end of man is to glorify God, as Paul explained: "They will glorify God for your obedience to the confession of the gospel of Christ through the proof provided by this service" (v. 13).

Our giving has theological significance that goes far beyond the meeting of physical needs or subsidizing a church budget. It is an act of worship that glorifies the Father and acknowledges Him as Creator/Owner and us as His stewards. Let's embrace the idea that the tithe is a good biblical place for beginning the journey of joyous giving, but that under grace and empowered by the Spirit, we can move beyond the tithe.

CHAPTER 3

Response to Ken Hemphill and Bobby Eklund
David A. Croteau

Praises for Hemphill and Eklund

Ken Hemphill and Bobby Eklund demonstrate that they have a very high view of Scripture. Their arguments are typically developed from the texts they discuss. For example, their tracing of the argument of Hebrews 7 is very well done. This kind of analysis will lead to more clarity in the discussions over the applicability of the tithe to Christians. They also emphasize grace and joy in giving. Promoting these concepts is commendable and biblical. Finally, the motivations for their arguments appear to be pure. They want all Christians to honor and glorify God with their possessions. Some people argue that those who promote tithing are simply greedy and after more money; I did not find a hint of this in their argumentation. I truly believe that they hold to their views based on their understanding of the biblical texts and their desire to see God glorified through biblical stewardship.

The Problematic Position Statement

However, in their position statement, Hemphill and Eklund make several declarations and assumptions that cannot go without challenge. The second sentence of their chapter "asserts" that Adam received instructions about giving from the Father, but this is not written in Scripture. What is the basis for this belief? Why should anyone assume that Adam was told how to give? Later on in their chapter they state: "Both Cain and Abel learned from their parents that giving back to the Creator is a natural and normal response of those created" and "Adam's sons, in obedience, thus gave back 'some' or 'a portion' as they had seen their father do." What is the biblical justification for saying that they learned this from Adam?

Later on in that same sentence, they claim that the tithe was "established" prior to the giving of the Mosaic law. What exactly do they mean by "established"? It seems as if they mean that before Moses gave the law, the tithe was already enacted by God as a permanent ordinance. Since there are only two passages that explicitly mention the tithe prior to the Mosaic law, and only one passage where someone is described as giving a tenth, this is a tall order for those passages. Can it really be said that God established tithing as a permanent law before Sinai on the basis of Genesis 14 and/or Genesis 28?

In Genesis 14 Abram was functioning in a unique circumstance: he was trying to get back his nephew Lot from some pagan kings who had taken him. Before he went on his expedition, Abram promised God that he would not keep any of the spoils of war if he should be victorious. After his success, he gave 10 percent to Melchizedek and the rest back to the owners. Abram is never described as giving a tenth again, and this passage is only an example of someone giving 10 percent from an unusual source of income: spoils of war.

Genesis 28 is an even more difficult passage to utilize to support their view. They say that "the entire context indicates a subdued man who was overwhelmed with the promises of God to provide the Abramic blessing through him and his descendants." In their analysis of the context, they fail to wrestle adequately with the life story of Jacob up to this point, his conversion being in the future, and the use of "fear" (Hb. *yare*) in Genesis 28. Jacob is never described as giving this tithe, and, if he did keep his word, it means that he did not tithe for the twenty-plus years between the promise and the fulfillment. They also neglect to mention that Jacob's tithe was a vow, something the Mosaic law prohibits (see Lev 27:26 and comments below).

Hemphill and Eklund declare that Jesus "assumed" that his followers would tithe. I have no problem with that statement. However, the issue is the definition of this tithe. If Jesus only assumed they would tithe, he must have assumed that they would be following the Jewish understanding of the day, which would be two or three tithes annually. In other words, Jesus' disciples would not be giving 10 percent, but 20 or 23.3 percent. This is the percentage they would be giving from the items listed in the Mosaic law. The tithe in the Mosaic law is defined as the act of giving one out of every ten items produced from the land (i.e., crops, whether grain or fruit) or from the herd. This would have been the understanding of the disciples. What about a fisherman? If Peter caught 100 fish, did he have to give 10 (or 20) of them for his tithe? No, because nothing in the Mosaic law declares fish to be liable to the laws of tithing. So if Jesus assumed His followers would tithe, they would be working off a radically different definition of the tithe than Hemphill and Eklund.

When Hemphill and Eklund state that Paul "taught and practiced biblical giving," they include a footnote which says that Paul declared himself to be a Pharisee in Acts 23:6. They claim that Paul would never have claimed to be a Pharisee unless he was a tither since tithing was required of Pharisees. The problem here, again, is about the definition of tithing. Ancient Jewish sources like the Mishnah, Tobit, and Josephus all say that the Jews in general (and Pharisees in particular) held to multiple tithes and that only agricultural items and animals from a herd were subject to tithes. Paul was not a farmer; Paul was a leather worker.[1] There is nothing in the Old Testament and nothing in the Jewish writings around the time of Christ that indicates a tradesman was required to tithe from his earnings. As stated in my chapter below, F. C. Grant discovered that tradesmen and Jews outside Palestine (both of which could describe Paul) did not pay tithes on anything. Therefore, the Pharisees present in Acts 23:6 would have had no problems with someone claiming to be a Pharisee when he did not pay tithes on income from leather work, especially when done outside Palestine.

Another response is needed for that footnote. Hemphill and Eklund claim that it is inappropriate to argue that, because Paul never specifically taught tithing, he did not think it was necessary. They believe that is similar to the argument some make regarding hell: Paul never mentioned hell because he did not believe in hell. First, the argument I made in *You Mean I Don't Have to Tithe?*[2] is not

---

1. See P. W. Barnett, "Tentmaking," in *Dictionary of Paul and His Letters*, eds. G. F. Hawthorne and R. P. Martin (Downers Grove: InterVarsity, 1993), 925–27; and M. J. Harris, "Tent," in *The New International Dictionary of New Testament Theology*, ed. C. Brown (Grand Rapids: Zondervan, 1978), 3:812–13; cf. J. S. Jeffers, *The Greco-Roman World of the New Testament Era: Exploring the Background of Early Christianity* (Downers Grove: InterVarsity, 1999), 27–28.

2. D. A. Croteau, *You Mean I Don't Have to Tithe? A Deconstruction of Tithing and a*

that silence demonstrates that Paul did not teach tithing, but that his description of giving in some passage, specifically 1 Corinthians 9, is *at odds* with tithing. The financial support Paul discussed in 1 Corinthians 9 was not a requirement; he said that he has the right to receive support, but he forgoes that right. Therefore, the Corinthians were not obligated to give it. This would mean that tithing would be required (*if* this passage were talking about tithing) in circumstances where the minister wants it, and it would not be required if the minister did not want it.

Finally, the last sentence of their introduction is another assumption that needs to be tested. Hemphill and Eklund believe that a Christian would never give less under grace than those who had lived under the Mosaic law. This is a common statement made by tithing proponents. In response it should be noted that Hemphill and Eklund seem to be advocating, based on this sentence, minimum giving to begin at about 20 percent. While they are clear later in the article that they believe Christian giving begins at 10 percent, this does not logically cohere with the statement that those under grace should give more than those under law.

Problematic Interpretations

Now that the introduction has been examined, some thoughts on some interpretations are in order. Regarding the infamous "storehouse" of Malachi 3, they state: "The storehouse clearly refers to God's house, the place of worship for His children and for present-day believers, that place would describe the meeting place of a local congregation. There is no provision made for another 'place or storehouse' in which tithes would be deposited." They cite two verses in favor of reading the "storehouse" as "God's house": Deut 12:5–7 and 26:2. While those verses do reference the temple in Jerusalem, the storehouse to which Malachi referred was not built until the time of King Hezekiah (2 Chron 31:6–11), which was seven centuries after Moses. In vv 10–11, the chief priest Azariah explained that there was so much brought into the house of God that there was food left over in piles. Hezekiah then commanded special rooms ("storerooms" in the NET; Hb. *lishkah*) be built in the house of God to store the tithes and offerings. When Malachi referred to the "storehouse" (Hb. *otsar*), he was referring to these storerooms

---

Reconstruction of Post-Tithe Giving. McMaster Theological Studies (Eugene, OR: Pickwick, 2010), 145, esp. n. 81.

in the temple area (i.e., the temple treasury). In other words, the storehouse does not refer to the temple or God's house in general, but the place where tithes and offerings were stored. By generalizing what the "storehouse" was, Hemphill and Eklund try to claim that this location would now be what we call "the church." Not only is the interpretation faulty, but this analogy falls short as well.[3]

It is not uncommon for tithing advocates to cite Abram's tithe as the basis for the Mosaic laws on tithing. Hemphill and Eklund conclude: "If Abram tithed as a spontaneous response to the goodness of God, then the later codification of the tithe through the Mosaic law would reflect Abram's response to the gracious activity of God who had given him victory over Chedorlaomer." The problem with this statement is that the commanded offering prescribed in the Mosaic law for spoils won in battle was not 10 percent but 0.2 percent (1 out of every 500; see Num 31:27–29). Therefore, Abram's actions apparently were *not* codified into law. Furthermore, the first statement made about tithing in the Mosaic law (Lev 27:30–33) is in the context of things *not* liable to vows.[4] Therefore, both the aspect of giving the spoils of war and the connection to a vow is different in the Mosaic law.

In another point about Abram and tithing, Hemphill and Eklund say: "If it can be established that Abram offered a tithe to the one true God prior to the Mosaic law, it would certainly blunt the argument that tithing is a legalism that has no significance under grace." It appears again that much has been assumed. Why would the argument be blunted? Their citation of Stuart Briscoe does not give the reason as to the "why." Does this mean that requiring circumcision would not be legalistic? What about requiring the law of levirate marriage to be kept? Would that not be legalistic? The fact that something occurred before the Mosaic law was given does not make that law permanent for God's people of all time.

Regarding the specifics on tithing in the Mosaic law, Hemphill and Eklund conclude that "there is not total agreement on how many tithes were required, but that is really not pertinent to the question of whether we should still be teaching tithing as a biblical principle for the Christian." Actually, this is a crucial question about tithing for Christians. If the Israelites were giving more than 10 percent of their income, then how could someone argue that Christians are required to give (only)

---

3. See ibid., 219–22, for how the temple was fulfilled in the New Testament.

4. Note that the context of Lev 27:2–25 is of things liable to vows. In v. 26, the text begins with a contrast ("however"). What follows vv. 26ff., are therefore not liable to vows.

10 percent? Why not lower it to 5 percent? If you are going to use the tithe passages from the Mosaic law in applying tithing to Christians (i.e., Malachi 3), you should not just ignore the specifics of the law. This is a *real* problem that many tithing advocates try to brush away or simply ignore. Saying it is not pertinent does not make it not pertinent.

Conclusion

Hemphill and Eklund resort to the kind of argumentation that is all too common in the current debate: *ad hominem.* "Most of those persons employed this argument as an excuse for why they gave less than a tithe. We found it perplexing that someone who had experienced grace made available through the cross would desire to do less than someone did under the Mosaic law. Such, to us, was a disgrace to grace!" Why is it that tithing advocates typically assume that those who believe 10 percent giving is not required under the new covenant also assume that those arguing for this are fighting for a lower standard of giving? The fact that post-tithe advocates do not start with "I must give 10 percent or I am in sin" does not mean they are arguing for giving less than 10 percent. In fact, most post-tithe advocates that I encounter want the (artificial) standard removed so that those who are wealthy do not think they have satisfied the requirements of scriptural giving by tithing! Those Christians who make millions of dollars a year are not living in conformity with New Testament principles if they are only giving 10 or 15 percent of their income to the local church. If they come face to face with the principles in the New Testament, if they recognize that their giving is a reflection of their love for God, if they recognize the need for the spreading of the gospel, if they recognize the need for missions, and if they recognize the plight of fellow believers around the globe, then they would only be demonstrating cold hearts and the idolatry of greed by giving 10 percent. Tithing advocates need to cease trying to guess the motives of those in the post-tithe camp, such as claiming that they are stingy; reality does not support this.[5] Greediness and stinginess are sins encompassing much of Christianity today, and it is not post-tithe advocates who have a corner on those sins.

---

5. In another place they say, "Why would anyone think that living under grace should grant us permission to do less than man was required to do under the Mosaic law?" This statement explicitly affirms that Christians *must* give over 20 percent, not over 10 percent (once one accepts the reality of the multiple tithes in the Mosaic law). So, in a sense, it proves too much!

CHAPTER 4

Response to Ken Hemphill and Bobby Eklund
Gary North

Ken Hemphill and Bobby Eklund are supporters of tithing. So am I. They insist that God rewards people who tithe. That is my personal experience. They say that tithing is not enough. I ask: "Not enough to do what?" Tithing is quite enough to meet the judicial requirement for tithing. I keep coming back to this idea. The tithe is 10 percent of your net income—no more, no less. You should feel guilty if you do not tithe. You should not feel guilty if you do tithe.

The writers begin their chapter with these words: "We assert that tithing is the foundational base from which believers can and must be challenged to become grace-givers." They present their case for tithing as preliminary—"the foundational base"—to what they call grace-empowered giving. They insist repeatedly that Christians must be cheerful givers. The problem I have with this approach is this: the assignment for this book was to discuss the Christian doctrine of the tithe. If the case for tithing is to be authoritative, it must be exegetical and theological. It must stand alone. I argue that the tithe is not part of a program of giving. The tithe is a legal requirement established by God. It has no more to do with giving than taxation does.

The writers assert, "Language describing giving as 'legalistic' or an 'obligation' is not the principal theme of any biblical discussion of giving." I agree entirely. But the language of legal obligation is exegetically mandatory for any Bible-based case for the tithe. Again, the tithe has nothing to do with giving.

Tithing and grace are related, because everything and grace are related. Everything that anyone possesses is by God's grace. James wrote, "Every generous act and every perfect gift is from above, coming down from the Father of lights; with Him there is no variation or shadow cast by turning" (Jas 1:17). There is special grace: eternal life, which is a gift unmerited by the recipients, and therefore grace. There is common grace: temporal life, which is a gift unmerited by the recipients, and therefore grace. It is all of grace.[1] Therefore, invoking grace in relation to tithing begs the question. What is the question? This: "How much, if anything, are Christians required by God to pay, and why?"

My answer to the first part of the question is this: Christians are required by God to pay 10 percent of their net income to the local congregation in which they are communicant members. This is a simple answer.

My answer to the second part of the question is this: Christians are required by God to make this payment because they are members of God's royal priesthood (1 Pet 2:9), and as lower priests, they owe a tithe to the high priest, Jesus Christ. He collects this exclusively by way of payments made to the local institutional church. This is a simple answer, but it is not intuitive. Therefore, I wrote a book, *The Covenantal Tithe*,[2] and my chapter in this volume.

I argue that the first example of the God-mandated tithe in history was Abram's payment to Melchizedek (Gen 14:17–20). As the priest of the Most High God (v. 18), Melchizedek served a communion meal of bread and wine to Abram (v. 18), and then he blessed Abram (v. 19). In this covenantal-judicial act, he spoke as God's intermediary to Abram, as a priest must. Then he blessed the Most High God, who delivered Abram's enemies into his hand (v. 20). In this covenantal-judicial act, he spoke as Abram's intermediary to God, as a priest must. This was the first tithe, because this was the first time that a lower priest of the Most High God increased his net wealth within the ecclesiastical jurisdiction of a higher priest of the Most High God.

This argument would be speculative, though exegetically possible, if the only evidence we had were Genesis 1–14. But we have other evidence. The most important evidence is Hebrews 7. Hebrews 7 is by far the most important passage in the Bible relating to the priest-

---

1. G. North, *Dominion and Common Grace* (Tyler, TX: Institute for Christian Economics, 1987); see http://bit.ly/DomCom.
2. Published by GaryNorth.com, Inc. Found at http://www.deliverancefromdebt.com/CovenantalTithe.pdf

hood. It presents Jesus Christ as the high priest of God. His priest-hood is after the order of Melchizedek (v. 17). Jesus was from the tribe of Judah, which was not the priestly tribe (v. 14). Hebrews 7 makes the point that Melchizedek's priesthood was superior to the Levitical priesthood, because Abram tithed to Melchizedek (vv. 4–10). This was covenantal subordination: point two of the biblical covenant model.[3] Abram represented Levi, for he was superior to Levi, as the patriarch. The point is, *Abram represented Levi as a priest*. As the founding pa-triarch (v. 4), he was a priest in God's only family of priests. Melchize-dek was not part of a family, for he was "without descent" (v. 3).

We come to the famous bottom line: *Christ changed the Mosaic priesthood*. This is the author's primary point. He then said, "For the priesthood being changed, there is made of necessity a change also of the law" (v. 12). Here, more than any other passage in the New Testa-ment, we should expect to find an announcement of a change in the law of the tithe if the tithe is no longer an aspect of the new covenant. We do not find it. We find only that the Levitical priesthood has been superseded. We must conclude that the Mosaic laws governing the priestly tithe are therefore annulled. Levi has been superseded by the new Melchizedek, Jesus Christ. There is now no tribal priesthood that is owed the tithe. There was under Moses (Numbers 18). Neverthe-less, there is also no announcement here that the principle of the Melchizedekan tithe has been annulled. What principle? This one: *A lower priest of the Most High God owes a tithe to the high priest of the Most High God*. The argument of Hebrews 7 rests on the legiti-macy of the payment of such a tithe. This is therefore the essence of our obligation to Christ. This payment is exclusively a priestly obliga-tion. It always was.

Hemphill and Eklund invoke Cain's payment as an example of tithing—tithing with a bad conscience. This is a misunderstanding of Cain's act. He brought an offering, but God rejected it. Why? Because it was an offering for sin. The Bible announces: "And almost all things are by the law purged with blood; and without shedding of blood is no remission" (Heb 9:22). Cain offered an agricultural sacrifice. Abel of-fered an animal sacrifice. Abel's sacrifice alone was acceptable. If this had been a tithe, Cain's payment would have been acceptable. There was no tithe to pay, because both men were priests. Both offered sac-rifices. They were not under a higher priest.

---

3. R. R. Sutton, *That You May Prosper: Dominion by Covenant*, 2nd ed. (Tyler, TX: Institute for Christian Economics 1992), chap. 2; see http://bit.ly/SutCov.

Hemphill and Eklund also discuss Abram's payment to Melchizedek. They discuss the issue of the Levitical priesthood as subordinate to Melchizedek's priesthood. They discuss Jesus as High Priest. But they do not follow the logic of the text in Hebrews 7. They do not discuss Abram as a household priest paying to a superior priest. Yet this was the essence of the Levitical priesthood's legal claim on the tithes of the other tribes' net output of rural land, which Levites could not own. The kingdom of priests owed tithes to the designated tribe of higher priests, who in turn owed tithes to the temple priests, who were members of this tribe. *This was a system of priestly hierarchy.* Hemphill and Eklund write, "If Abram tithed to Melchizedek, would it not follow that the Christian would offer tithes to the great high priest who is greater than Melchizedek?" The answer is categorically *yes.* But on what judicial basis? They do not pursue this. My answer: because Christians are members of God's royal priesthood. There is still a hierarchy of priests, not in the sense of men who offer blood sacrifices, which Jesus Christ ended with His sacrifice, but in the sense of Melchizedek, who gave bread and wine to Abram, and who then blessed him in the name of God, and blessed God in the name of Abram. I think this is the Bible's answer to the question: "On what judicial basis does God impose on His redeemed saints the obligation of tithing?" What do you think?

Contrary to Hemphill and Eklund, the tithe is not about giving. The tithe is about lower priests making a legally obligatory payment to higher priests, who serve as God-ordained guardians of the ecclesiastically mandatory sacraments. It is about the support of the institutional church.

Hemphill and Eklund go out of their way to denounce what they call the language of legalism and obligation. That means me. Think of my chapter and responses as a room. To enter this room, you must pass through a door. On the front of the door, there is a sign: Tithing Is a Legal Obligation. On the other side of the door is another sign: Exit Here, but Only After You Have Paid Your Tithe.

CHAPTER 5

Response to Ken Hemphill and Bobby Eklund

Reggie Kidd

I know a number of individuals who testify to the benefits of operating with a formula like the one Hemphill and Eklund advance: take the tithe "as a normative starting point from which believers can move to Spirit-empowered or grace giving." In practice, I have found my own life journey to take a shape similar to the position they stake out. And I know a number of pastors who find it tremendously helpful to teach such a pattern: (1) pastors find it is simple for believers to grasp: if you are below the tithe, aim for it; if you are at or above it, seek the grace to move beyond where you are; and (b) pastors understand that it is likely that fewer churches would be in such dire straits if more believers gave at least a tenth of their income to their church.

But I find I'm not sounding a great "Huzzah!" Why is that?

One reason is that there's a lot of shaming language in this chapter. It is possible for the rhetoric of promoting grace and battling legalism to mask precisely the opposite. Such is my response to sentences like: "Why should anyone think that living under grace should grant us permission to do less than man was required to do under the Mosaic law?" Frequently, Hemphill and Eklund remind us of the need for giving to come from the heart, and that those hearts should be enlivened by the saving grace of God. But then they make the (unsubstantiated) claim that most of the people who argue that tithing is legalism are merely offering "an excuse for why they gave less than a tithe," thus doing "a disgrace to grace." For all the language of grace, there's not a lot given here. Despite a lot of carrot phrases in this chapter, there's more stick in actuality.

I do believe, with Hemphill, Eklund, and North, and against Croteau, that the shape of redemption means the principle of tithing carries over into the new covenant era. I believe, with Croteau and against Hemphill, Eklund, and North, that the casuistry of the tithe does not. I believe that Hemphill and Eklund in particular stretch the biblical evidence to make it look as if a self-evident pattern is in play from the beginning. They imagine God teaching Adam about stewardship and then Cain and Abel learning about it from their parents. They are entirely too confident that Abram's example establishes that "the concept of giving a portion back to God as an offering of gratitude is understood and defined as 10 percent."

It is to their credit that Hemphill and Eklund see Jesus' fulfilling of the Law and Prophets to be a matter of intensifying and internalizing God's commandments rather than of weakening them. It is heartening, moreover, to see them recognize that it will be the coming of the Holy Spirit (as anticipated in Ezek 36:26) that would enable the sort of obedience that Jesus had in mind.

I would have preferred that Hemphill and Eklund not drop the narrative strand of the work of the Holy Spirit in energizing Jesus' earthly ministry and then in continuing His heavenly ministry post-Pentecost. I would have liked to see them acknowledge the utter grace of anyone's response to the gift of God's grace in Jesus Christ—and along with that the sheer wonder and joy of forgiveness and the mystery of finding a Father's delight in the tiniest baby steps of Spirit-enabled obedience. As it is, they talk of tithing as mere duty, the minimum that Christians must do, and then reserve the language of "grace" and Spirit-enablement for what believers give after they have tithed. To the contrary, giving is about Spirit-enablement from beginning to end. If our giving doesn't end with the tithe, as Hemphill and Eklund maintain, God's grace doesn't begin there either.

PART II

CHAPTER 6

The Post-Tithing View
GIVING IN THE NEW COVENANT

David A. Croteau

Introduction

The requirement of the tithe as the standard for Christian giving is the assumed position for most of evangelical Christianity in America. The debate on this topic can get quite heated, and logical arguments are sometimes avoided in lieu of personal attacks. For example, one book advocating tithing raised some great theological and hermeneutical questions. But when one looked for the answers to these issues, the questions were evaded and the author proceeded to assume that those who raised those points wanted to avoid giving sacrificially. He never defended his stance biblically!

Rather than succumb to *ad hominem* arguments, this essay provides an analysis of the major passages of Scripture, both Old and New Testament, that shed light on the applicability of the tithe for Christians. Finally I address the fulfillment of the tithe, which is followed by the post-tithing view of giving.[1]

---

1. For further explanation and support for all of the following interpretations, details, and background information, see D. A. Croteau, *You Mean I Don't Have to Tithe?*

What Does Scripture Say?

One of the main problems in current discussions on tithing is a lack of knowledge about the description of the tithe in the Old Testament. Understanding the specific laws on the tithe reveals the tithe's relationship to both the two explicit narratives that reference the tithe before the Mosaic law (i.e., Abram and Jacob) and the context for the three passages in the New Testament that mention the tithe.

Tithing Before the Mosaic Law

The first passage that refers to the tithe before the Mosaic law is Gen 14:18–20. Many have read this passage and wondered who Melchizedek was. Concrete answers remain a mystery. We do know that he was a priest and the king of Salem, but besides that, not much information is available. Another issue is, Who gave a tithe to whom? While this text remains somewhat ambiguous, Heb 7:1–2 is abundantly clear that Abram gave a tenth to Melchizedek. A third issue is the source of Abram's gift. Did he give a tithe from the spoils of war or from his own possessions? Genesis 14:20 says he gave a tenth "of everything." Here is where context becomes important. Genesis 14:21–24 is unambiguous in saying that Abram gave the tithe from the spoils of war. These verses contain the oath he had sworn, that he would not keep any of the spoils of war. In fact, he gave 10 percent to Melchizedek and the rest he gave away, *all as part of a vow*. Technically, Abram did not give just 10 percent; he gave 100 percent. Abram's vow was part of a vow for making war in the ancient Near East; it was common to offer something to a god before going to war to try to get the deity to aid in victory. These are called spoils of war vows. So the context of the war and the following conversation with the king of Sodom make the spoils a more compelling source for the tithe. Finally, Heb 7:4 says that Abram gave Melchizedek a tenth "of the plunder" (ἀκροθίνιον; *akrothinion*). This text unambiguously says the plunder was the source of the tithe.

One of the most perplexing issues is determining why Abram gave 10 percent. While some try to argue from silence that God must have commanded the tithe previously, a surer ground can be found in background information: tithing was very prevalent in surrounding

---

A Deconstruction of Tithing and a Reconstruction of Post-Tithe Giving, McMaster Theological Studies (Eugene, OR: Pickwick, 2010).

cultures. The specifics of all the different cultures[2] and rules they had about tithing cannot be discussed here. But one key to understanding how these data impact one's interpretation of Genesis 14 is the differences the practices in these cultures had from each other. First, they differed in the amount given. One might wonder how the amounts could differ if it was a tithe (10 percent). The laws in these cultures required a single tithe or a double tithe depending on the product and the circumstances of its cultivation. Second, the voluntary nature was different. Some cultures viewed the tithes as mandated and others as purely optional. Third, the time of the year varied for when the tithe was to be given. Various cultures required the tithe to be given at different times and seasons. Fourth, where the tithe was to be given was diverse. In certain cultures the tithe was given in the capital cities and in others at places of worship. Fifth, sometimes the common people (such as those who did not own land) did not have to pay tithes. For example, citizens in Arabia were required to pay tithes on frankincense they harvested. However, if the ground was not watered by their own irrigation system but by rain (i.e., Baal), then 20 percent was due. Here is the key principle: the diversity of the practices of these cultures was greater than the consistency. This information (and more to follow) argues against Abram's tithe originating from God; instead, Abram borrowed the practice of tithing from the surrounding cultures

To summarize: (1) Abram's giving of a tithe was directly connected with his vow to God that he would keep none of the spoils. (2) Abram's tithe was a borrowed practice from the surrounding cultures. (3) There is no evidence that Abram was commanded to tithe. (4) There is no evidence that Abram consistently tithed.[3] (5) Abram gave voluntarily, and Genesis never says he gave a tithe from the increase of his possessions.

One more important issue is whether Abram observed a command to tithe that was consistent with tithing in the Mosaic law. The answer is, Absolutely not! According to Num 31:28–29, the Israelites were commanded to "set aside a tribute for the Lord from what belongs to the fighting men who went out to war: one out of every 500

---

2. The following ancient cultures practiced some form of tithing: Roman, Greek, Carthaginian, Cretan, Sicilian, Phoenician, Chinese, Babylonian, Akkadian, Egyptian, Assyrian, Canaanite, Ugaritic, Morrocan, Persian, Lydian, Syrian, Sumerian, and South Arabian.

3. The circumstances that precipitated the giving of this tithe were not common. This passage is not describing Abram's everyday practice.

humans, cattle, donkeys, sheep, and goats" and to give it to the priest as an offering to God. Therefore, the stipulated amount required by the Mosaic law for spoils won in battle is *different* from what Abram actually offered Melchizedek in Genesis 14.

The second passage that directly mentions tithing before the Mosaic law was given is Gen 28:13–22. This passage is problematic because it is difficult to determine how Genesis is portraying Jacob. Did Moses portray Jacob as someone offering reverential worship or as a faithless and conniving man? Before we answer that question, God's promises to Jacob and his response need to be examined.

God promised Jacob six things: (1) to give Jacob the land on which he rested, (2) that his descendants would be great in number, (3) that his descendants would bless the families of the earth, (4) that God would stay with Jacob, (5) that God would keep Jacob safe in his journeys, and (6) that God would bring him back to the land on which he rested. God reassured Jacob that these things would happen and that God would not leave him. Jacob had two responses: he was fearful, and he made a conditional vow.

In Gen 28:17 the Hebrew word (usually) translated "afraid" is יָרֵא; (*yare*), which can mean "reverential awe" or "scared." Which meaning is being used here? The next three occurrences of the Hebrew word all refer to Jacob as being "scared" or "afraid," not as one engaged in reverential worship (see 31:31; 32:7,11). Being fearful appears to be a characteristic of Jacob; reverential worship does not.

The second response was his conditional vow. After God had promised him the list given above, Jacob said that "if" God did what Jacob asked, "then" Jacob would respond in a positive way. The *conditions* Jacob placed on God are as follows: (1) if God would stay with Jacob, (2) if God would keep him safe on his current journey, (3) if God would provide him with food and clothes, and (4) if he returned home safely (Gen 28:20–22). God had already promised to fulfill three of these four conditions, and the fulfillment of the fourth seems to be assumed. The "then" part of Jacob's vow indicates that (1) Yahweh would be his God, (2) the pillar would be God's house, and (3) Jacob would give a tenth (i.e., a tithe) of all that God gave him.

In interpreting Old Testament narratives, it is important to remember that the people are not always portrayed in a positive light. For example, David and Solomon had many wives. This should not be read as an encouragement for polygamy. When Abram heeded his wife's words and slept with Hagar, that should also not be understood as a positive portrayal of Abram. And this account does not present Jacob positively. The biblical interpretation principle holds true here: description does not equal prescription.

Jacob's response in Gen 28:22 could be understood as Jacob's attempt to bribe God. He seems to have been a specialist in the area of negotiation, as Gen 25:29–34; 29:18 demonstrate. Also, Jacob does not appear to be converted *yet* in Genesis 28. His lack of conversion can be discerned because: (1) his reaction to God's presence was terror or fear, not awe; (2) he proclaimed himself ignorant of God's presence (Gen 28:16); (3) the conditions he placed on God speak against Jacob having been converted; and (4) Jacob's conversion appears to have taken place when he wrestled with God (Gen 32:24–30), not in his dream (Gen 28:10–15).

There is one final reason to view Jacob negatively in Genesis 28—the narrative in Genesis 32. In the latter passage, Jacob returned to the land of his fathers Abram and Isaac. As he journeyed home, he heard that Esau was coming out to meet him. Even though God had promised to return him safely home, Jacob reacted in fear. He split up his entourage in order to keep some safe in case Esau attacked. More importantly, rather than trusting God to protect him, Jacob sent gifts to bribe Esau—gifts intended to placate Esau's anger against Jacob. These actions demonstrate that Jacob still did not trust God's promises in Genesis 28.

One final problem for tithing advocates needs to be pointed out. In Gen 28:21–22 Jacob said that he would give a tenth of all that God gave him if he returned safely to his father's house. Therefore, Jacob was not going to give this tenth until the conditions were met. Genesis 31:38 says, "I've been with you these 20 years. Your ewes and female goats have not miscarried, and I have not eaten the rams from your flock" (cf. v. 41). Nowhere does it say that Jacob tithed during the interim. In fact, Scripture is clear that God (materially) blessed him despite his lack of paying tithes during these 20 years. So in the context, Jacob's vow that he would "give to You a tenth of all that You give me" (Gen 28:22) is best understood as Jacob's conditional promise of a *one-time gift* to God upon his safe return home; it was *not* a promise of perpetual action.

Two passages have been analyzed to understand tithing before the Mosaic law. Abram tithed off the spoils of war, not his own possessions. His tithe was based on a previous vow, and the idea for him to tithe probably originated from the surrounding cultures. Jacob also promised to tithe based on a vow. His tithe may be connected to an attempt to bribe God in a response of fear, not faith. Finally, Jacob did not tithe for at least 20 years, and the text never describes him as giving the tithe—even after he returned home. This time period contains no command for anyone to tithe and no *real* description of anyone giving 10 percent of the increase.

Tithing in the Mosaic Law

The Mosaic law contains three major passages related to tithing (Lev 27:30–33; Num 18:20–28; Deut 14:22–29). Each one aids in understanding how the tithe functioned in ancient Judaism. This section probably contains the most important information for understanding the applicability of the tithe to Christians. The key to determining how many separate tithes have existed in the Mosaic law is in the details of these passages.

Leviticus 27 contains a general introduction to tithing. The purpose of this passage is to assimilate tithing practices from the surrounding cultures into Judaism. Although the discussion on tithing begins in v. 30, it is important to begin reading the chapter at v. 1. The reason is that a shift takes place at v. 26 away from what can be vowed (the subject of the previous verses) to what is not liable to vows. Three categories are then explained that are not liable to vows: the firstlings of animals, any devoted thing, and the tithe of the land. Therefore, tithes in the Mosaic law are distinct from vows.

Three categories are also explained as being liable to tithes: seed of the land, fruit of the tree, and every tenth animal of the herd or flock. All three of these categories are connected to the Holy Land (i.e., Israel). When an Old Testament law is connected to the land, this fact has implications for its applicability for Christians. The land was a shadow (cf. Col 2:16–17) and does not *directly* apply to Christians. Furthermore, only items falling within these categories are liable to tithes; nothing else is.

Some have protested at this point that money is not mentioned because Israel was an agricultural society. While it is entirely true that Israel was an agricultural society, this does not mean that they did not have money or did not deal in money. In Genesis alone, money is referenced 29 times.[4] The typical Hebrew word used in these verses is *keseph* ("silver" or "money"). Originally a shekel was not a unit of coinage, but rather a measure of weight. In fact, *shekel* is the Hebrew

---

4. See Gen 17:12,13,23,27; 31:15; 33:19; 42:25,27,28,35 (2x); 43:12 (2x),15,18,21 (2x), 22 (2x),23; 44:1,2,8; 47:14 (2x), 15 (2x),16,18. The HCSB, ESV, and NASB typically read "money," while the NIV sometimes says "silver."

word for weight.[5] Even though the minting of coins did not begin until the late seventh century BC, money was available and used in trade long before this. The references to money in Genesis demonstrate this. Before the Mosaic law mentions tithing, it refers to money about 38 times. Leviticus 25–27 makes up the last section of the book. This section of Leviticus contains an interesting reference to money (or silver): "You are not to lend him your silver with interest or sell him your food for profit" (25:37). The last section of the book contains a reference to an ancient banking system rule *before* a reference to tithing is made. Therefore, Israel used money before the giving of the Mosaic law. This means that it is significant that money was never liable to tithes. Simply stating that Israel was an agricultural society does not provide a complete explanation for the situation.

One of the vexing problems of Leviticus 27 is that it never says who the recipients of the tithes were; it simply says they belong to Yahweh. This is because Leviticus is not directly compatible with Numbers 18 or Deuteronomy 14; it is simply an introduction to tithing in the Mosaic law. The other passages are intended to clarify the tithe for Israel. However, the tithe of animals is not mentioned in the other passages. This animal/cattle tithe is very difficult, but 2 Chron 31:5 seems to indicate that it was another tithe from the Israelites to the priests.

While Leviticus 27 contains a general introduction of the tithe, Num 18:20–24 explains the details of the Levitical tithe. In the Mosaic law, the Levites stood between Israel and God while offering daily sacrifices for sin. Numbers 18:20–24 declares that the Levites would receive the entire tithe for their services of bearing this burden and for not getting an inheritance in the land. This is an important aspect of the tithe as it relates to the Levites and priests: they did not receive it as a *wage* but as an *inheritance*. This offering was compulsory and was used for the livelihood of the Levites. Numbers 18:25–30 discusses the priestly tithe, but v. 31 turns back to the Levites and instructs them that they may eat the tithes anywhere.

The priestly tithe (Num 18:25–28) was a sub-tithe of the Levitical tithe: the Levites received the tithes from the Israelites and then gave tithes to the priests. There were basically two instructions for the priestly tithe. First, the amount was prescribed as one-tenth of all the Levites received as gifts. Second, the quality of the offering was to be the best of what they had received.

---

5. Archaeological evidence indicates that a shekel of silver (from limestone weights) was around 11.4 grams.

Deuteronomy 12:17–19 introduces the festival tithe. This is the second tithe required of the Israelites, and it is more fully explained later (14:22–27; see 26:10–16). Deuteronomy 12 contains several important details. (1) This tithe was not to be eaten within their own gates. (2) This tithe was to be eaten in the place where God would choose; eventually this would be Jerusalem. (3) The Israelites were commanded not to forget the Levite; Deuteronomy 14 provides additional details. (4) The givers of the tithe were actually the recipients; they were to eat it themselves and share with the Levites. This means that the ownership of the tithe remains with the giver of the tithe. (5) The purpose for this tithe was "so that you will always learn to fear the Lord your God" (Deut 14:23). The differences between the Levitical tithe and the festival tithe are interesting:

Table 1. The Levitical Tithe Compared with the Festival Tithe

	Levitical Tithe	Festival Tithe
Location	Eat anywhere	Jerusalem
Recipients	Levites	All of Israel
Owner	Levites	Original owner
Purpose	Replace land inheritance	Teach fear of the Lord

Some have claimed that it was unlikely that the festival tithe was instituted without introduction or clarification. How would the Israelites have understood the relationship between the two tithes? In response, both Deut 12:19 and 14:27 exhort the Israelites not to neglect the Levites. These verses are a reference to the Levitical tithe since that is the tithe that provided for the Levites and guaranteed they would not be neglected. Thus these verses (Deut 12:19; 14:27) contain references to the Levitical tithe, a clarification to the Israelites that even though another tithe (the festival tithe) was being instituted, they are still responsible for the Levitical tithe.

Finally, Deut 14:28–29 describes the charity tithe. This third tithe can be distinguished from the previous two in two ways. First, it was offered every third year while the other tithes were offered yearly. Second, it was intended for the Levite, foreigner, orphan, and widow. The Levitical tithe was for the Levites and the festival tithe was for all of Israel.[6]

---

6. Further, the Hebrew of Deut 14:27 marks the end of a paragraph, thus separating vv. 27 and 28.

Table 2. The Distinction of the Charity Tithe

Previous Tithes	Charity Tithe
Given every year or during feasts	Given every third year
Levitical Tithe	Charity Tithe
Mostly for the Levites' sustenance	Not for the Levites only; for foreigners, orphans, and widows

Was there really *another* tithe burdening the Israelites? Yes, the charity tithe was a third tithe required every third year. If, as some claim, the charity tithe *replaced* the Levitical tithe every third year, then how were the Levites sustained that year? Also, if the charity tithe replaced the festival tithe every third year, did the Israelites just ignore the prescribed feasts in those years? Theories that claim the charity tithe replaced the Levitical or festival tithe create more problems than they solve. Finally, the mention of "the year of the tenth" in Deut 26:12 appears to corroborate this conclusion.

How much did the Israelites give in tithes every year? The answer to this question is impossible to determine. For example, since the tithe demanded that they give every tenth animal that passed under the rod, how many animals did they give if 17 passed under the rod? Only one! Therefore an exact calculation is impossible. However, from the produce of the land they were supposed to average 20 percent yearly in tithes (not including other offerings and mandated contributions).

Table 3. Israelite Tithes from Produce by Year in a Seven-Year Cycle

Year	Tithes Given	Total Percentage	Average at this point
1	Levitical; Festival	20%	20%
2	Levitical; Festival	20%	20%
3	Levitical; Festival; Charity	30%	23 1/3%
4	Levitical; Festival	20%	22.5%
5	Levitical; Festival	20%	22%
6	Levitical; Festival; Charity	30%	23 1/3%
7	Sabbatical Year	0%	20%
	Seven-Year Average	20%	

Different scholars have different calculations. Regardless of the total, the tithe laws are clearly more complicated than a mere

10 percent; also, the Israelites were required to give more than 10 percent from the land. Nowhere is there a command to tithe from income.

Historically speaking, Judaism around the time of Christ understood the Old Testament as *prescribing* multiple tithes. Three sources attest to this. The apocryphal book of Tobit, while not authoritative for Christian doctrine or practice, remains a valid source for history. Tobit 1:6–8 describes Tobit as paying three distinct tithes. Josephus, the Jewish historian who wrote in the late first century, explained that Jews were supposed to tithe three times in years three and six of the seven-year cycle.[7] The Mishnah, a collection of rabbinic debates spanning from before the time of Christ until about AD 200, disagrees with both Tobit and Josephus. In the section on tithes, the Mishnah appears to say that the Mosaic law describes three distinct tithes, but only two were paid in any given year. While the Mishnah differs from both Tobit and Josephus, all three sources hold to multiple tithes. The view taken here is that there are three basic tithes, but a total of five. They are all distinct from one another: Levitical tithe, festival tithe, charity tithe, animal/cattle tithe, and priestly tithe (the sub-tithe of the Levitical tithe).[8]

Though some may dispute whether Judaism around the time of Christ was correct in its understanding of the Old Testament prescriptions regarding tithing, it should be noted that this understanding is never challenged in the New Testament. If the New Testament writers considered tithing as consistent with the new covenant era, then their understanding (most likely) would have been that of two or three tithes. No document has been located that suggests that first-century Judaism held to a single tithe.

Tithes were given from the increase of *the land*. The Mosaic law never directed the Israelites to give of their increase; it specified particular products that were liable to tithe laws, and these products were always connected to the land. There was a very strong connection of products liable to tithes to the land; originally, only products produced from Israel were included. In the New Testament period, artisans, fishermen, and tradesmen did not pay tithes on their income, and Jews outside Israel (those in the Diaspora) did not pay tithes on anything.[9] Furthermore, priests and the poor (who owned no land or animals) were exempt from tithes.

---

7. Josephus, *Antiquities*, 4.8.22.
8. If one includes the *totally distinct* tithe in Amos, then the total comes to six.
9. F. C. Grant, *The Economic Background of the Gospels* (London: Oxford, 1926), 95n.1.

A final issue is whether the tithe in the Mosaic law was a tax. A tax is a required contribution for the support of government; a religious contribution is a voluntary offering to support religion. Therefore, the tithe is really part tax and part religious contribution since it contains aspects of both.

Comparing Pre-Mosaic Law Tithing to Mosaic Law Tithing

Abram's tithe and the Mosaic law tithes are described in very different terms (see Table 4 below). Abram's tithe was directly connected to a vow; Leviticus 27 says that tithing and vows were to be distinct. There was a specific situation that precipitated Abram's tithe, which leads to the conclusion that it was an occasional tithe. The Mosaic law demands systematic tithing. Abram gave his tithe to Melchizedek (a priest), while the Mosaic law tithes were (mostly) for the Levites. Abram gave voluntarily and not from his own possessions; the Mosaic law tithe was compulsory and was on the increase of possessions connected to the land. Abram gave 10 percent to Melchizedek (though his gift was really 100 percent) and the Mosaic law tithe averages about 20 percent. Finally, there is no evidence that Abram was obeying some revelation from God prior to the Mosaic law. Numbers 31:27–29 says that the Israelites were to take one five-hundredths (0.2 percent) of the spoils of war and give it to the priest as an offering to Yahweh.[10] Therefore, the stipulated amount required by the Mosaic law for spoils won in battle is significantly less than what Abram offered Melchizedek in Genesis 14.

Table 4. The Differences between Abram's Tithe and the Mosaic Law Tithe

Abram	Mosaic law
connected to a vow	not subject to vows
occasional	systematic
for Melchizedek (a priest)	(mostly) for the Levites
voluntary	compulsory
not of his possessions	tithe on increase of possessions
10 percent	averages 20 percent
taken from spoils of war	taken from produce of the land

10. Numbers 31 likely does not prescribe a tenth because spoils of war are not connected to the land.

Jacob's tithe is also described in different terms than the Mosaic law tithes (see Table 5 below). As with Abram, Jacob's tithe was connected to a vow while tithes in the Mosaic law are not connected to vows. Jacob's tithe was apparently an occasional tithe; the Mosaic law tithes are supposed to be systematic. Jacob's terminology seems to point to a tithe on general increase, but in the Mosaic law only specific products are liable to tithes. Jacob's tithe was voluntary; the Mosaic law tithes are compulsory. While Jacob vowed to give 10 percent, the Mosaic law tithes average about 20 percent per year. Finally, there is no record that Jacob actually gave this tithe to God. The lack of a description of Jacob fulfilling his vow is puzzling.[11] Jacob even returned to Bethel, made an altar, and poured a drink offering and oil on it, but there is no reference to his fulfilling his vow to tithe (see Genesis 35).

Table 5. Jacob's Tithe and the Mosaic Law Tithe Compared

Jacob	Mosaic law
connected to a vow	not subject to vows
occasional	Systematic
on general increase?	specific products liable
voluntary	compulsory
10 percent	averages 20 percent

Evidence is lacking that either Abram or Jacob were obeying the Mosaic law of tithing as a direct revelation from God. They were more likely functioning according to the tithing paradigm from their surrounding cultures. Even if Abram and Jacob both gave one-tenth to God, the actual law of tithing as contained in the Mosaic law was *more* than one-tenth. Regardless of the exact percentage prescribed in the Mosaic law, Abram and Jacob were not obeying the Mosaic tithing laws.

Finally, it is unclear to whom Jacob would have given his tithe. While this is not (overly) problematic for the Abram narrative (see Heb 7:1–10), it is for Jacob's since there is no indication of a possible recipient of the tithe; only speculation can answer that question. The texts that discuss tithing prior to the Mosaic law do not portray tith-

---

11. Jews in the second century BC seemed to be concerned with this issue as it was addressed in *Jubilees* 32, a pseudepigraphal work written around 150 BC. That chapter in Jubilees says that Levi was at Bethel when he had a dream that he was made a priest. Therefore, when Jacob woke from his sleep, he was able to tithe to his son Levi.

ing as a systematic and continual practice, but as an occasional, even exceptional, form of giving.

The evidence from the period prior to the Mosaic law suggests that no system of tithing was in place. Scripture records no command to tithe, and thus the evidence that any systematic tithing existed prior to the giving of the law is scarce. What is more, all giving discussed prior to the Mosaic law was voluntary. In fact, many passages throughout the Old Testament discuss voluntary giving. In conclusion, the diversity between the accounts of Abram and Jacob versus the Mosaic law tithe is greater than the similarities.

Malachi 3

By answering the following six questions, a proper understanding of Malachi 3 can be reached and applied to the issue of tithing. (1) What was the purpose of Malachi 3 in the context of Malachi? (2) To what do "offerings" refer? (3) To what does the "storehouse" refer? (4) Is the "testing" universal? (5) What is the promised reward? (6) Are Christians robbing God if they fail to tithe?

The main purpose of Malachi 3 is a call to repentance and a reminder of God's faithfulness, which Malachi illustrated with the specific issue of tithes and offerings. In spite of the people's sins, God loved them and patiently waited for them to return to Him. Keeping this context in mind can help restrain interpreters from misapplying this text.

One fact that may explain why this passage is frequently misapplied is that not many interpretations of this text deal with the question of how to define the term "offerings." Verhoef commented that the offering "was not taken from the cereal offering, or from the sin offerings, these being most sacred, but from the peace offerings and other sacred gifts, in the form of the breast of the wave offering, the thigh of the ram of ordination (Exod 29:27,28; etc.), cakes of leavened bread, etc. (Lev 7:14). It was one of the chief sources of the priests' livelihood."[12] Like tithes, these were *compulsory* contributions required by the Mosaic law for the temple staff. In other words, "offerings" do not refer to tipping God, and they were not optional.

The "storehouse" does not refer to local churches. It was an actual building used by the Levites to store all they received, like grains and livestock. The Levites would either use or sell these items as they

---

12. P. Verhoef, *The Books of Haggai and Malachi*, NICOT (Grand Rapids: Eerdmans, 1987), 305.

saw need. This storehouse was not part of the Mosaic law but was added for storage purposes. Its purpose and construction are mentioned in 2 Chron 31:10–12:

> Azariah, the chief priest of the household of Zadok, answered him, "Since they began bringing the offering to the LORD's temple, we eat and are satisfied and there is plenty left over because the LORD has blessed His people; this abundance is what is left over." Hezekiah told them to prepare chambers in the LORD's temple, and they prepared them. The offering, the tenth, and the dedicated things were brought faithfully. Conaniah the Levite was the officer in charge of them, and his brother Shimei was second.

It is unusual (though not unheard of) in the Old Testament for man to test God. There is great danger in testing God when our hearts are not right (see Mal 3:15) or when doing so on one's own initiative. However, Malachi did not state this testing in universal terms but limited it to the current situation by the phrase "test Me in this" in the middle of v. 10. The expression "in this" most likely limits this test to the current situation.

The promised reward for tithing is threefold: (1) the windows of heaven would be opened, (2) God would prevent the devourer, and (3) the vines would bear fruit. An examination of each of these rewards is helpful for an understanding of this passage. The first promise refers to *rain*. The combination of the Hebrew word *arubbah* and *shamayim* as a phrase occurs elsewhere (see Gen 7:11; 8:2; 2 Kgs 7:2,19) and *always* refers to rain. This is an appropriate promise to make in Mal 3:10 since Israel depended heavily on agriculture for food and commerce. Thus, "rain" was the promise, and nothing else. The second promise refers to keeping locusts from destroying Israel's crops. The third promise states that Israel's vines would bear fruit, a reference to abundant crops. God promised to provide rain, stop the locusts, and give them abundant crops. All three promises are directly related to an agricultural society and are deeply connected to Israel's inheritance of the land. In summarizing the issue of the rewards, Smith noted: "It may be that this passage in Malachi should be understood as a one-time, special act on God's part to renew the fires of faith in an age of skepticism and indifference. If so, then this is not an open-ended promise to bless in a material way anyone and everyone who tithes his possessions."[13]

Some have claimed that Christians are robbing God if they fail to tithe. Paul Fink, in the *Liberty Bible Commentary*, provides an excellent response to this. He says, "Each believer is independently accountable to God for the allotment of the money God entrusts to him. . . . The principle holds true today. God blesses His children not because they give 10 percent (or more), but because in their cheerful giving keeping with the measure that God has blessed, they are giving testimony of their obedience, subjection to, and dependence upon God."[14]

Parallels to Tithing in the Old Testament

Some have argued by analogy to other laws that tithing still directly applies. Several proposals have surfaced in the search for an appropriate parallel to the law of tithing in the Old Testament: adultery, murder, circumcision, and Sabbath. A good parallel would be a law that was obeyed before the giving of the Mosaic law, incorporated into the Mosaic law, and then discussed in the New Testament. Adultery and murder both seem to fit this description, but they are explicitly prohibited in the New Testament and, as shown below, no explicit command to tithe occurs in the New Testament. The Sabbath has been the center of controversy between many God-honoring Christians; it would take an entire monograph to cover this issue. Circumcision would be a fairly good parallel except that it is explicitly abrogated in the New Testament and tithing is not.[15] But there is a good parallel—the levirate law.

The levirate law can be seen before the Mosaic law (Gen 38:6–26), it is incorporated into the Mosaic law (Deut 25:5–10; cf. Ruth 4), and it is discussed in the New Testament (see Matt 22:23–32; Mark 12:18–27; Luke 20:27–38). Using the logic of those who advocate tithing, an argument could be made for the continuing validity of the levirate law.

The levirate law requires that when brothers live together and one of them dies without an heir, one of the surviving brothers takes

---

13. R. L. Smith, *Micah–Malachi*, WBC (Waco: Word, 1984), 32: 334.

14. P. Fink, "Malachi," in *Liberty Bible Commentary: Old Testament*, ed. J. Falwell (Lynchburg, VA: The Old-Time Gospel Hour, 1982), 1860.

15. Unless one interprets Heb 7:12 like early Baptists in England did. See B. R. White, *Association Records of the Particular Baptists of England, Wales and Ireland to 1660*, 3 vols. (London: Baptist Historical Society, 1974), 1:44–45,48,151; 3:153–57.

his widow as his wife, and the firstborn of this new marriage is regarded by law as the son of the deceased. The purpose of this law is so that the line of the deceased brother does not end; this was an important practice for Israel.

Regarding Tamar's marriages to the sons of Judah (see Gen 38:6–10), one should note that the law is introduced without justification or reasoning; it was not a new concept or a new law. It seems fairly clear that Onan understood the repercussions of his father's command: the child would not legally be his. Furthermore, the law appears to be binding since v. 8 refers to fulfilling or performing the *duty* of the levir. Significantly, when Judah was caught, he referred to Tamar (who pretended to be a prostitute and slept with Judah) as more righteous than he was (v. 26). This practice, like tithing, was widespread and the origin is unknown. It was practiced by the Assyrians, Hindus (in India), some Brazilians, Ugaritans, Moabites, Elamites, Hittites, New Caledonians, Mongols, Afghans, Abyssinians, and some later Native Americans.[16] However, rather than tracing this command back to God, every scholar consulted traced it back to other sources for various reasons.

Deuteronomy 25:5–10 is different from Genesis 38. Three modifications of the practice should be noted. First, the duty of the levir was limited to a blood brother living close to the deceased brother. Second, the duty was not binding, for the (humiliating) ceremony of *halizah* could release the prospective levir from fulfilling the obligation. Third, the levir married the widow. This is how the widespread practice was incorporated into the Mosaic law. That this was practiced in Judaism can be seen because of the narrative in Ruth 4 and the references to it in Judaism shortly following the time of Christ.[17]

Furthermore, the Sadducees asked Jesus a question concerning levirate marriage and the resurrection (Matt 22:23–32; Mark 12:18–27; Luke 20:27–38). This question gave Jesus every opportunity to abrogate or abolish the levirate law. However, Jesus was much less concerned about the continuation or abrogation of this law than He

---

16. W. R. Smith, *Lectures on the Religion of the Semites*, new edition (London: Adam and Charles Black, 1914), 245–46; S. R. Driver, *A Critical and Exegetical Commentary on Deuteronomy*, ICC (New York: Scribner's, 1903), 169; D. W. Manor, "A Brief History of Levirate Marriage as It Relates to the Bible," *Restoration Quarterly* 27 (1984), 3:130–31; R. de Vaux, *Ancient Israel: Its Life and Institutions*, trans. J. McHugh (New York: McGraw-Hill, 1961), 38; O. J. Baab, "Marriage," in *The Interpreter's Dictionary of the Bible*, ed. G. A. Buttrick (New York: Abingdon, 1962), 3:282.

17. See the Mishnah (especially tractate *Yebamoth* ["Sisters-in-law"]).

was about the Sadducees' unbelief. Table 6 summarizes the similarities between the levirate law, the tithe laws, and circumcision.

Table 6. Similarities Between the Levirate Law, the Tithe Laws, and Circumcision

	levirate law	tithe laws	circumcision
Introduced without reasoning/ justification	X	X	
Practiced before the Mosaic law	X	X	X
Obligatory before the Mosaic law	X		X
Widespread; origin unknown	X	X	
Codified, with changes, into the Mosaic law	X	X	
Practiced outside the Pentateuch (in OT)	X	X	X
Received a tract in the Mishnah	X	X	
New Testament never explicitly abrogates	X	X	
Jesus discussed and never abrogated	X	X	X*

*See John 7:22–23. Circumcision was incorporated into the Mosaic law, but no significant changes were made (though see Deut 10:16; 30:6).

The study of these passages demonstrates two things. First, the existence of a practice prior to the giving of the Mosaic law as well as subsequent to it does not *necessarily* prove that it was meant to continue into the new covenant era. Second, the assertion is unfounded that, because tithing existed prior to the giving of the Mosaic law, it must continue to be practiced by God's people in later periods.

Tithing in the New Testament

A proper understanding and definition of the tithe in the Mosaic law is crucial background information for the practice in the New Testament. Now that the relevant texts have been analyzed, a biblical definition of "tithe" can be reached. Tithing is the act of giving one out of every ten items produced from the land (crops such as grain from the soil or fruit from the trees) or from the herd. It only applied when the Israelites lived in the Holy Land and never referred to earned income. While it is important to recognize two important categories on this issue, only one discussion can take place at this time: the three passages in the New Testament that directly reference the tithe (Matt 23:23 [cf. Luke 11:42]; Luke 18:9–14; Heb 7:1–10).[18] Two conclusions should be evident in the following analysis. (1) None of these passages have tithing as their primary subject. If a subject is mentioned in a passage, that occurrence does not mean it is the primary subject of the text; these two things are entirely different. The goal of interpreting these texts is to look for the author's intent. (2) None of these passages command tithing for Christians. Commanding tithing and mentioning tithing are *not* the same thing. Furthermore, commanding tithing for the Jews does not automatically command it for Christians.

In Matt 23:23, Jesus did not condemn the act of tithing, but He did consider tithing to be a less central aspect of the Mosaic law; it was still part of the Mosaic law—he did *not* abrogate it. But the appropriate question is, What is the main point of this verse? Jesus meant that justice, mercy, and faithfulness are required and basic responses to God (cf. Mic 6:8). Does that *alone* negate the tithing requirement? No, since Jesus also said, "These things should have been done without neglecting the others" (v. 23). Why does He say that? Tithing was prescribed in the Mosaic law; all Jews were commanded to give tithes. Jesus did not *prohibit* tithing, but He condemned the wrong *attitude* and *motive* of those who were tithing under the old covenant.

This verse should not be used to argue for the continuation of tithing based on the clear fact that Jesus' statement about tithing was for the scribes and Pharisees who were still under the old covenant. Significantly, in Matt 23:2–12 Jesus was talking to the crowds and His disciples, but in v. 13 Jesus' audience changed to the scribes and Pharisees. Jesus' command to Jews who were still functioning under the old covenant does not necessitate that the command applies to Christians. One example of this should suffice. The hermeneutical maxim that description in the Gospels does not equal prescription should be heeded. Matthew 8:1–4 provides a good example:

> When He came down from the mountain, large crowds followed Him. Right away a man with a serious skin disease came up and knelt before Him, saying, "Lord, if You are willing, You can make

---

18. The other issue, passages in the New Testament that some *say* refer to the tithe but do not explicitly reference it, is discussed in Croteau, *You Mean I Don't Have to Tithe?* 138–49. The passages discussed are Matt 22:15–22; 1 Cor 9:13–14; 16:1–4; 2 Cor 8:8; 9:7; Gal 6:6.

me clean." Reaching out His hand He touched him, saying, "I am willing; be made clean." Immediately his disease was healed. Then Jesus told him, "See that you don't tell anyone; but go, show yourself to the priest, and offer the gift that Moses prescribed, as a testimony to them."

Must Christians demonstrate their purity so they may enter a church on Sunday for worship? What about the offering? Is the gift prescribed by Moses in Leviticus 14 also required of Christians? The answer is unequivocally no. These commands were given to Jews functioning under the old covenant. The differences between the old covenant and new covenant cannot and must not be ignored. Therefore, those who advocate tithing based on Jesus' endorsement of it to the scribes and Pharisees are endorsing (at least) a 20 percent contribution, not 10 percent. Furthermore, if one uses Matt 23:23, then: (1) Christians must give at least 20 percent; (2) this includes items from a personal garden; and (3) to tithe correctly you would have to live in Israel. Whether or not one advocates tithing based on the New Testament, it must be based on other passages, but not Matt 23:23.

Luke 18:9–14 contains the parable of the tax collector and the Pharisee. Parables can be difficult texts to interpret if the reader does not understand the proper methodology for interpreting such texts. Therefore, as a reminder to correct methodology, there is one main point for every major character in a parable. This parable contains two main characters: a tax collector and a Pharisee. This parable is not about tithing or stewardship; neither of these topics is the main point. From the Pharisee the lesson is that the one who exalts himself will be humbled; from the tax collector the lesson is that the one who humbles himself will be exalted.[19] Tithing is not prohibited by this text, but it must be pointed out that Jesus never said that the one who was justified, the tax collector, had tithed. Therefore, it would be inappropriate and tenuous to attempt to draw any concrete conclusions concerning the continuation (or discontinuation) of tithing from this parable.

Hebrews 7:1–10 is a great text to sharpen the interpreter's use of three principles of sound biblical interpretation. First, an interpreter is always to seek the author's intent; he needs to attempt to lay aside his own agenda. Second, the primary meaning(s) needs to be the focus of interpretation; secondary (or tertiary) meanings can

---

19. C. L. Blomberg, *Interpreting the Parables* (Downers Grove: InterVarsity, 1990), 258.

be identified, but should not be the focus of the interpretation. Third, the interpreter must remember that only primary meanings build doctrine. If a text has an implication (a secondary meaning) that appears to support a certain doctrine, a text should be located that has as its primary meaning that doctrine. Then the secondary meaning can be used to validate the text that has that doctrine as its primary meaning.[20]

How does Heb 7:1–10 fit into the context of the argument of Hebrews and what is the argument of Hebrews? The author of Hebrews explained that Jesus' sacrifice is superior to the sacrifices of the old covenant, and therefore the Jews should not turn back to their former ways. The argument of Hebrews is as follows:[21] (1) Jesus is superior to the angels, even though he was temporarily made lower than them. (2) Jesus was temporarily made lower than the angels so his priesthood could be made superior to the Levitical priesthood. (3) Jesus' priesthood is greater than Aaron's based on election (Heb 5:1–10). (4) Melchizedek's priesthood is greater than the Levitical priesthood. (5) Jesus' priesthood is of the same kind as Melchizedek's. (6) Since Melchizedek's priesthood is greater than the Levitical priesthood, Jesus' priesthood is greater also. (7) Thus, since Jesus' priesthood is superior to the Levitical priesthood, the sacrifice He offered is a superior sacrifice. Therefore, *Hebrews 7:1–10 demonstrates that Melchizedek's priesthood is superior to the Levitical priesthood* (#4 above). That is the main point.

Hebrews 7:1–10 can be broken into two sections: vv. 1–3 say that Melchizedek remains a priest forever; vv. 4–10 provide the proof of his superior priesthood. Three proofs are offered. First, Melchizedek is greater than Abram because Abram gave him an offering (v. 4). This is the central argument of the three. Second, Melchizedek is greater because he blessed Abram (v. 7). The third argument needs a little historical background. Levitical priests typically served only after a certain age (20, 25, or 30—depending on the source consulted). After a certain age, they stopped ministering. Eventually, of course, they would die. Now for the third argument: while Abram's descendants paid tithes to priests who would die, Abram paid his tithe to a priest who lives on—Melchizedek (v. 8). Therefore, since Melchizedek was

---

20. G. D. Fee and D. Stuart, *How to Read the Bible for All Its Worth: A Guide to Understanding the Bible* (Grand Rapids: Zondervan, 1982), 108.
21. This analysis is somewhat dependent on G. H. Guthrie, *The Structure of Hebrews: A Text-Linguistic Analysis* (New York: Brill, 1994).

able to perform the functions of a priest without being in the Levitical lineage, Jesus is also able to be a priest without the necessary lineage.

The one theological truth the author intended is: *Melchizedek was greater than Abram and thus greater than the Levitical priests.* Hebrews 7:1–10 is a stepping stone to 8:1–2 which proclaims that Jesus, a superior high priest, rendered a superior sacrifice. This is the author's primary meaning and what he intended to communicate.

The argument from this passage for tithing usually focuses on Heb 7:8: "In the one case, men who will die receive tenths, but in the other case, Scripture testifies that he lives." The question is, Who is the "he" that lives? Some say the "he" is Jesus and thus Jesus is proclaimed to have received tithes. However, the word "he" does not occur in the Greek.[22] It is implied in the Greek, but *not* stated. Furthermore, the implied "he" (or "one") is not a reference to Christ but to Melchizedek. The author did not turn his attention to Jesus until v. 10. Everything before v. 10 is about Melchizedek.

The main objection for the use of Hebrews 7 for the continuation of tithing for Christians is that the author of Hebrews was not attempting to argue for a continuation of the practice of tithing in this passage. His purpose was to prove the superiority of Melchizedek's priesthood to the Levitical priesthood. To prove tithing from the New Testament, a passage must be produced that has as its *primary* purpose to advocate tithing. This reference to tithing is illustrative and descriptive.

Besides these three passages discussed above, no other passages explicitly mention tithing. None of the above passages command Christians to tithe. Therefore, all references to tithing in the New Testament are incidental. The two conclusions from these passages in relation to the continuation of tithing are that (1) none of the passages have tithing as their primary subject, and (2) none of the passages command tithing for Christians.

The Fulfillment of the Tithe

One weakness in nearly every analysis that concludes the tithe is not directly applicable to Christians is that the specific ways in which the tithe has been fulfilled in the new covenant are hardly mentioned. Therefore, an extremely abbreviated discussion on how each of the

---

22. The phrase "receive tithes" does not occur in the Greek text either.

three main tithes is fulfilled in the New Testament helps explain exactly *why* this law is no longer directly applicable.

There are three ways in which the Levitical tithe has been fulfilled in the New Testament. First, the Levitical tithe was for the support of the Levites and priests. The Levites worked at the temple so the priests could function as mediators between God and Israel. While some preachers have proclaimed that the clergy are in the line of the priests, the New Testament indicates that every Christian is a priest. This doctrine is known as the priesthood of all believers. It is probably most clearly discussed in 1 Pet 2:9 where Christians are described as a "royal priesthood."[23] Priests and Levites served two to three weeks per year in the temple; it was not a full-time job. Most American evangelical pastors serve full time. The analogy falls flat.

A second area of fulfillment is that of inheritance. The tithe was an inheritance given to the Levites instead of their receiving land. Just as the Israelites needed to keep the law in order to keep their inheritance (the land), the Levites needed to fulfill their obligations in order to keep their inheritance (tithes). Levites did not *earn* tithes; they were an inheritance. However, tithes were not their only inheritance, since they also received 48 cities, 2,000 cubits of land for the cities, and various offerings. When the New Testament mentions the believers' inheritance, it refers to their future salvation (see Eph 1:14). Acts 20:32 is particularly important since it is addressed to the elders in Ephesus. Paul told the elders that they would receive an inheritance, as well as all Christians. Therefore, while in the Old Testament the Levites' inheritance consisted of tithes and 48 cities, the elders of Ephesus were told that their inheritance was *just like* the inheritance of all Christians, not distinct from it. Therefore, the underlying aspect of inheritance has been fulfilled in the (future) salvation that belongs to those who believe.

Finally, the Levitical tithe has been fulfilled because the temple has been fulfilled. The primary way[24] that the temple has been fulfilled in the new covenant is through Christians, both corporately and individually. Paul told the Corinthians "you [plural] are God's sanctuary" (1 Cor 3:16–17). Since the "you" is plural, Paul is most likely saying that the corporate body of believers is the temple. However, in 1 Cor 6:19, Paul said, "Don't you know that your body is a sanctuary of the

---

23. Cf. Rom 12:1; Heb 10:22; Rev 5:20; 20:6.
24. For another way in which the New Testament declares the temple fulfilled, see Croteau, *You Mean I Don't Have to Tithe?* 220.

Holy Spirit who is in you, whom you have from God?" In this text Paul appears to be referring to each individual, not to the church as a whole.[25]

The Levitical tithe is fulfilled since the three aspects connected to this tithe are fulfilled in the New Testament. The priesthood is fulfilled by all Christians. The concept of "inheritance" now refers to salvation. The temple is fulfilled since Christians (both individually and corporately) are referred to as the temple of the Holy Spirit.

The fulfillment of the festival tithe is much less complex. The festival tithe was the financial undergirding for the celebration of the three feasts of Israel (Passover, Pentecost, and Tabernacles), and each of these feasts is described as fulfilled in the New Testament. Passover has been primarily fulfilled in Christ, our Passover lamb (1 Cor 5:7). While the specific way in which Pentecost has been fulfilled is hard to say with certainty, that it has been fulfilled seems certain. The fulfillment of Pentecost (or the Feast of Weeks) is best summarized by Tremper Longman: "The many converts on Pentecost, thus, were the firstfruits of the harvest of people who would turn to Christ."[26] Finally, Tabernacles contains three feasts, but only one is discussed here. The Day of Atonement (see Lev 16; 23:26–32) is fulfilled in Christ's work on the cross. When the high priest imparted the sins of Israel onto the scapegoat (Lev 16:21), this pointed to Christ's becoming sin on behalf of Christians (see 2 Cor 5:21). The main difference is that rather than being offered year after year, Christ offered a once-for-all sacrifice that covered the sins of all who believe in him.

The fulfillment of the charity tithe is slightly different from the other two tithes. The charity tithe had many recipients: Levites, aliens, orphans, and widows. While the Levites were a temporary group created for the maintenance of the temple (see discussion above on their fulfillment), the other three groups are discussed in the New Testament, and the concern for their care continues. Hebrews 13:2 exhorts Christians to be hospitable to strangers (i.e., aliens). Widows and orphans are both a concern in Jas 1:27. The underlying principle to these three groups (aliens, widows, and orphans) is a concern for the poor. The New Testament is very clear—both in the teachings of Jesus (Matt 6:2–3; 19:21; Luke 14:13) and among the apostles (James, Peter,

---

25. See D. E. Garland, *1 Corinthians*, Baker Exegetical Commentary on the New Testament (Grand Rapids: Baker, 2003), 238, for a justification for this.

26. T. Longman, III, *Immanuel in Our Place: Seeing Christ in Israel's Worship*, The Gospel According to the Old Testament (Phillipsburg, NJ: Presbyterian & Reformed, 2001), 196.

and John are also said to be concerned for the poor in Gal 2:10; cf. Jas 2:1–13)—that Christians should care for the poor.

Each of the three main tithes has been fulfilled in the New Testament. The Levitical tithe, the festival tithe, and the charity tithe are no longer binding on Christians because they are fulfilled. This is not to say that the New Testament has left Christians with no guide for giving. Far from this, the New Testament contains a plethora of principles that are extremely helpful and convicting.

Toward an Understanding of New Covenant Giving: The Post-Tithing View

Some might notice that the phrase "grace giving" has not been used up to this point. As far as I can tell, grace giving is a term that was used to separate those who advocated tithing from those who did not. However, those supporting tithing also use it, so a new phrase might be helpful. When I refer to my view as the "post-tithing view," I mean this in two ways—historically and theologically.

Historically, this work is a call to move past *and* build on the conclusions of the tithing renewal movement.[27] Some of the problems this movement sought to address were worthy and some were somewhat solved. Ministers were paid very poorly before the tithing renewal; that is not as much of a problem in contemporary evangelical American Christianity. However, as proposed in this chapter, the strategy for fulfilling the financial issues connected to the Great Commission has not been a biblical strategy with the employment of the Old Testament tithe.

Theologically, God's plan through history is still progressing and His character never changes. All Old Testament laws have eternal principles underlying them, and these principles are sometimes obvious and sometimes not. The underlying eternal principles of the tithe should not be discarded, but the wholesale acceptance of the tithe by many Christians today is misguided.

The two categories for giving that are discussed here are the foundations for giving and the issue of the amount to be given.[28] While all believers should take part in giving and give on a regular basis (1 Cor

27. See Croteau, *You Mean I Don't Have to Tithe?* 48–59.
28. In ibid., 238–59, I discussed 20 principles for giving broken into five categories: (1) The Foundations for Giving, (2) The Details of Giving, (3) The Amount of Giving, (4) The Motivations for Giving, and (5) The Attitude of Giving (and Possessions).

16:2), the amount that should be given remains controversial once the 10 percent figure is cast aside.

One of the most important aspects of giving is the foundations for giving: what drives Christian giving. In 2 Corinthians 8–9 Paul provided some principles for new covenant giving. In commenting on these two chapters, Craig Blomberg said that "grace is the entire theme of this entire two-chapter section."[29] That being said, what Paul is describing here is *grace-driven giving*. In 2 Cor 8:5 Paul laid the foundation for all the principles for giving: "they gave themselves especially to the Lord, then to us by God's will." Giving must not only be grace driven, but *relationally driven*. Christians should place their relationship with Christ above all other aspects of their lives. Scott Hafemann concluded that the "greatest expression of God's grace in a person's life is not its demonstration toward others, but its response to God and his cause."[30]

Since giving is connected to one's relationship with God, it is not surprising that Paul said generous giving proves the genuineness of a Christian's love for God (2 Cor 8:8). Then in v. 9 Paul provided a motivation for giving in the way he prescribed: Jesus gave of Himself. The mention of love in v. 8 prompted this thought. Giving should be compelled by love. *Love is a foundational motivation for giving in the new covenant.* Therefore, giving should be *love driven*. Giving everything one has without love results in nothing (see 1 Cor 13:3). The ultimate demonstration of God's love was Jesus' death on the cross (see Rom 5:8; 1 John 4:9–10). Mueller concluded, "It is only at the foot of the blood-stained cross of Calvary that the believer learns the art of Christian giving."[31] Generous and sacrificial giving occurs when the motive is love.

Table 7. The Foundation for Giving

Principle	Description	Location
Relationship Driven	Giving is based on one's relationship with the Lord and the receiver of the giving.	2 Cor 8:5
Grace Driven	Giving is a response to the grace of God shown to believers.	2 Cor 8–9
Love Driven	Giving is a demonstration of Christian love.	2 Cor 8:8–9

---

29. C. L. Blomberg, *Neither Poverty nor Riches: A Biblical Theology of Possessions* (Downers Grove: InterVarsity, 1999), 191.

30. S. J. Hafemann, *2 Corinthians*, NIVAC (Grand Rapids: Zondervan, 2000), 333.

31. J. T. Mueller, *Christian Dogmatics: A Handbook of Doctrinal Theology for Pastors, Teachers, and Laymen* (St. Louis: Concordia, 1934), 415.

God has revealed in both Testaments that He desires giving to be based on the amount determined in one's heart. Paul said, "Each person should do as he has decided in his heart" (2 Cor 9:7). While some who have heard this teaching have scoffed at it as mystical or too loose, when one bases the amount on the grace that God has showed him, as can be seen in the narrative in Exodus 35–36, giving will not be stingy. God wants believers to have a relationship with Him. He does not want them simply punching numbers into a calculator or just moving a decimal point. This principle, combined with the three that follow, leads to God-honoring giving.

The value of the gift should be related to the income of the offerer. Paul stated, "I testify that, on their own, according to their ability and beyond their ability. . . . For if the eagerness is there, it is acceptable according to what one has, not according to what he does not have" (2 Cor 8:3,12). Those who make more should give more; this is typically referred to as proportionate giving. Someone making $100,000 per year should be giving a higher percentage than someone making $20,000 per year. So one's income needs to be taken into account when the amount of the gift is being considered.

Christians are not just commended, but commanded, to meet the needs of those ministering to them and of fellow saints. In 1 Corinthians 9, Paul argued for the right of ministers of the gospel to receive support for their ministry.[32] This is not to say that all ministers should live in luxury, but that their needs should be met. Paul was equally clear in 2 Cor 9:12 that saints should fully supply the needs of the other saints. Taking this into consideration is not very difficult today. Believers in our context can simply look at the church budget and give accordingly (assuming that the pastor is getting paid and a fund for the poor is included in the budget). Of course, giving outside of the regular church offering should be encouraged to fulfill this New Testament obligation of caring for ministers of the gospel and fellow saints.

Finally, believers are commanded to give generously. Paul desired a generous gift from the Corinthians for the poor saints in Jerusalem (2 Cor 8:2–3). However, he did not want them to give to the point where an offering was needed for them.[33] Paul also praised the Philippians as being generous givers (Phil 4:17–18).

---

32. It should be noted that in the context, Paul used this as an illustration of forsaking rights, like doing without food sacrificed to idols (cf. 1 Cor 8). Therefore, the meaning above is the *secondary* meaning of the text.

33. Note especially the NLT's clear translation of 2 Cor 8:2–3,13.

Table 8. The Amount of Giving

Principle	Description	Location
Heart Based	Giving is based on the amount determined in one's heart.	Exod 25:1; 35:5,21–22; 36:6; 2 Cor 9:7
Income Based	The value of the gift is expected to be related to the income of the offerer.	Deut 16:16–17; 1 Cor 16:2; 2 Cor 8:3,12
Needs Based	Meet the needs of those ministering and of fellow saints.	1 Cor 9:1–14; 2 Cor 8:13–14; 2 Cor 9:12
Generous	Give generously, but not to the point of personal affliction.	2 Cor 8:2–3,13; Phil. 4:17–18

Conclusion

While tithing should not be advocated as a minimum contribution based on Scripture, the affluence of our country is such that giving at least 10 percent, for the *majority* of Christians, would be the natural application of the principles above. Affluent Christians giving 10 percent should not think that they have fulfilled the giving requirements of Scripture. John Piper said, "My own conviction is that most middle and upper class Americans who merely tithe are robbing God."[34] Christians should be giving generously out of concern for God's glory, in response to the grace and love He has shown them, and from a desire to see ministers of the gospel and the poor have their basic needs met. Nothing written here should be understood as an excuse for not giving; rather, Christians should be freed from the 10 percent model so they can embrace the model endorsed in the New Testament.

---

34. J. Piper, "I Seek Not What Is Yours but You: A Sermon on Tithing," sermon delivered on January 31, 1982 <http://tinyurl.com/ydg528g> (accessed March 5, 2010).

CHAPTER 7

Response to David A. Croteau
Ken Hemphill and Bobby Eklund

David Croteau's chapter seems to support a view of giving as the norm for believers today, but reveals a great reluctance to accept tithing as a biblical mandate despite Jesus' affirmation of the practice in Matt 23:23 and Luke 11:42. Most curious is the stance that "each of the three tithes has been *fulfilled* in the New Testament . . . . This is not to say that the New Testament has left Christians with no guide for giving. Far from this, the New Testament contains a plethora of principles that are extremely helpful and convicting." These convicting principles are left to the reader's imagination but would provide insight into Croteau's eventual conclusion that modern-day believers should be generous (but not tithers).

As a whole, this view fails to take into account God's approach in teaching mankind, not just the Israelites, whereby He reveals truth, adding complexity and richness until the whole fabric is revealed. The concept of a Savior, Messiah, and Redeemer is a perfect example, beginning in Genesis and culminating in the earthly life, death, and resurrection of Christ. Thus, to understand giving, and specifically the tithe before codification of the Mosaic law, Abram's story cannot be the beginning place. The garden of Eden is the beginning place where God Himself taught Adam and his family the concept of man (the created) giving back a portion of his God-provided resources to the Creator and Owner of all—God.

Failure to see this connection results, in our opinion, in excessive attention to the *mechanics* (some might say legalism) of giving rather than the *reasons* behind giving in general and the tithe in particular. And it is precisely this point that makes giving and tithing relevant for modern-day believers. The author has given an excellent analysis of the mechanics of Old Testament tithing practices employed in an agrarian society, but insufficient attention, we believe, to the very roots of man's recognition of God's ownership of everything and everyone created, and to man's living out his God-directed stewardship role.

As an example, in an attempt to link Abram's tithe to practices of other cultures in the ancient Near East and thus concluding it (the tithe) was a one-time event, he fails to recognize that Abram's tithe was given *in response to* the victory given by God Most High, and it was given to the priest of God Most High (Gen 14:18–20). This voluntary tithe and freewill offering of the balance of the spoils that were rightfully Abram's were nowhere described as a "pre-war gift to guarantee victory" or "previous vow" as Croteau suggests. This is speculation; perhaps it is informed speculation, but speculation nevertheless.

Abram's tithe was given to God's representative, a priest, but the tithe belonged (then and now) to God. This question—to whom does the tithe belong?—comes up throughout the text and particularly with respect to accounts of God's tithes being given back to the people to eat and enjoy in His presence. It is within the divine prerogative to prescribe both man's worship and the use of tithes offered. The tithe, in any case, does not belong to the giver, but to God.

Speaking to the issue of eternal principles found in Scripture, Dr. Paige Patterson has said,,

> To me, the *coup de gras* to the unfortunate idea that we are not obligated to tithe is found in the seventh chapter of the book of Hebrews. There are laws such as the day of atonement and the Passover that are fulfilled in Christ or else preceded by more important practices, such as the Lord's Supper as a memorial of the cross rather than the Passover as an anticipation of the cross, but there are other practices from Judaism that are incorporated in the law, but stand as eternal principles. One of those is the eternal principle of the Sabbath day.

We must agree with our colleague who declared:

> While we worship on the first day of the week in honor of Christ's resurrection, the principle of the Sabbath has never altered. One-seventh of one's time is to be devoted completely to the

Lord. This includes worship, our personal devotional walk with God, Bible study, our witnessing and mission effort etc., but one-seventh of our time is due to the Lord. That principle just never changes, not even under grace. By the same token, a tenth of what He gives us we are to give back to Him by way of recognition of His grace and kindness. Now see this worked out in Hebrews 7:7 and following. Abraham, who is the lesser, is blessed by Melchizedek, the better. On earth, mortal men receive tithes, but there Melchizedek received them of whom it is witnessed simply that he lives. While I believe that to be a theophany or a christophany, to be more technically correct, whatever one's interpretation, the idea of *perpetuity* is definitely in the text. . . . The practice of tithing precedes the law and is simply an eternal principle that was incorporated in the law. This, to my way of thinking, is an absolutely irrefutable position.[1]

Since Scripture is silent about Abram's overall tithing and giving, there is no basis at all to the suppositions and conclusions that he tithed "only" from spoils and not his possessions, or that his giving originated in surrounding cultures.

The fact that other cultures practiced some form of tithing, and we certainly do not dispute this, does not dictate the reasons behind Abram's voluntary, spontaneous tithe. Since all cultures sprang from one family, and that family was instructed in giving by God Himself, it is hardly a surprise that giving/tithing would be characteristic of other cultures.

While no one would argue that Jacob is presented in an unfavorable light in several passages, this fact does not negate the simple fact that he offered a tithe. Scripture does not present men and women of Scripture as they should be, but truthfully, as they are.

In any case, trusting fully in God's promises is not a prerequisite for following His commands. The fact that Jacob did not trust God fully only makes him human as we are. "Nowhere does it (Scripture) say that Jacob tithed during the interim" is neither a safe nor a logical conclusion. We could say with equal certainty, "Nowhere does it say that he did not tithe during the interim." Such assumptions or conclusions do not inform but rather obfuscate the meaning intended.

In the Malachi discussion, Croteau correctly identifies the real subject of God's displeasure with His people—their unfaithfulness,

---

1. P. Patterson, president of Southwestern Baptist Theological Seminary, unpublished, used by permission.

which was expressed in their marriages and in their giving. Far from describing a one-time event, God declared, "'Since the days of your fathers, you have turned from my statutes; you have not kept them. Return to Me, and I will return to you,' says the LORD of Hosts" (Mal 3:7). The first example of their disobedience is "by not making the payments of 10 percent and the contributions." God then proceeded to demand, "Bring the full tenth into the storehouse" (v. 10). We must ask, How can this demand not be construed as a command?

As to the unsupported position that "storehouse" in Mal 3:10 refers specifically (and only) to a special room in the temple designated to hold tithes and offerings, the principle is the same. The gifts (tithes and offerings) belong to God; they are used and administered by His representatives (in this instance, those charged with disbursing funds) to carry out the work of the kingdom. While the "storehouse" designation certainly may be hermeneutically applied as "a place of gathering," we must insist that the focus is on the tithe given and on the intended recipient, God, and not the place of storage or gathering.

In comments related to Leviticus 27, described as the general introduction to tithing, we cannot agree that the writer's intent was to "assimilate tithing practices from the surrounding culture into Judaism." In our opinion, the intent was to describe Judaism as significantly different from other cultures.

Croteau's research in untangling the complex system of tithes and offerings and the uses thereof is most helpful. Once again, however, the mechanics seem to dominate such that mistaken assumptions lead to erroneous conclusions, namely that the promises God made concerning the blessings were appropriate and limited to "an agricultural society and are deeply connected to Israel's inheritance of the land."

There is much to be said for the commentary on Matt 23:23, especially where Croteau states that "Jesus does not prohibit tithing, but he condemns the wrong attitude and motive of those who were tithing under the old covenant." Precisely! This is the same issue that Cain faced in making his offering—the wrong attitude and motive. But when he states that "this verse should not be used to argue for the continuation of tithing based on one main fact: the command to tithe was for the scribes and Pharisees who were still under the old covenant." This statement begs the question: When is the requirement under grace ever less than the requirement under the Mosaic law? And the second question would be, who is the true audience in this discourse? Was it truly the scribes and Pharisees, or was it Jesus' disciples and the band of followers who stood listening? Jesus' own statements about the inability of the spiritually blind and deaf scribes and Pharisees to grasp the truths of the gospel lead us to conclude the real and intended audience was the followers of Jesus.

Croteau, in our opinion, does his best work in describing a proper motivation for giving. In a word, it is love—love as a response to a gracious and loving God. While we must agree to disagree on the ongoing requirement of a tithe (10 percent) as the beginning point for obedient giving, we most heartily agree that the believer who gives as God directs will never be stingy. The natural consequence of loving God is not to be "freed from a 10 percent model" but to be free to give generously under the leadership of His Spirit.

CHAPTER 8

Response to David A. Croteau

Reggie Kidd

I once had a friend whose Lutheran upbringing and dispensational seminary training put us at different places with regard to the place of the Mosaic law in the believer's life. One day he was explaining that although he was comfortable calling on believers to be "holy," he was not comfortable invoking the law. I said I thought Calvin's "third use of the law" made sense: if we understand that after the law convicts us of sin and drives us to Christ ("first use of the law"), it becomes (with adjustments for post-death and post-resurrection factors) what the psalmist embraced it to be: "a light on my path" (Ps 119:105—"third use of the law").

"That's all well and good," he countered, "but I've known too many Reformed pastors who claim that view, and they're all driven legalists."

In the moment, I decided not to pursue the argument. I knew that even though my friend's statement was hyperbolic, there was enough truth in it to give at least this Presbyterian pastor pause.

What I came to appreciate about my friend's ministry was the way his teaching portrayed the loveliness of Christ and the grace of His appearing. He made the *indicative* of Christ's person and work attractive and compelling. People under his ministry seemed to grasp the *imperative* of the Christian life without the need for a lot of hammering on duty, duty, duty.

I never really changed my theological grid, but I did find myself thankful for my friend's pastoral instinct for inculcating an obedience that grows out of a profound sense of being loved by the Master. In David Croteau's chapter I hear a voice similar to my friend's. There are a number of premises and statements I do not agree with, but I am glad for the pastoral instinct to help believers know the joy of giving from the heart. But there are some hermeneutical—or methodological—questions I wish to explore.

Primary Meaning and Doctrine?

I am not as insistent as Croteau that doctrine be built on primary meanings. It's altogether conceivable that massively important doctrinal matters are implicit rather than explicit. There is no word "Trinity" in the Bible, nor "incarnation." But the church found it necessary to coin them in order to crystalize implicit biblical truths. Croteau himself infers "eternal principles" underlying OT laws whose primary meanings he says we are to jettison. Further, Croteau acknowledges he derives the obligation to support church workers from the secondary meaning of Paul's instructions about meat sacrificed to idols.

There is a shape to the biblical story that seems to me to include tithing principally, even if the specific shape of redemptive history calls for an adjustment in application in the new covenant situation. I find I cannot accept Croteau's burden of proof for the continuation of tithing. Thus, it is not as significant to me that tithing passages are "incidental," nor fail to have tithing "as their primary subject."

Further, I do not think that, hermeneutically, it is the final word on the relevance of Abram's and Jacob's tithes to note that they are pre-law or that they emerge in narrative rather than prescriptive portions of Scripture, as though there were some sort of neat "test" for normativeness. Richard Hays argued, and rightly I think, that the Christian moral vision is shaped not only by the Bible's explicit prescriptive and proscriptive statements (such as "present your offerings" and "do not rob God"), but also by the Bible's paradigms and patterns (e.g., the incarnational pattern of Christ's coming among us), as well as principles (e.g., proportionality and voluntarism).[1] Especially if Croteau is going to place high value on the voluntary nature

1. R. B. Hays, *The Moral Vision of the New Testament: Community, Cross, New Creation, A Contemporary Introduction to New Testament Ethics* (New York: HarperSanFrancisco, 1996).

of giving under the new covenant, one would think that Abram's and Jacob's precedents would be exceedingly instructive. It is insufficient to dismiss the pre-law tithe as something merely borrowed from surrounding culture, or, at least in Jacob's case, stemming perhaps from a dishonorable desire to bargain with God. The former assertion (that tithing existed in ancient Near Eastern cultures) could lead, I think, to reflection on whether "surrounding culture" bears the mark of the image of God in regard to acknowledging deity's claim over us. The latter suggestion (Jacob's ambivalent motives—not to mention the text's ambiguity about his follow-through) merely reminds us of the numerous indicators in the patriarchal accounts of the human frailties in spite of which and because of which God works redemption.

Tithing in Matthew 23

As to whether tithing is ever commanded of Christians, I differ with Croteau on the intent of Matthew 23. Despite Jesus' literal second person address to the scribes and Pharisees, those people are mere foils for Jesus' instruction to His disciples and the crowds. I think the Rorschach effect is in play here, and there is a different construal of the shape of the biblical story that sends Croteau (and others) in one direction and me in another. The effect of this negative denunciation of the scribes and Pharisees is to provide positive instruction ("all that I have commanded you") about discipleship for those who are to be baptized "in the name of the Father and of the Son and of the Holy Spirit" (see Matt 28:18–20).

Is "Fulfilled" a Univocal Notion?

I appreciate the way Croteau connects the dots between the Levitical tithe and the fulfillment of the Levitical ministry in the new covenant (e.g., support of the temporary mediaries between God and us; the provision of an inheritance for them; the maintenance of a temporary physical building to "house" God's presence in anticipation of a new temple made of "living stones"). Similarly, I salute his seeing the festival tithe as pointing to Pentecost, and the charity tithe to the new covenant provision for the poor.

But I would lobby for a more robust typology and a less simplistic sense of what it is for the old covenant to find fulfillment in the new covenant. The "fulfillment" of circumcision, for instance, is more a matter of its transformation than of its dismissal. Every believer in Christ is circumcised, by virtue of union with Christ, as pictured in baptism (Col 2:11–12).

The church is, I agree, the temple come into its own. By our Holy Spirit baptism, we are all teachers and prophets — indeed, a kingdom of priests. But precisely because the Spirit we all share dispenses his gifts variously and makes "one" of "many," some believers may be gifted and set apart to carry on those teaching and prophetic and priestly functions in a more focused way in the church — God's new temple — on behalf of all the rest of us. If that be the case, then perhaps the tithe itself does not so much wither away, as undergo a deepening, an intensification, an internalization.

I think that in practice, Croteau seeks to promote just such giving. Such giving is "post-tithe" in that the old temple is gone. But precisely because in the new covenant era what it means to be "bought with a price" comes into its own in the life of the new temple, so does the principle of tithing when unpacked in terms of proportionality, generosity, intentionality, and love.

CHAPTER 9

Response to David A. Croteau
Gary North

David Croteau begins with an assertion: "The requirement of the tithe as the standard of Christian giving is the assumed position for most of evangelical Christianity in America." If true, this assumption is wrong. The tithe is not the standard of Christian giving. It has nothing to do with giving. The tithe is the God-mandated payment by God's royal priesthood to higher priests who are formally ordained to defend the church and the sacraments, as surely as the Mosaic temple priests were formally ordained to protect the temple and the sacrificial system.

Croteau says that Abram's tithe to Melchizedek was part of a vow. He offers no verse to prove this. He refers to, but does not quote, Gen 14:21–24, and comments: "These verses contain the oath he had sworn that he would not keep any of the spoils of war himself. In fact, he gave 10 percent to Melchizedek and the rest he gave away, *all as part of a vow.*" In fact, the passage proves the opposite of what Croteau says it proves.

First, Abram had made a specific vow, as he told the king of Sodom: "I have raised my hand in an oath to the Lord, God Most High, Creator of heaven and earth, that I will not take a thread or a sandal strap or anything that belongs to you, so you can never say, 'I made Abram rich'" (Gen 14:20–21). No gifts! This vow referred only to the king of Sodom. It did not refer to Melchizedek. Abram did take gifts from Melchizedek: bread and wine (v. 18) and a blessing (v. 19).

After presenting his argument regarding Abram's vow, Croteau points out that Abram paid his tithe only from the plunder. He expects the reader to believe that the tithe was a special case. It was indeed a special case. It was the only case where Abram profited while being under the geographical jurisdiction of Melchizedek. Whenever he was outside this jurisdiction, he did not see Melchizedek or accept bread and wine from him or receive a blessing from him. So, whatever he accumulated on his own outside Melchizedek's jurisdiction was his own since he was the household priest for his family. There was no local priest above Abram to whom he could tithe.

Croteau also argues that Abram's payment of a tithe was a practice borrowed from other cultures. He offers no textual proof of such practices or borrowing. In any case, evidence from pagan cultures has no judicial bearing on what God requires from those under His covenant of redemption. What heathens paid to their priests has no covenantal bearing on what Christians, as a royal priesthood, owe to ecclesiastically ordained men above them.

Croteau's next argument refers to the only other example of a tithe in Genesis: Jacob's vow to tithe to God, a vow made when he was on the run from Esau at his mother's recommendation (Gen 28:20–22). To prove his point, he argues that Jacob was an unconverted covenant-breaker who had never been redeemed by God: "His lack of conversion can be discerned because: (1) his reaction to God's presence was terror or fear, not awe; (2) he proclaimed himself ignorant of God's presence (Gen 28:16); (3) the conditions he placed on God speak against Jacob having been converted; and (4) Jacob's conversion appears to have taken place when he wrestled with God (Gen 32:24–30), not in his dream (Gen 28:10–15)." This is a very strange argument—unique.

I have responded to this line of reasoning in my chapter,[1] but I offer only this here: this incident was *an act of covenant renewal*. It had to do with the promised covenantal inheritance. Jacob was not arguing like this: "If you don't protect me, I will not tithe to you." He was arguing like this: "If you don't protect me, I cannot tithe to you." If you do not accept my explanation, then you are stuck with the idea that Jacob, the heir to the promise given to Rebekah before Jacob's birth (Gen 25:23), remained a heathen for the first 97 years of his life.[2]

---

1. See chap. 14 under the heading "Tithing and Inheritance."
2. 97 years = 130 years (47:9), minus 39 years at Joseph's birth, plus 6 years (29:29–30; 31:38).

Croteau devotes much space to a consideration of the tithes of the Mosaic law. He makes an observation regarding the nature of the Levitical tithes. Regarding the tithe from rural land's net output, which went to Levites, "they did not receive it as a *wage* but as an *inheritance*." However, this is irrelevant to Christians. The new covenant tithe goes to the institutional church, because the new covenant tithe rests covenantally on the tithe Abram paid to Melchizedek. Hebrews 7 says the Levites paid this tithe representatively to Melchizedek.

Croteau argues that the storehouse in Malachi 3 does not refer to local churches. "The 'storehouse' does not refer to local churches. It was an actual building used by the Levites to store all they received, like grains and livestock." This is the logical equivalent of arguing that the church is not the recipient of the tithes of its members, because the money is kept in a bank. I am not saying this for rhetorical purposes. This really is what his argument means in a modern setting.

Under the heading, "Parallels to Tithing in the New Testament," Croteau goes on at some length about the levirate marriage, where a brother living close to another brother who died with no male heir had to father a child with his sister-in-law (Deut 25:5–10). I have devoted a chapter to this passage in my commentary on Deuteronomy, *Inheritance and Dominion*. This law had to do with preservation of the family name, not the tithe. Jesus was born in the covenant line of Boaz, who was a levir: the closest relative of Ruth's deceased husband who was willing to marry her.

With respect to Matt 23:2–12, the passage regarding what the Pharisees did and did not do, Croteau makes this statement: "A command given by Jesus to Jews who are still functioning under the old covenant does not necessitate that the command applies to Christians." I agree completely. This is why I have rested my case for the tithe on Hebrews 7.

We come to his exposition of Hebrews 7. Croteau writes, "First, the interpreter is always to seek the author's intent; he needs to attempt to set aside his own agenda." Whenever you read a statement like this, rest assured that the interpreter is about to apply his agenda to his opponent's agenda.

Croteau says we should look at the text's primary meaning and summarizes his version of the argument of Heb 7:1–10. He says that the text's primary meaning is that "Jesus' sacrifice is superior to the sacrifices of the old covenant, and therefore the Jews should not turn back to their former ways." This is not the text's primary meaning. The primary meaning is that Jesus' office as high priest rests on His restoration of Melchizedek's priesthood, which was superior to Levi's, for Abram, representing Levi, tithed to Melchizedek. This is made clear in v. 9: "Levi himself . . . paid tithes through Abraham." This is a covenantal argument—the argument from representation, point two of the biblical covenant model.[3] The text's entire argument for the superiority of the new covenant rests on the argument that Levi tithed to Melchizedek through Abram. *Tithing is central to this argument.*

Oddly, Croteau then admits the following, which refutes his previous argument regarding the primary meaning of the passage: *"Hebrews 7:1–10 demonstrates that Melchizedek's priesthood is superior to the Levitical priesthood. . . . That is the main point."* My suggestion is for Croteau to decide what the main point is and then stick with it. Do not offer two main points regarding the same passage. When you do, it indicates confusion.

Croteau then says that tithing was merely "illustrative and descriptive," not fundamental. The author of Hebrews was trying to prove the superiority of the new covenant priesthood with an illustration. "To prove tithing from the New Testament, a passage must be produced that has as its primary purpose to advocate tithing."

So the central argument of the passage regarding the superiority of the new covenant over the old covenant rests on the covenantal issue of tithing, which is a judicial issue. But once the author of Hebrews made this covenantal point—central to Christ's office as high priest—then tithing is no longer a judicial issue. *Melchizedek was judicially entitled to Abram's tithe, but Jesus, as the covenantal replacement of Melchizedek, is not judicially entitled to a tithe.* The tithe disappears judicially from God's covenant. This makes no sense theologically.

---

3. R. R. Sutton, *That You May Prosper: Dominion by Covenant*, 2nd ed. (Tyler, TX: Institute for Christian Economics, 1992), chap. 2.

PART III

CHAPTER 10

Tithing in the New Covenant?

"YES" AS PRINCIPLE, "NO" AS CASUISTRY

Reggie Kidd

When I tell friends I'm writing about tithing, I've come to expect one of two responses: either "I hope you won't let people off the hook and say it's merely optional," or "I hope you're not going to lay a lot of legalistic guilt on those of us who are struggling to make ends meet." Tithing gets a rise out of everybody I talk to. Some think that the church's finances are in the toilet because Christians are avariciously living for themselves—many beyond their means. According to this view, tithing is a matter of fundamental obedience, the way out of personal financial disaster, and the only way to ensure that the body of Christ can be what it's called to be and do what it's called to do. Others are concerned that an insistence on tithing detracts from the grand story of a God who has purchased us at no small price. They insist it would be folly—and pastorally unwise—to monetize what we owe in return. Worse, to do so would inevitably give the well-off the false security of thinking their 10 percent is enough!

Writing about tithing has prompted a lot of soul-searching for me as well. I try not to think about money a whole lot because either avarice, greed, or discontentment is always an unguarded thought away. Dante's *Divine Comedy* has been much on my mind. Dante's inferno is populated with people whom God has given over to their consuming passions: lovers eternally locked in unsatisfying liaisons, gluttons stuffing themselves on filth, soul-devourers trapped in eternally cannibalistic embrace with their earthly enemies. Dante described avarice as "the sin that eats the race" (*Purgatorio* XX.6). I can imagine all my possessions attaching themselves to me like leaden, parasitic growths of mistletoe, draining the life from my body while I have to drag them around forever.

The upside of the *Divine Comedy*—after all, it is a comedy—is that there is a paradise for the repentant. Much of what Dante has to offer about the right use of wealth lies in his portrait of Francis of Assisi, who gave up wealth and privilege to become a preacher of repentance and a minister to the poor (*Paradiso* XI). Dante adopted Francis as a model to inspire him. He was convinced that God does not call everyone to mimic Francis, but rather to learn from him. In his own life, Dante had been successful as a poet and a politician. Later, his fortunes reversed. His political party was ousted from Florence and his writings came under papal ban. Dante discovered he was able to cope because Francis had already taught him to love God and to be free from possessions (with them or without them).

I find myself striving for something like that: freedom from avarice, freedom in loving God—whether with or without a lot of money and "stuff." The question before the house is whether and if and how God intends tithing to be a part of such an equation.

Since I have but a chapter and not a whole book to provide my basic view of tithing, I'm going to key off of one text, Matt 23:23–24 (and its parallel Luke 11:42)—the one place where the New Testament speaks of tithing in anything like a prescriptive fashion. It seems to me that tithing is like a Rorschach test of biblical interpretation. What we see in tithing passages depends a lot on what we already bring with us, and our conclusions tell a lot about how we construe the whole of the Christian life. Like Rorschach blots, tithing passages appear against a large backdrop. Happily, unlike true Rorschach blots, they do not appear against a backdrop of blank paper. The backdrop of Israel's (and the church's) story promises that their meaning is not arbitrary. Nonetheless, the backdrop is large and the passages have proven difficult to place.

The truth is, the passages speak provocatively and suggestively, but not with such clarity that their significance is beyond question. The variety of approaches that have emerged in the history of the believing church is evidence in itself that there's no slam-dunk case to be made exegetically for how they are to be interpreted and applied. If there were, writers of such close spiritual kinship and overall theological consensus as are contributing to this volume would be in agreement from the start.

The event recorded in Matt 23:23–24, the one time[1] Jesus mentioned tithing in a prescriptive fashion, illustrates the point well:

> Woe to you, scribes and Pharisees, hypocrites! You pay a tenth of mint, dill, and cumin, yet you have neglected the more important matters of the law—justice, mercy, and faith. These things should have been done without neglecting the others. Blind guides! You strain out a gnat, yet gulp down a camel!

Ben Witherington waved off the tithe reference as just so much old covenant flotsam:

> Intuitively, even Christians who are not very biblically literate know that we are not under the Mosaic covenant anymore. We don't live our lives on the basis of the Mosaic law given to the Hebrews so many centuries ago. We are under the new covenant inaugurated by Jesus, and it has many commandments, *but tithing is not one of them.* The basic rule of guidance about such things is that if the Old Testament commandment is reaffirmed in the New Testament for Christians, then we are still obligated to do it. If it is not, then we are not. . . .
>
> [In Matt 23:23] Jesus is instructing the Pharisees, not his own disciples, much less Christians after Easter. Jesus wants the Pharisees to be consistent if they are going to keep the Mosaic covenant, which they have promised to do. Clearly the Mosaic covenant commands tithing. But it is striking that nowhere does Jesus tell his disciples to tithe. In fact, what he tells them is something more radical than giving a tenth of their income.[2]

R. T. Kendall stated with equal certainty that Jesus' endorsement of the tithe in Matt 23:23 solidly anchors it in new covenant living:

---

1. This includes its parallel in Luke 11:42.
2. B. Witherington III, *Jesus and Money: A Guide for Times of Financial Crisis* (Grand Rapids: Brazos Press, 2010), 21–22.

Tithing was so deeply imbedded in the Jewish conscience . . . that it needed virtually no mention in the New Testament. Tithing was an assumption in Israel when Jesus came on the scene. . . . Our Lord, I say, might have made light of their tithing of "mint, dill and cumin." . . . But He *took the care Himself* to sanction such bother to tithe, provided that it was done in the context of judgment, mercy, and faith. . . .

He attacked the Pharisees because of their distortion and lack of balance with respect to religion. And yet Jesus honored that part of the law with respect to tithes! . . . If tithing was a part of the law that would or could be dropped under the New Covenant this is the place our Lord would have done it. He did not.[3]

To one interpreter it is clear that tithing is not a command for followers of Jesus under the new covenant, but to the other it is equally clear that tithing is a command for us. Perhaps one writer sees too little here and the other too much. Then again, perhaps both have a point. Regardless, for both of these writers, it seems to me, the interpretation of this passage turns on a prior understanding of the way the Christian story works.

Understanding One's Own Pre-Wiring

In the interest of full disclosure, I should tell more of my own story and the way my understanding of the Christian story pre-wires me to read tithing passages. As I come to these texts late in the sixth decade of my life, I do so as one who has consciously walked with Jesus for four of those decades. It's hard for me not to read them now in light of the way they took shape for me early in my Christian pilgrimage, and thus in light of the way they have already shaped me as I write now.

I grew up in a mildly liberal Presbyterian church. The gathering of tithes and offerings in the worship service followed the sermon. The offertory always felt odd and uncomfortable. I thought this was when you paid the pastor for the sermon. I remember thinking, "That's a lot of pressure for a preacher." It was only after I went off to college that Jesus Christ became a real person to me.[4] My new spiritu-

3. R. T. Kendall, *Tithing: A Call to Serious, Biblical Giving* (Grand Rapids: Zondervan, 1982), 29–30.

4. I tell my story in short compass in R. M. Kidd, *With One Voice: Discovering Christ's Song in Our Worship* (Grand Rapids: Baker, 2005), 35–40, 44–46.

al environment was the full-bodied Calvinism of the defenders of "Old Princeton" who founded Westminster Theological Seminary and the several Presbyterian denominations under the banner of J. Gresham Machen's call to arms in his book *Christianity and Liberalism*. My spiritual mentor was Mort Whitman, who was planting a church on behalf of the Orthodox Presbyterian Church in my college town. Mort introduced me to the spiritual voices that were shaping him: Francis Schaeffer, Cornelius Van Til, John Murray, Abraham Kuyper, and, behind them all, John Calvin.

Those spiritually formative years came during the height of the Jesus Movement. I realized pretty quickly that one thing distinguishing the voices that were shaping me was their attitude toward the Mosaic law, and their sense of what was new about the new covenant. The believers of the local charismatic fellowship characterized themselves as a "new covenant" church and us Calvinists as an "old covenant" church. They were experiencing the newness of the Spirit, and in their view we were still trying to grind it out under the Mosaic law. Leading dispensationalist teachers were afraid that stressing things like the Ten Commandments and the Sermon on the Mount in the age of grace would lead to works-based righteousness. (I found it to be poetic justice that precisely into that vacuum and almost entirely to those churches spoke Bill Gothard with his wildly extra-biblical *Institute in Basic Youth Conflicts*.) While a supposed prophecy expert like Hal Lindsay was dating Jesus' return (meaning we wouldn't need to worry about the Mosaic law much longer anyway), the cautiously amillennialist Cornelius Van Til was talking as though the City of God might call for a longer view of things (meaning we might have to keep wrestling with the question of the Mosaic law in society and in life).

All the while, Mort Whitman was teaching me a Reformed hermeneutic that spoke of both covenant eras as being characterized by grace-preceding-law, the difference being that forgiveness is no longer a mere promise in the new covenant, nor is the ability to obey. Grace has come with the consolation of guilt borne and shame taken away. Grace has come with the transforming power of the Spirit to write God's law on our hearts.

I was taught, in sum, Calvin's "third use of the law." To be sure, the Mosaic law convicts us of our sin and teaches us our need of a Redeemer (the "first use of the law"). But the law also outlines—calling for epochal adjustments to account for the difference between a theocracy and a Christocracy—principles for civic and social life (the "second use of the law").[5] In addition, at bottom the Mosaic law has always reflected the correlation between God's character and that of those called to bear His image. As a result, redeemed people who no longer have reason to fear its curses—and in this sense no longer stand "under the law"—find the law to serve as a positive aid in their growth in grace, that is to say, in their sanctification (the "third use of the law").

Theologically, so Mort and others taught me to believe, the Mosaic law reminds us that we have been folded into Israel's story. The psalmist declared that "his delight is in the law of the LORD" (Ps 1:2, KJV), and he celebrated the promise of ethical congruity between God's heart and ours. A parable of the whole dynamic lies in the fact that John Calvin taught his congregation in Geneva to sing the Ten Commandments during the worship service—not just to sing them, but to sing them *after* the confession of sin and with one of the celebratory "Geneva jigs."[6] And so I find that I have learned a certain way of doing theology, thinking about the Christian life, and how to worship that differs from many of my fellow evangelicals.

To accept as a general rule the notion that a command has to be reaffirmed in the new covenant if we are still obligated to keep it feels atomistic and casuistic. Rather, it seems to me a better question is more organic and holistic: "How does Christ's coming allow the true significance of old covenant features to come to the surface in the new covenant?" A singular blood sacrifice has completed all requirements for the shedding of blood—thus our initiation rite no longer requires the cutting of the foreskin, and our Passover meal does not include lamb meat. We don't circumcise anymore because Christ is our circumcision and because by virtue of our baptism we are in fact included in his circumcision (the point of Col 2:11–12). We don't sacrifice a Passover lamb, because "Christ our Passover

---

5. I note merely in passing that an important dimension of the tithing question has to do with the times and places in the history of the church when "tithing" has amounted to an "ecclesiastical tax."

6. Note the difference between the 1539 *Strasbourg Psalter* version of the Ten Commandments, set to the minor mode feeling tune OYONS LA LOY, punctuated throughout with "Kyrie eleison," and the spritely, rhythmic major key version, set to the tune LES COMMANDEMENTS DE DIEU, which appeared in the 1547 *Genevan Psalter* (no. 724 in the *Trinity Hymnal* and no. 153 in the *Psalter Hymnal*). The custom in Geneva was to sing the "first table" of the Ten Commandments, to offer a prayer that acknowledged our shortcomings and asked for renewal, and finally to sing the "second table." I expand here on the discussion in B. Thompson, *Liturgies of the Western Church* (Minneapolis: Fortress, 1961), 191.

has been sacrificed" (1 Cor 5:7). Ethics measured by the grandeur of the exodus ("remember that you were strangers, aliens, and slaves") yields to ethics measured by the greater grandeur of the cross ("as I have loved you").

In each case, the new is not lesser — if the old is not repeated, it is not because the old is too specific or too demanding, but because it could never specify or demand enough. In some cases, new covenant application means old covenant practices pass away (circumcision, the Passover slaughter). In other cases, new covenant application sweeps up an old covenant practice and carries it over in its wake (loving one another includes caring for the dispossessed).

I am aware of one other factor shaping my approach to the tithing question: witnessing the folding of the church planting venture that brought Mort Whitman and me together during my college years. Simply put, there weren't enough people paying the bills. After that experience, I recall reading the celebrated sermon by Clement of Alexandria (third century), *The Rich Man's Salvation*.[7] Pastoring a wealthy congregation, Clement wrestled with whether Jesus' challenge to the rich young ruler was universal or specific. Clement concluded that anyone who renounced wealth itself but not love of wealth was no better off, nor would the church be well served if everyone gave away all his possessions: "For what sharing [*koinōnia*] would be left among men, if nobody had anything?" (chap. 13). Clement led me to consider Christ's differential calls on people's lives. He called some to divest and follow him.[8] He called others to stay home[9] or take "talents" and invest them.[10] He called some to minister as itinerants,[11] some along the way,[12] some from home.[13]

There is, I came to see, a deep dynamism in the biblical story that underlies Jesus' posture. There is both a "go" and a "stay," both a "give freely" and a "give prudently."

Abram was called to "go" to a new land, which he would inhabit only as a stranger. His offering (a tenth of the spoils from his military

---

7. Clement of Alexandria, *The Rich Man's Salvation* (LCL, no. 92, translation by G. W. Butterworth, 1979).

8. The rich young ruler (Matt 19:16–22 = Mark 10:17–22 = Luke 18:18–23).

9. The man healed of blindness in two stages outside Bethsaida (Mark 8:26); the Gerasene demoniac in Mark 5:1–20 = Luke 8:26–39.

10. Though a parable rather than a narrative, the parable of the talents presupposes a certain social nexus (Matt 25:14–30 = Luke 19:11–27).

11. The Twelve, at least, but then also the Seventy.

12. The benefactresses (Luke 8:1–3).

13. Mary and Martha come readily to mind (Luke 10:38–42; cf. John 12:1–3).

victory) to God Almighty whom Melchizedek served (Gen 14:17–20) appears to have been spontaneous. It certainly was not mandated by the Mosaic law, since the law did not yet exist.

By contrast, Israel, rescued out of Egypt and ushered into the land of promise, was called to see itself as a "kingdom of priests" and a "holy nation" (Exod 19:6). The "tenth" became part of the Mosaic law—a symbolic and sustaining aspect of Israel's "constitution" as God's people. The tenth gave stability to the community, allowing it to stay in the land—to be more than a nomadic, purely amorphous and theoretical "idea" of God's kingdom of priests.

I became aware of two economic patterns embedded in Israel's life that were designed to further the interests of governance, worship, and relief for the poor. They were the Sabbath cycle (including the Sabbath day, the Sabbath year, and Jubilee)[14] and the tithing system.

The tithing system made provision for worship by ensuring regular financial support of the ministry of the tabernacle and then the temple (Num 18:21–23) and by calling on all Israelites to come together for a feast "in the presence of the LORD your God" (Deut 14:22–23). The tithing system also safeguarded just governance by demanding that support of the sanctuary and its personnel trumped governmental claims to a tithe (see 1 Sam 8:15,17) and by ensuring adequate compensation for Levites and priests whose call to service precluded their share in landed estates (Num 18:20–21). Further, the tithing system ensured relief for the poor, mandating a "third year tithe" that went to foreign residents, orphans, and widows as well as to the Levites (Deut 14:28–29). It seemed that there was a profound dynamism in the call both for a grand vision of what it is to be God's people and for a down-to-earth program for realizing the vision in real life.

Similarly, after the demise of the work that Mort had set out to accomplish in his church plant, I concluded two things. First, Jesus calls each of us to ponder and live out "the more important matters of the law—justice, mercy, and faith" (Matt 23:23). Second, I concluded that Jesus does not intend "the more important matters" to float above everyday life in a romantic fog, but to be grounded in maintenance structures supported by a tithe—even down to, as Clar-

---

14. Regrettably, I do not have the leisure to explore the relationship between the Sabbath pattern and the tithe in this chapter.

ence Jordan so masterfully paraphrased it, "your pennies, nickels, and dimes."[15]

So I began, as best I was able, to let my giving begin at the tithe, desiring thereby to support "the more important matters." And this brings us back to Jesus and Matt 23:23 (and Luke 11:42).

Tithing? No, It's about More Important Matters

First, I would like to address the substantive helpfulness of a view like Witherington's, that is, to the inadequacy of a focus on tithing in the new covenant. Jesus does indeed call for something more radical than a tenth of our income. He calls for everything.

When I first trusted Christ, someone gave me a tract about "one priceless pearl" (Matt 13:46). In the tract, heaven (or a relationship with God) was portrayed as a possession so valuable that to try to purchase it would diminish its value and insult God who wishes to give it freely. Nice lesson about God's grace. But that is not what the parable means. The parable says the kingdom of heaven is like a merchant who finds one valuable pearl (apparently in some marketplace) and goes, sells all he has, and purchases it. In the parable, there is "one priceless pearl" up for purchase. The question is, what is it going to cost you, and are you willing to pay it? The pearl does not cost 10 percent. It costs everything. The question of a measly tithe pales beside the realization that Jesus' coming presses the more important questions of justice, mercy, and faith with respect to our money, financial assets, and possessions.

Jesus' coming calls for a response of "justice," that is, doing right by others, furthering God's right ordering of relationships according to His fairness (Matt 23:23; Luke 11:42). A case in point is Jesus' pronouncement, "Today salvation has come to this house," when chief tax collector Zacchaeus promised to give half his goods to the poor and to make fourfold restitution to those he has defrauded (Luke 19:1–9). In another place, Jesus railed at the injustice of refusing to support one's parents in the name of religion (Matt 15:4–9; Mark 7:6–13).

Without any prompting, the most down and out and desperate seemed to understand that Jesus embodies God's mercy. "Have mercy," they ask over and over again.[16] And so Jesus' coming presents

---

15. C. Jordan, *The Cotton Patch Version of Matthew* 23:23; see http://www.rockhay. org/cottonpatch/scriptdex.htm#matthew.

16. Matthew 9:27 (two blind men); Matt 20:30–31 = Mark 10:47–48 = Luke 18:38–39 (the blind men/man outside Jericho); Matt 15:22 (the Canaanite woman); 17:15 (the

the demand of "mercy," that is, the call to display a surprising love that goes beyond what is merely "due," even (depending on the circumstances) withholding a retribution that is "due." The inquisitorial lawyer recognizes that the Good Samaritan's generosity of time and resources is a study in showing "mercy" (Luke 10:37). Receiving mercy creates an obligation to identify with others who have wronged you, and to extend to them what has been extended to you, as the king said to the unforgiving servant in Jesus' parable: "I forgave you. Shouldn't you also have had mercy . . . as I had mercy on you?" (Matt 18:32–33).

Jesus' coming fundamentally raises the question of "faith" (Matt 23:23) or "love for God" (Luke 11:42). Which will you serve, God or Mammon? Because you can't serve both (Matt 6:24; Luke 16:13). Where will you lay up treasure for yourself, heaven or here (Matt 6:19–21; Luke 12:33–34)? Will you entrust your future to your labors and your fortunes, or to the God who provides (Luke 12:13–21)? To whom are you loyal? Caesar? Self? God? (Matt 22:15–22). This is the implicit question that sent the rich young ruler packing: "Whom do you love, your money or God? What do you believe in, it or Him? Will you belong to it, or will you belong to Me and to those who are Mine?" There are no halfway—much less "10 percent"—answers to any of these demands.

Matthew 23 sets up the "scribes and Pharisees, hypocrites" as foils, examples of how not to be a disciple.[17] In the first Beatitude Jesus proclaimed that those whose poverty of spirit causes them to trust and depend on God are "blessed" (Matt 5:3), but in Matthew 23 he pronounced "woe" on those whose faith is defined by pride of title and prestige.[18] He cursed those who, rather than mourn the failings of those who do not obey the law, withhold help and instead pour on more demands.[19] Jesus cursed those who, rather than live out Abram's call to bless the nations by telling God's story in meek-

---

father of the epileptic).

17. C. Keener, *A Commentary on the Gospel of Matthew* (Grand Rapids: Eerdmans, 1999), 536. Contending that the fivefold structure of Matthew's teaching sections are reminiscent of the Pentateuch, N. T. Wright likened the Beatitudes in the Sermon on the Mount to the blessings of Mount Gerazim and the woes against the scribes and Pharisees to the curses of Mount Ebal (*The New Testament and the People of God* [Minneapolis: Fortress, 1992], 386–87). For the sake of his followers and uncommitted onlookers, Jesus portrayed the way of life versus the way of death. I borrowed Wright's architectural observation; the pairings of the "Beatitudes" and the "woes" are my own.

18. Cf. Matt. 5:3 with 23:5–12.

19. Cf. Matt. 5:4 with 23:4.

ness, go across the sea to make proselytes "twice as fit for hell as you are!"[20] While Israel's teachers should have been models of purity of heart, they were corrupt to the core of their being.[21] Their pretense at being sons of peace belied their hostility to God's true prophets; when called to stand with prophets whose truth-telling brings persecution, they flip and join the murderers. "Woe," Jesus said to them seven times over.

At the critical midpoint[22] of Jesus' woes on the scribes and Pharisees stands his condemnation of hypocritical tithing. Rather than bespeaking a hunger and a thirst for God's righteous rule over them and all else, their giving betrays a slothful disengagement from the burning matters that the tithe had been instituted to promote: God's justice and mercy, as well as faith in Him.[23] Their gardens may be dedicated, but their affections, their minds, and their bodies were not.

The Pharisees' scrupulousness at tithing masked a fundamental lack of generosity, for they preferred giving a fixed percentage of crops to the more demanding, more radical, and more important use of their resources to pursue justice and mercy and love for God (Matt 23:23; Luke 11:42).[24] Theirs was religiosity that technically looked right because they were coloring inside the lines, doing as much as was formally, legally, contractually required. But Jesus shattered this pretense.

Matthew invited his readers to share Jesus' angle of vision on those who failed to "get it"—but then to look back upon themselves and reflect on the way that the life of "blessing" rather than of "woe" should characterize them. In this way, Jesus refocused the question of giving around "the more important matters of the law—justice, mercy, and faith." As a whole, the New Testament places the emphasis precisely where Jesus did: "justice, mercy, and faith" and "love for God."

Consequently, New Testament voices do seem generally reticent about a literal tithe. It's almost as though they were bashful, almost as though it would be insulting to have to specify a ceiling or a floor, almost as though there's a refusal to begin measuring who owes what to

---

20. Cf. Matt. 5:5 (see Ps 37:11) with 23:15.
21. Cf. Matt. 5:8 with 23:25–28.
22. This is the fourth of seven woes.
23. Cf. Matt. 5:6 with 23:23–24.
24. Generous Giving, "Frequently Asked Questions," "Questions about Tithing," No. 9, "Will God really 'throw open the floodgates of heaven' if I start to tithe?" http://library.generousgiving.org/ (accessed Feb 3, 2010).

whom. It's almost like Doc's last words at the end of the first *Back to the Future* movie: "Roads? Where we're going, we don't need roads!"

There is perhaps no better exemplar of Jesus' attitude toward giving than that most notorious of Pharisees, Saul, whom we come to know by his Roman name Paul. Paul was doubtless from a background of privilege. You can almost see him puff out his chest as he explained that he was from Tarsus in Cilicia, "a citizen of an important city" (Acts 21:39), and that, no, he had not had to purchase his Roman citizenship, "I was born a citizen" (Acts 22:28). Not only was he a "Hebrew born of Hebrews" (Phil 3:5), but he was the beneficiary of no doubt the finest education available to a Jewish man of his day, trained in Jerusalem "at the feet of Gamaliel" (Acts 22:3).

Paul thus stepped down and across a deep social divide when he accepted God's call to minister among Gentiles. He did so in voluntary conformity with the pattern of the self-impoverishment of Jesus, whose grace Paul summed up in this manner to the Corinthians (arguably one of the wealthiest of his congregations):[25] "Though He was rich, for your sake He became poor, so that by His poverty you might become rich." (2 Cor 8:9). And he placed that self-impoverishing pattern before these same Corinthians (1 Cor 4:11–13,16):

> Up to the present hour we are both hungry and thirsty; we are poorly clothed, roughly treated, homeless; we labor, working with our own hands. When we are reviled, we bless; when we are persecuted, we endure it; when we are slandered, we respond graciously. Even now, we are like the world's garbage, like the dirt everyone scrapes off their sandals. . . . Therefore, I urge you, to imitate me.

Paul nearly tripped over himself not to play the normative card with the Corinthians when it came to the money they had voluntarily promised for the Jerusalem collection. In 2 Corinthians 8–9 he used every term he could think of to talk about money without talking about money. Though he could have appealed to duty, he did not want to do so. He painted his portrait of Christ's becoming poor to make many rich, and then urged the Corinthians to understand that "God loves a cheerful giver" (2 Cor 9:7).

When early church fathers like Irenaeus and Justin Martyr and Tertullian placed a premium on the voluntary, rather than coercive,

---

25. R. M. Kidd, *Wealth and Beneficence in the Pastoral Epistles: A "Bourgeois" Form of Early Christianity?* (Atlanta: Scholars Press, 1990), especially 67–69.

nature of Christian giving, they were picking up on the New Testament's notion that true obedience to God's law can only be present where it is existential; it can arise only out of a love that God has written on a heart He has redeemed.[26]

Congruently, when Basil the Great fretted over why he should keep anything and John Chrysostom excoriated the rich for being generous toward church buildings rather than toward a Christian neighbor in whom Christ really dwells, they resonated with Jesus' own challenge that the kingdom costs not a mere 10 percent, but everything we are and have.[27]

Tithing? Yes, It's about "Not Neglecting the Others"

Conversely, I now address my view of what is correct in a perspective like Kendall's, one that sees the tithing principle carrying over into the new covenant era.

To be sure, while Jesus puts the focus on "the more important matters," He nonetheless concluded that "these things should have been done without neglecting the others" (Matt 23:23). These are sobering words. I don't see how we can dismiss them.

---

26. Irenaeus (*Against Heresies* IV, XVIII [*ANF.*1, 484f], in Lukas Vischer, *Tithing in the Early Church* [Minneapolis: Fortress, Facet Books, 1966], 14): "[B]y the very oblations, the indication of liberty may be set forth. . . . [The Jews] had indeed the tithes of their goods consecrated to Him, but those who have received liberty set aside all their possessions for the Lord's purposes, bestowing joyfully and freely"; Tertullian (*Apologeticus* 39.5 [LCL, no. 250], trans. T. R. Glover and G. H. Rendall and discussed in Martin Hengel, *Property and Riches in the Early Church: Aspects of a Social History of Early Christianity* [Minneapolis: Fortress, 1974], 66–69): "Even if there is a chest of a sort, it is not made up of money paid in entrance fees, as if religion were a matter of contract. Every man once a month brings some modest coin—or whenever he wishes, and only if he does which, and if he can; for nobody is compelled; it is a voluntary offering. You might call them the trust funds of piety"; for Justin Martyr, see below.

27. Basil (Ep. 223 *Against Eustathius of Sebasteia* [*NPNF.*2 8:263], as cited in C. Paul Schroeder [ed.], *St. Basil the Great on Social Justice* [Crestwood, NY: St. Vladimir's Seminary Press, 2009]): "Then I read the Gospel, and I saw there that a great means of reaching perfection was the selling of one's goods, sharing them with the poor, giving up all care for this life, and the refusal to allow the soul to be turned by any sympathy to things of earth"; John Chrysostom (*Homiliae in Matthaeum 50.4* [*NPNF.*2 ad loc.], as cited in Rodney A. Whitacre, *A Patristic Greek Reader* [Peabody: Hendrickson, 2007], 254): "And also consider this concerning Christ: whenever he goes about as a wanderer and a stranger, needing a roof, and you yourself, neglecting to receive him, beautify pavement and walls and capitals of columns, and you fasten gold chains through lamps, but him, bound [with chains] in prison, you do not want to see."

It is inadequate to observe that Jesus was addressing scribes and Pharisees rather than post-Easter Christians.[28] Even though he addressed His "woes" in the second person, Jesus considered the scribes and Pharisees to be beyond instruction. The disciples are the true audience—in fact, the audiences for the Sermon on the Mount and the denunciations of the scribes and Pharisees are one and the same: "His disciples" and "the crowds" (5:1; 7:28; 23:1). Matthew 23:23–24 is a part of Matt 28:19–20's baptismal life, part of "everything I have commanded you."

It is inadequate to say that if we're going to enforce the tithe, we need to enforce usury laws as well.[29] We certainly should not be lending to others—whether brothers and sisters in Christ or not—to their disadvantage.

It is inadequate to observe that the original tithe was addressed only to original landowners in the Promised Land and that it only covered agricultural produce. Even the Mosaic law provided a "cash for cabbage" program so agricultural assets could be liquidated and presented in the temple (Lev 27:31–33; Deut 14:24–25). In the typological advancement of redemption past an agricultural economy and past a people defined by the geography of Palestine, surely Christians can figure out the implications of concepts like "firstfruits" and "tithe" in the post-Easter situation and in economies of manufacturing and services.

It is inadequate to dismiss the possibility of an obligation to tithe in view of the fact that it appears there were two tithes every year and a third tithe every third year, meaning Israelites were essentially tithing 23.3 percent.[30] Maybe we should be talking about 23.3 percent. Then again, maybe "tithe" isn't supposed to be taken with pedantic literalism.[31]

In a host of ways, Matthew expected his readers—including us, I submit—to make appropriate adjustments. Indeed, in the new covenant situation, cleansed lepers need neither to present themselves to a priest nor to offer a sacrifice[32]—their great high priest has already

28. D. A. Croteau, *You Mean I Don't Have to Tithe? A Deconstruction of Tithing and a Reconstruction of Post-Tithe Giving*, McMaster Theological Studies Series (Eugene, OR: Pickwick, 2010), 129–30.

29. Witherington, *Jesus and Money*, 22–23.

30. Croteau, *You Mean I Don't Have to Tithe?* 107.

31. Without arguing the case, I register here my appreciation for J. M. Baumgarten's thesis that the tithe isn't always necessarily a literal 10 percent ("On the Non-Literal Use of ma'ăśēr/dekatē," *JBL* 103 [1984]: 245–51).

32. Croteau, *You Mean I Don't Have to Tithe?* 130.

declared them cleansed by virtue of his perfect, once-for-all sacrifice. For 2,000 years we've understood that in the new covenant, just as in the old covenant, God does not want us to bring a polluted offering to Him. Where lack of reconciliation creates cracks in the walls of the new temple of the Spirit, it is certainly incumbent upon parties involved to seek each other out, embrace in forgiveness, then bring their gifts to "the altar" (Matt 5:24).

The challenges of issues like these do not obviate the obligation of the tithe. In view of Jesus' apparent lack of interest in spelling out what "without neglecting the others" involves, I do not believe He meant for us to replace His day's casuistry with a new one. But I do believe He taught that the tithing principle stands. It carries symbolic freight, and in my view symbols are significant! We offer a proportion of our wealth as the Lord's rightful due in view of His claim on all that we are and all that He has entrusted to us.

To understand the carry-over of the tithing principle, I think it's helpful to return to the dynamism of Jesus' call: a "go" and a "stay." "Follow me," Jesus said, not just to select Galilean fishermen and tax collectors, but to all. What "follow me" looks like is principial abandonment—heart-abandonment—of all by all. For some, it means packing our bags. For others, it means staying home.

Similarly, "sell your belongings and give to the poor, and . . . follow Me" (Matt 19:21) means exactly the same for all. "It is no great gain to be poor in possessions but rich in passions," as Clement of Alexandria sagely and pastorally observed.[33] What Jesus demanded is that we surrender our passions to Him. For some, it means moving to a monastery or a mission apartment or a manse. For others, it means remaining right where we are, "having as not having" and "using as not using up" (1 Cor 7:30–31).

Indeed, people like Paul and Basil and Chrysostom and Francis leave us with probing questions about why any of us should hold on to anything. But the fact is—or it certainly appears to be—that Jesus doesn't call everybody to do what the rich young ruler refused to do or what Paul was willing to do. Many of us He leaves at home like Mary and Martha, or like Zacchaeus. He calls us to live vested, mundane lives, and to use resources He provides in the service of His church and His work.

The tithe principle is an enormous help for those of us called to "stay." It's congruent with the "earthiness" of the Mosaic law that

---

33. Clement, *Rich Man*, 15.

Jesus mentioned a tithe of garden plants. The Mosaic law brought huge principial concerns down to earth. The Mosaic law precisely mirrored the three great values that Jesus pointed to—justice, mercy, and faith. The Levitical tithe ensured just provision for ministers of Israel's cultus. The poor tithe extended God's redemptive mercy to aliens and orphans and widows. The feast tithe occasioned all Israel's celebrating its common faith. New covenant giving no less than Old should concretely aim to further God's great values: justice, mercy, faith, and (to use Luke's term) love of God.

James, Jesus' half brother, called us "the firstfruits of His creatures" (Jas 1:18). In doing so, he invited us to reflect on the way that Deuteronomy 26 conjoins the firstfruit offering (Deut 26:1–11) and the tithe (vv. 12–15). Together these acts of worship serve as a dual capstone to the sort of giving that God's generosity calls forth. Israel was in promise what the church is now in reality: a vanguard that signals God's renewal of the human race. All of us can confess—whether of Jewish or Gentile extraction—that we are children of "a wandering Aramean" who have been delivered "with a strong hand and an outstretched arm." Now we worship before the Lord, and through our firstfruits and tithes we care for the alien and orphan and widow, and we submit to His constitution of us as "His special people . . . a holy people" (Deut 26:5,8,10,12,18,19).

Some of us live that "firstfruits" life radically and incarnationally. We "go" like the desert fathers in the ancient church and the monks of the medieval church. Others of us live out no less a challenge as we "stay": we live ordinary lives, many of us surrounded by tremendous wealth, with access to luxuries the human race has never seen before. We are called to stay in our families, our cities, our schools, our workplaces, and be "firstfruits" of the as-yet unclaimed, yet-to-be-harvested whole. We tell and live the story of the world's rightful King and Lord. We own minivans, but we are not owned by minivans. We are "in" suburbs, but we are not "of" them.

It is with an eye, I think, to those of us called to follow Jesus while we stay that He said, "These things should have been done without neglecting the others." Part of the way we help ourselves to inhabit this duality of following while "staying" is to say, "This tithe—*Your* tithe—is my reminder that it's all Yours." To borrow a line from G. K. Chesterton, it is a means of participating in the "romance of orthodoxy." It is a way of keeping our fingers but loosely attached to the things still held in trust. It is even a way of remaining ready to join the fellowship of those called to sell all, give to the poor, and follow Christ. And it is a way of carrying a share of the cost of furthering God's kingdom, of helping to give shape to the house He is building as His dwelling.

What Matters: Keeping God's Commands

Thus it is worth taking another look at Paul's attitude toward finances and the church. There's an almost scary multivalence to the Bible's approach to normativeness—to the concept of law.[34] That is especially true when it comes to Paul. To the Galatians he sounded nearly antinomian: "Christ has liberated us to be free. . . . don't submit again to a yoke of slavery. . . .what matters is faith working through love" (Gal 5:1,6). To the Corinthians he sounded nearly legalistic: we must try "not to exceed what is written" because "what matters is the keeping of the commandments of God" (1 Cor 4:6; 7:19, NASB).

With respect to Paul we need to understand what kind of instruction a particular time and place called for. To the Galatians, who failed to see how much we live now in the age of fulfillment, Paul stressed existential and situational considerations: not law, but "faith working through love" (5:6); not law, but "new creation" (6:15). To the Corinthians, who failed to see that we are not yet "as the angels" in the eschaton and who overemphasized Paul's "everything is permissible" sayings, Paul asserted that God's commandments still stand.[35] He struck a note of normativeness. He nuanced it wonderfully and extraordinarily—we relate to the law through Christ, after all (1 Cor 9:21). Thus, Paul illustrated the continuing claims of the "commandments of God" for believers not with a list of rules, but with a reminder of the way redemption reorients self-understanding: "You

---

34. In the following, I use the terminology of "normative," "situational," and "existential" in accordance with John Frame's tri-perspective explanation of God's lordship: His authority to command, His sovereign control over all things, and His personal presence within his creation (e.g., J. Frame, *Salvation Belongs to the Lord: An Introduction to Systematic Theology* (Phillipsburg, NJ: P&R, 2006). Much of Frame's work is accessible at http://www.frame-poythress.org/.

35. I agree with the way A. T. Lincoln (*Paradise Now and Not Yet: Studies in the Role of the Heavenly Dimension in Paul's Thought with Special Reference to His Eschatology* [Cambridge: University Press, 1981, 2004], 33–35) assessed the Corinthian situation: "These Corinthians believed that the kingdom was already here and that they were already enjoying the eschatological blessings of freedom and fullness associated with the consummation. . . . [T]he apostle has to show that Christian existence at present involves suffering and that 'the church is as yet before the angels and that it is not yet as the angels' (4:9)."

were bought at a price; do not become slaves of men" (1 Cor 7:23). The apostle did not back down from his premise that the believer's new situation is one of living as "a new creation" (2 Cor 5:17). This is still the "acceptable time . . . the day of salvation" (2 Cor 6:2).

But Paul wanted the Corinthians to understand there are important caveats to his teaching that "everything is permissible." He followed that statement with "not everything is helpful . . . not everything builds up" (1 Cor 6:12; 10:23)—that is, my freedom is freedom only to the extent that it expresses itself in love for my neighbor, especially my Christian neighbor. "I will not be brought under the control of anything" (1 Cor 6:12)—that is, my freedom is only freedom to the extent that it participates in my ongoing deliverance from dominance by things like avarice, lust, injustice, anger, idolatry, foolishness.

Moreover, Paul strongly countered the Corinthians' pretense at being "already full" and having already "begun to reign" (1 Cor 4:8). Instead, the Corinthians needed to learn from Israel's wanderings (1 Cor 10:1–13). Their situation "between the times" (delivered from sin and death, but not yet resurrected) meant that falling was yet possible, and that they—even in the new covenant—needed positive instruction from Israel's story and the commandments issued to her. "Now these things happened to them as examples, and they were written as a warning to us, on whom the ends of the ages have come" (1 Cor 10:11).

It is in this regard that we should consider Paul's likening of financial support for gospel ministers to the financial support the Mosaic law had required for temple workers. Paul called the Corinthians "God's building" (1 Cor 3:9), indeed "God's sanctuary," the "sanctuary of the living God" (1 Cor 3:16; 2 Cor 6:16). The church's obligation, therefore, to support its ministers is more than a matter of general reciprocity—of the sowing of "spiritual things" rightly yielding a return of "material things" (1 Cor 9:11). Paul likened gospel ministers to Levites and priests of the old covenant who "perform the temple services" and thus "eat the food from the temple" (vv. 13–14).[36]

---

36. Though there is some conversation in the commentaries about the matter, there's no question to me that, despite the fact that he had to correct confusion about trafficking with pagan temples in Corinth, the model that Paul placed before the Corinthians for the kind of temple in terms of which they are to define their own identity was Israel's temple and its practices. The various options for Paul's temple allusion at 1 Cor 9:13 are nicely laid out by A. Köstenberger and D. Croteau ("Reconstructing a Biblical Model for Giving: A Discussion of Relevant Systematic Issues and New Testament Principles" [http://biblicalfoundations.org/pdf/pdfarticles/bbrtithing2.pdf]), and I think their conclusion is correct: "Paul probably has in mind the Jerusalem temple" (12n.61).

Implicitly, Paul applied the typological significance of temple tithes in support of Jesus' directing that "those who preach the gospel should earn their living by the gospel" (v. 14).

If his own Jewish background gave him a tithe as a personal standard of giving or as one to promote among his churches, he did not explicitly tell us so. From Luke's description of Paul as continuing to be a practicing Jew,[37] it is not difficult to imagine that Paul practiced normal giving as a Jew. He may very well have done so, and taught Gentile believers a similar pattern. We can only guess. What he made clear is that giving should be patterned after Christ's, and it should be joyful.

In 2 Corinthians 8–9 Paul addressed the Corinthians' commitment to an occasional gift for Jerusalem. Their ongoing financial responsibility for worship, support of ministers, and care of their poor is simply not under discussion. Even here, though, he was not afraid to subtly remind them that they have given their word and that others in far less favorable financial circumstances are giving sacrificially; he even invoked a measure of the so-called Malachi "storehouse" logic: to paraphrase Paul, "Give and see if God doesn't give back" (2 Cor 9:6–14).

Paul's basic premise gives us the responsibility for assessing the pastoral situation in which we live. Where believers live under a Galatian mind-set, we may need to sound more like the Paul of Galatians. Where tithing, for instance, is perceived as an odious burden, or is thought of as a means of placating a God who may require payment beyond the blood of Christ, or, just as bad, it is commanded as a cynical mechanism for contractually binding God somehow to respond with financial blessings, it may be necessary to sound anti-tithing, to speak of "post-tithe giving," maybe even to introduce a concept like, oh, I don't know, "grace giving."[38]

Where believers live under a Corinthian delusion, we need to sound more like the Paul of the Corinthian correspondence. Where supposed freedom from the Moses law has resulted in lawlessness, we may need to turn to the commandments and tease out their

---

37. E.g., circumcising Timothy (Acts 16:3); keeping what appears to be a Nazirite vow (18:18); and underwriting such vows for others, including participating in temple rituals and offerings (21:23–26).

38. I think that Köstenberger and Croteau's "grace giving" principles embody a great deal of wisdom: that giving should be systematic; proportional; sacrificial/generous; intentional; motivated by love, equality, and a desire to bless; cheerful; and voluntary. None of these values would not characterize my own advocacy of a tithing principle, including voluntarism (God doesn't want begrudging obedience).

implications. It's not difficult for me to see how those "thinking Paul's thoughts after him" might apply Old Testament tithing legislation in settings where the spirit is antinomian, where God's generosity is being presumed on, where believers are acting as though they were financially autonomous and have no obligation for the welfare of their churches, for their Christian or non-Christian neighbors, or for the needs of a broken world. Thus, altogether understandably and not inappropriately, I think, *The Apostolic Constitutions* urge the bishop to receive "tenths and first-fruits, which are given according to the command, as a man of God; as also let him dispense in a right manner the free-will offerings which are brought in on account of the poor."[39] Far from lapsing into pre-Christian legalism, such an exhortation bespeaks a profoundly Pauline appreciation for what it is to live simultaneously in the age of fulfillment (the tabernacle was, after all, "fore-appointed for a testimony of the Church") and in an age in which we must be on guard against presuming on God's promises, and thus must "use the things which belong to the Lord, but do not abuse them."[40]

How Much?

I submit that from Jesus' denunciation of the Pharisees we are not to tithe the way so many of us pay our taxes—making sure to give as much as required and no more. In this regard, one concern of the anti-tithe or post-tithe voices is laudable. Securing autonomy over the other 90 percent by relinquishing claim on 10 percent is the economy of the Devil. It is to turn God's economy on its head.

As clear as Jesus was that we are not to neglect "the others" (Matt 23:23), a reference to the tithe, he did not say much about how to do that. He did not say whether and how to bridge the gap between Israel's agricultural tithe and other economies; that is, He did not say what artisans or bankers are obligated to do with the tithe principle. He gave us no calculus to determine with certainty what the original Mosaic formula was, much less what it was in His day, or how to re-

---

39. *Constitutions of the Holy Apostles* (*ANF* 7, 408–9; http://www.ccel.org/schaff/anf07/ix.iii.iv.html).

40. I believe L. Vischer's (*Tithing in the Early Church*, 11–30) reading of the reemergence of a theology of tithing in the early church is insufficiently attentive to the typological rather than allegorical and pragmatic lenses through which his sources (principally, *The Apostolic Constitutions*, Origen, and John Chrysostom) read the Old Testament. Regretfully, I do not have time or space to pursue the question here.

configure it for modern Western democracies. He did not say whether to tithe from gross or net, or whether to tithe from stock dividends or tax refunds, or whether the idea of "proportionality" in giving is simply a heart thing, or a community-derived thing, or whether it's our church's business or ours to work out simply before God, or whether it's supposed to go to officially constituted churches or para-church ministries.

It's as though Jesus expects us to discern, to exercise wisdom in dependence on the Holy Spirit. When you have finally learned to drive, you don't keep reading the driver's manual. You don't read it, not because it is no longer relevant, but because it's inside you. With the coming of Christ, God wrote His law on our hearts. He gave us the Holy Spirit, a Spirit of understanding, a Spirit that teaches discernment. We received the Spirit who assures us that our Heavenly Father proudly displays our feeblest attempts at obedience on His heavenly refrigerator. We have become His "works of art" (*poiēma* at Eph 2:10), and He delights in our grateful offerings regardless of how little they approximate true beauty. His vision is forever impaired by the lens of Christ.

Bringing an Offering: The Worship Dimension

As I have no doubt just made evident, I am reluctant to give specific answers to questions about tithing that many perceive to be vital, such as whether the tithe is a starting point or baseline. I don't think such questions are vital. I think they trivialize something tremendous. I don't think the Bible is a rule book for tithing. I think the Bible invites us to delve into a story and listen for where its plot line takes us. I think the Bible invites us to immerse ourselves in baptismal reality and to bring our wallets with us. Thus, I think there are some answers that are given only to the worshipper and only in the act of worship—*lex orandi, lex credendi* (to paraphrase: "show me how you pray, and I'll show you what you actually believe"). The writer to the Hebrews wonderfully explained that Jesus—our high priest, the sacrifice and the sacrificer—has provided an altar from which we have the "right to eat," and we respond with a "sacrifice of praise . . . the fruit of our lips that confess His name" and thus we are compelled "to do what is good and to share, for God is pleased with such sacrifices" (Heb 13:10,15–16).

The church my family and I attend takes up a weekly offering and offers weekly communion, following the *Book of Common Prayer*: "Representatives of the congregation bring the people's offerings of bread and wine, and money or other gifts, to the deacon or celebrant." The pattern is ancient, and embodies profound truth.[41] The offering begins the Ministry of the Table, which follows the Ministry of the Word. Ushers pass plates, then, on behalf of the whole congregation, they bring forward a dual offering: the elements for the Table and the monetary donations for the church. (In other times and places, the donations might include livestock or produce or handiwork.)[42] The prayer of Great Thanksgiving that follows celebrates God's attributes and rehearses his creative and redemptive acts. Then the prayer asks the Lord to bless the gifts we have brought—explicitly the bread and wine, and implicitly the monetary donations. Thus, the money takes its rightful place in the commemoration of that grand transaction in which the Giver gives grace upon grace.

Both the communion elements and the money come from a combination of God's work and our own. Bread and wine result from divine produce and human manufacture; in many churches, families bake the communion bread. Our money is no less a result of God's providential care and our labors. In worship, bread and wine establish no merit, but they mean more than their mere physical composition would otherwise suggest. So it is with our money. Our money at the altar is not a payment, but (to paraphrase Luke Timothy Johnson) a symbolic expression of ourselves.[43] It is as much our presenting ourselves to God as the bread and wine are ultimately the Lord's presenting Himself to us.

Further, the Table reminds us of God's lavish generosity. Holding nothing back, Jesus came and made the one offering that counts for our rescue and redemption. "The Messiah also loved us and gave Himself for us, a sacrificial and fragrant offering to God" (Eph 5:2).

---

41. Earliest indications are that the people would bring the wine and the bread, which B. Thompson said were symbols "of the inward offering of themselves" (*Liturgies*, 5). The presider would then offer a prayer of thanksgiving over the bread and the wine—each the result of a combination of God's produce (grain and grapes) on the one hand, and human nurture and manufacture (agriculture, baking, and winemaking) on the other.

42. The fading of the offering of goods in favor of money appears to have been complete by the twelfth century in the West. I have not had leisure to trace the development as closely as I'd like, but see Thompson, *Liturgies*, 44; D. Cloud, "The Theology of the Offertory Collection," in J. D. Chrichton, ed., *The Mass and the People of God* (Collegeville, MN: Liturgical Press, 1966), 117.

43. L. T. Johnson, *Sharing Possessions: Mandate and Symbol of Faith* (Minneapolis: Fortress, 1981), 40.

Jesus, the offering and the offerer, is our model and our leader in worship (Heb 8:2). Thus our offerings imitate Jesus' offering, and we find convergence between "the more important matters . . . without neglecting the others." The liturgy embodies a lovely picture of it all—our offering is about so much more than paying a preacher!

In the Old Testament, living in covenant with the God of rescue required that the Israelites "must love the foreigner, since [they] were foreigners in the land of Egypt" (Deut 10:19).[44] In the New Testament, Jesus commanded, "I give you a new commandment: love one another. Just as I have loved you, you must also love one another" (John 13:34). The generosity of the exodus with "a strong hand and an outstretched arm" (Deut 26:8) yields to the generosity of the incarnation with arms stretched out on a cruel cross. It is no accident that the eucharistic table attracted to itself a second kind of offering, one for the poor. Justin Martyr described the close of the eucharist:

> And the distribution and the participation by each one in those things for which thanks has been given (*ta eucharistēthenta*) take place, and through the deacons it is sent to those who are absent. And those who are well off and who are willing, each according to his own choice, give what they want, and that which is collected is put aside by the leader. And he himself helps the orphans and widows, and those who are in want because of sickness or for some other reason, and those who are in bonds, and the sojourning strangers, and, in a word, he is guardian (*kēdemōn*) for all who are in need.[45]

Small wonder that the early church was known for its generosity. He who was offerer and offering had come. The first church of Jerusalem broke bread together and made sure their poor were cared for (Acts 2:42–47; 6:1–7). Because Christ the Passover lamb has been sacrificed, Paul invited Gentiles to Israel's feast and offered, as his own priestly service, the Gentiles to God. He took up a collection from the Gentiles for the Jews, but the offering was not so much the money as the Gentiles themselves (Rom 15:16; 1 Cor 5:7–8; see Isa 66:20). The one true offering has occasioned our sub-offering.

---

44. Israel's legislation provided special protection for the disadvantaged (e.g., Lev 19:35; 25:38,42,55), and this was explicitly grounded in what the Redeemer God did for his people when they were similarly disadvantaged (e.g., Exod 23:9; Lev 19:34; Deut 10:19; 15:15; 16:12; 24:22).

45. Justin Martyr, *First Apology* 675b–6, with text and translation in Whitacre, *Patristic Greek Reader*, 78, 219.

In his day, the believing Tertullian could proclaim that pagans marveled: "Behold, how they love one another."[46] In his day, the unbelieving Julian, apostate emperor and nephew of Constantine, complained: "They care not only for their poor, but for ours as well!"[47] Calvin made it a practice to take up such an offering for the poor— and many churches still take up a "deacon's offering" in association with communion.

Summary

The Table is where, in the convergence of God's gift and ours, we taste what it is to be swept up into the eternal self-giving of Father, Son, and Holy Spirit. We "become what we eat,"[48] so that when we return to our callings in the world we may "leave a trail of crumbs back" to this very place.[49]

Also, at this Table we taste a portion of a final banquet at which an ultimate reconciliation among estranged brothers and sisters will take place. Perhaps no more important thing can emerge from this conversation about tithing than the realization that we all need to appreciate the merely partial nature of the truth any of us perceives, the certainly errant nature of some portion of what any of us believes, and the attendant necessity, as Paul might put it, to "wait for one another" (1 Cor 11:33).

Dante comes to mind again. In his vision of paradise, the Dominican St. Thomas Aquinas, one of the great promulgators of Christian theology, spoke the praise of St. Francis of Assisi, champion of heart-repentance and care for the poor (*Paradiso* XI). Conversely, the Franciscan St. Bonaventure praised St. Dominic, founder of Thomas's order (*Paradiso* XII). Thus, in heaven's symphony of love, orthodoxy lauds orthopathos and orthopraxy. Orthopathos and orthopraxy laud orthodoxy. In glory, complementarity is everywhere, and even back here on earth, where it is easy to yield to competition and opposition, Dante would urge us, I think, to pray "on earth as it is in

---

46. Tertullian, *Apologeticus* 39.7 (LCL).
47. Julian the Apostate, *Epistle* 22, *To Arcacius* (LCL, no. 157), 3.69.
48. As R. Webber (*Ancient-Future Worship: Proclaiming and Enacting God's Narrative* [Grand Rapids: Baker, 2008], 146) riffed on a leading motif in A. Schmemann's *For the Life of the World: Sacraments and Orthodoxy* (Crestwood, NY: St. Vladimir's Seminary Press, 1997).
49. A. Tate, "Take to the World" (Cumbee Road Music, 2002).

heaven." In heaven, enemies embrace and oppositions show themselves to have been ultimately mutually supportive.

If for some of us it seems a trivializing of matters to insert the language of "His tithes" into the equation of our giving, then may we at least make sure our giving is as concrete as the incarnation and the resurrection and our neighbor's and the church's need. If for others of us it seems a vaporizing of matters to paint the picture of God's generosity in Christ and to let folks follow "the Spirit's leading," then may we at least make sure our hearts follow the tithes we offer with lives wholeheartedly given to "justice, mercy, and faith" (Matt 23:23) and "love for God" (Luke 11:42).

CHAPTER 11

Response to Reggie Kidd
Gary North

If you read all the chapters that introduce each section before you read any of the responses, you will have a major advantage with my chapter. You will know exactly what I am saying. This clarity comes at a price. I do not leave you much wiggle room. I am telling you that you own 10 percent of the net increase in your wealth whenever you receive that increase in the form of either money or consumer goods as a result of an economic exchange. I do not argue that if your investment doubles one day and you do not sell it, you owe a tithe on the increase. It may fall tomorrow. The Israelite farmer did not owe a tithe on the market appreciation of his farm if he did not sell it. He did if he leased it. You owe the tithe when you sell it, just as you owe the tax collector.

This is the new covenant tithe. You owe all of it to your local congregation. Why? Because you are a member of God's royal priesthood (1 Pet 2:9). You are therefore an heir to the covenant oath of the Israelites, who constituted a kingdom of priests (Exod 19:6). As a nation of priests, they owed a tithe to members of the priestly tribe, Levi, the tribe that represented them ecclesiastically before God. Your local congregation's bank account is the judicial equivalent of the Mosaic covenant's storehouse, to which the tithes were brought by the Israelites (Mal 3:10). Not to bring them was the judicial act of robbing God (v. 9). I am warning you not to rob God. If you rob God, you will answer for this on judgment day. You will answer even more to your detriment after you have read this book. To whom more is revealed, more is expected (Luke 12:47–48).

If you do not believe in the accuracy of my exegesis of Hebrews 7, the chapter on the new covenant priesthood, then you come under the judgment of one or more of the other three chapters. Take your pick. These chapters tell you that you may owe God a lot more than 10 percent. Why? Because God may be calling you to give more. I do not know how much God is calling you to give. I do know what God requires that you pay and to which institution you owe it on His behalf. My position is that the new covenant tithe, after the cessation of the Mosaic covenant at the fall of Jerusalem in AD 70, has nothing to do with giving. It has everything to do with paying. You do not owe a gift. You owe a tithe.

The other chapters reject my position. They all categorize the tithe under "gifts to God." The moment that an expositor does this, all limits are off. The issue of what you owe God moves from that which is judicially mandatory, but also judicially limited, to the notoriously unreliable world of self-examination. The world of self-examination is sometimes too lenient and sometimes too rigorous, but it is never fixed. There are no guidelines. There is no blueprint. There is, therefore, no peace.

Once you reject my position, you may cry peace, peace, but there will be no peace. I offer peace, not at any price, but at 10 percent of your net income when it is received in the form of money or consumer goods. This is a bargain. This is God's bargain.

I had hoped that Reggie Kidd would pursue the issue of Israel's status as a kingdom of priests. He writes, "By contrast, Israel, rescued out of Egypt and ushered into the land of promise, was called to see itself as a 'kingdom of priests' and a 'holy nation' (Exod 19:6). The 'tenth' became part of the Mosaic law—a symbolic and sustaining aspect of Israel's 'constitution' as God's people." But then he added this but with no explanation of it: "The tenth gave stability to the community, allowing it to stay in the land—to be more than a nomadic, purely amorphous and theoretical 'idea' of God's kingdom of priests." I am not sure what he means by this. I know how I would apply it. The land of promise gave them an inheritance. The Levites did not share in the distribution of rural, unwalled land; so God gave them the tithe as their inheritance (Num 18:21). But Kidd does not extend his remarks. He does not connect the Levites' tithe, as I do, to the land, inheritance, and Israel as a kingdom of priests.

Kidd moves from the Levitical tithe to Jesus and says, "Jesus does indeed call for something more radical than a tenth of our income. He calls for everything." Here, he moves the discussion of the tithe from a priestly function to a service function. What I ask—not rhetorically—is this seemingly obvious question: "Did God not call for everything under the old covenant?" This raises a corollary: "What evidence is there in the old covenant or Old Testament that God called for anything less than Jesus called for?"

The heathen under the old covenant was not required by God to tithe. Even the stranger living inside the land was not required to tithe. Yet God calls all men to worship Him all of the time. He calls for everything that a heathen has to offer. But He does not expect the heathen to tithe, nor is there any verse in the Bible that mandates this. Why not? Because no heathen is part of the kingdom of priests/royal priesthood. The tithe is a legal obligation of the lower priesthood to the higher priesthood: Abram to Melchizedek, Israelites to Levites, Levites to temple priests, and church members to their local congregations. *The tithe is a priestly function.*

Kidd joins the other commentators in his assumption that the tithe is in some way related to giving, to charity. This was not the case under the Mosaic law. I am speaking of the tithe owed to the Levites and the tithe owed by the Levites. *Tithing is not giving.* Tithing is paying what you owe to God by way of a local congregation. Tithing is not optional to members of God's royal priesthood.

There is a tendency for Christians to proclaim, "We're under grace, not law." Thank God that man's institutions are not under such grace. They are under God's law. Whenever their officers assert their institutional autonomy from God's law, they become tyrannical over time. God's law places them under constraints. The law of the tithe was designed by God to protect Christians from churches that would extract more than a tithe if they could get away with it. The law of the tithe places limits on the institutional church.

Kidd says that Jesus did not tell us what to do: "He did not say what artisans or bankers are obligated to do with the tithe principle." True, but Hebrews 7 surely does. The royal priesthood must tithe to a higher priesthood.

Kidd uses an analogy. "When you have finally learned to drive, you don't keep reading the driver's manual." Quite true. But Kidd and the other contributors also insist that there is no new covenant driver's manual on tithing. I say that such a manual is needed to limit the authorities. We do not want to drive on roads where traffic cops can make up speed laws whenever they have not met this month's quota of speeding citations.

Kidd asserts that "the kingdom costs not a mere 10 percent, but everything we are and have." This is a startling confusion of biblical categories. First, the tithe is what church members owe to their local congregations. The tithe finances the ecclesiastical-institutional aspect of the kingdom of God. Second, the other 90 percent of our net increase is supposed to finance the other 90 percent of our work in the kingdom of God. By equating (1) God's comprehensive claims of total service—100 percent—that are owed to Him by everyone—100 percent—in history with (2) the tithe, which is owed by royal priests to their local congregations, is to confuse the institutional church with the kingdom of God.

When members of the royal priesthood do not bring their tithes to the institutional church, they are stealing from God (Mal 3:9). The tithe was not voluntary under the Mosaic law. Why not? Because the Levites and the priests had a lawful claim on certain restricted forms of support: the tithe, the firstfruits, the firstborn males, and participation in required feasts. This has been reduced to just the tithe in the New Testament. Still, the priests complain. "We're under grace, not law." The guilt that this produces is enormous. There is guilt for having stolen from God. There is guilt for having not given enough.

Pay your tithe. End the guilt.

CHAPTER 12

Response to Reggie Kidd
Ken Hemphill and Bobby Eklund

Tithing in the New Covenant

Reggie Kidd uses an approach we could all strive to emulate as well as recommend to others whose interpretations and views do not necessarily align with those we hold. He is admirable in genuine efforts to present differing views, weighing and testing them against each other and providing insights into his reasoning.

We found it both interesting and thought provoking that the word "casuistry" was used in the title. According to Webster, casuistry is "the solving of cases of right and wrong in conduct by deciding how far circumstances alter cases; used disparagingly of subtle or false reasoning." If we understand him correctly, we take this to present a case for interpreting Scripture in the light of context. However, since the connection to the title and the whole of the text is not crystal clear, the reader must wonder.

We will focus our comments on the author's general approach, some of his interpretations, and finally the resulting conclusions.

General Approach

Kidd spends considerable effort in explaining his personal background and faith walk that influence and inform his position on tithing as scriptural under the new covenant. We find this both helpful and honest. Throughout the text he points out some of the common, albeit mistaken, views on tithing that all could acknowledge having heard in some form or other and that generally inform responses to those seeking a full understanding of references as well as the principles undergirding them. The clearest evidence of this is seen in his coupling of giving and heart attitude: "freedom from avarice, freedom in loving God—whether with or without a lot of money and 'stuff,'" while addressing the real question of "whether and if and how God intends tithing to be a part of such an equation."

Interpretations

In contrasting both well-articulated views on the "tests" of Old Testament scriptural mandates' applicability to New Testament practices, Kidd quotes Ben Witherington's view that "the basic rule of guidance . . . is that if the Old Testament comment is reaffirmed in the New Testament for Christians, then we are still obligated to do it. If it is not, then we are not," while others would say with equal confidence, "or if not specifically changed, then it applies." Referring to the Matt 23:23–24 passage, Kidd says that "the interpretation of this passage turns on a prior understanding of the way the Christian story works." He shines brighter in declaring the better approach as asking, "How does Christ's coming allow the true significance of old covenant features to come to the surface in the new covenant?"

The discussion regarding the two economic patterns embedded in Israel's life and designed to further the interests of governance, worship, and poor relief as being the Sabbath cycle and the tithing system is particularly helpful and seems to get at the very heart of God's intent. Tithing, we believe, cannot be separated from worship; the two are inextricably linked. Having settled the matter of giving a tithe for himself, the author guides us into thinking about "the more important matters" (Matt 23:23) and begins with the statement that "Jesus does indeed call for something more radical than a tenth of our income. He calls for everything."

We believe he paints an accurate and rich picture of just who Jesus addressed in the Matthew 23 passage—not the hypocritically tithing Pharisees upon whom He pronounced woes, but those who stood listening and learning—His disciples and the crowds that followed. The mirror that is held up for the Pharisees is equally our mirror: "Rather than bespeaking a hunger and a thirst for God's righteous rule over themselves and all else as well, their giving betrays a slothful disengagement from the burning matters that the tithe had been instituted to promote: God's justice and mercy, as well as faith in Him."

Sadly, Kidd concludes that New Testament voices are reticent, almost bashful about a literal tithe. But Jesus was neither bashful nor reticent when He declared, "These things should have been done without neglecting the others" (Matt 23:23). There is no ambivalence in this pronouncement. His is the voice of authority and, at the same time, the undisputed voice of love. Kidd states: "These are sobering words. I don't see how we can dismiss them." He has previously stated that the tithe is the beginning point for his own personal giving, and he provides further insight when he says, "I do believe He taught that the tithing principle stands. It carries symbolic freight, and in my view symbols are significant! We offer a proportion of our wealth as the Lord's rightful due in view of His claim on all that we are and all that He has entrusted to us."[1]

Kidd does us great service when he describes the way believers live out their calling to "follow Me"—which looks very different when viewed from person to person and place to place—since all aspects of our lives should be focused on a personal surrender of all that we have and are to Him. Giving tithes and offerings allows God's people to ensure just provisions for ministers, to extend God's redemptive mercy to aliens and orphans and widows, to occasion the celebration of our common faith, and to further God's great values of justice, mercy, faith and love for God.

Under the heading "What Matters: Keeping God's Commands," Kidd describes Paul's method of teaching in the context of the spiritual maturity (or lack thereof) in the churches he established, mentored, and cultivated. The parallels he draws between Old and New Testament practices (financial support for ministers of the gospel as seen in Old Testament support for priests and Levites, the Malachi logic applied to the Corinthians' gift to Jerusalem) are beautiful word pictures of living out and applying the fundamental concepts of giving taught from the beginning. Also, Kidd's argument that Paul emphasizes different sides of the issue based on the needs of the community (i.e., Galatians or Corinthians) is well stated and fits well with C. F. D. Moule's view in *The Birth of the New Testament.*

No one could argue with an approach that calls for spiritual leaders to take their followers' maturity into account as they preach and minister, but a word of caution might be in order lest the reader misunderstand and conclude that the demands of the gospel may not apply to all. Kidd clearly settles the matter when he discusses Paul's

---

1. Cf. Ps 24:1.

appreciation for what has gone before, even as he lives, as we do, in the present age—being aware of our obligation for the welfare of the churches, the unsaved, and the needs of a broken world. Thus an application might be that Paul taught the tithe to new believers because of their basic needs and grace giving to the more mature.

Conclusions

While Kidd can draw no clear conclusions about Paul's personal status as a tither, we submit that the very fact that he proclaimed himself "a Pharisee, a son of Pharisees" (Acts 23:6) settles the matter. He could not have made such a claim unless he tithed according to Mosaic law, nor could a man of such character teach and preach about something he did not practice personally. Kidd's testimony is this: "I began, as best I was able, to let my giving begin at the tithe, desiring thereby to support 'the more important matters.'"

We found refreshingly honest the discussion on the difficulty a Christian faces in living so that we do not neglect other important matters. These questions, indeed, are the ones that put people in knots! Yes, we can agree with Kidd (with a hallelujah!) that

> Jesus expects us to discern, to exercise wisdom in dependence on the Holy Spirit. When you have finally learned to drive, you don't keep reading the driver's manual. You don't read it, not because it is no longer relevant, but because it's inside you. With the coming of Christ, God wrote His law on our hearts. He gave us the Holy Spirit, a Spirit of understanding, a Spirit that teaches discernment.

Kidd returns to an earlier conclusion—appropriately linking giving to worship—in a most insightful way: "In worship bread and wine establish no merit, but they mean more than their mere physical composition would otherwise suggest. So it is with our money. Our money at the altar is not a payment but a symbolic expression of ourselves. It is as much our presenting ourselves as the bread and wine are ultimately the Lord's presenting himself to us." The only missing ingredient in this otherwise savory offering is a measure of obedience, preferable to God than sacrifice, He tells us.

There is much to learn from and admire in this thoughtful and thought-provoking statement of faith.

CHAPTER 13

Response to Reggie Kidd
David A. Croteau

Introduction

Reggie Kidd has made a valiant attempt to remove as much "law" from the tithe as possible, while apparently keeping 10 percent as a minimum. I can feel the tension in his thoughts as he wrestles with certain texts. For example, his discussion on Genesis 14 contains some good observations, though I'm not sure how he envisions the text applying to Christians. Kidd also does an exceptional job of placing giving in the context of worship. Whether or not one views the tithe as a minimum, it should be clear from all of Scripture that giving in the new covenant is a part of worship. However, several aspects of Kidd's chapter need to be discussed.

Misunderstandings of the Definition of the Tithe

Kidd makes the common mistake of consistently defining the tithe in the Mosaic law as a tenth. While the Hebrew word may mean this, the concept in the Mosaic law is different. For example, he says, "The 'tenth' became part of the Mosaic law—a symbolic and sustaining aspect of Israel's 'constitution' as God's people." As already discussed, the Israelites were not giving a tenth. Any consistent reference to the tithe in the Mosaic law to being a "tenth" is misleading; the repetition gives the reader the idea that it actually was 10 percent of their income.

The problem of defining the tithe in Scripture continues. Kidd claims, "It is inadequate to dismiss the possibility of an obligation to tithe in view of the fact that it appears there were two tithes every year and a third tithe every third year, meaning Israelites were essentially tithing 23.3 percent." At the end of that sentence, Kidd footnoted a previous work of mine. On that page all I am doing is arguing for the tithe being about 23 percent. There is no dismissal of any possibility of an obligated tithe. Now, it is true that I believe that one of the major problems with advocating a mandated giving of 10 percent is the 23 percent number. In other words, because the Israelites were required to give about 23 percent in tithes, it requires an interpreter to do hermeneutical gymnastics in order to find only 10 percent still mandated. The issue is consistency, not numbers. The tithe should not be *dismissed* because of the 23 percent number, just rethought and reconsidered.

Kidd continues, "Maybe we should be talking about 23.3 percent. Then again, maybe 'tithe' isn't supposed to be taken with pedantic literalism." If Kidd actually argued that Christians are obligated to start their giving with 23 percent of their income, then his argument would be far more consistent; we would still not agree, but I would applaud the attempt at consistency. The final sentence is an interesting suggestion. He footnotes a classic article by J. M. Baumgarten, who argues that the Hebrew and Greek words for "tithe" do not always mean a literal "tenth," but can be taken many times to refer to religious giving, regardless of the exact percentage. It is an interesting argument, one that I was very open to when first reading the article years ago. However, it is very unlikely that a nonliteral reading of the words for tithing could be applied consistently. Leviticus 27:32 is a good example: "Every tenth animal from the herd or flock, which passes under the shepherd's rod, will be holy to the LORD." What meaning makes most sense of the word translated "tenth"? The text is referring to counting, a specific number, not some generic and nonspecific religious gift.[1] One of the biggest general problems surrounding the tithing debate is the lack of attention given to the detailed prescriptions in the Mosaic law. And regarding "pedantic literalism," we would all do well to pay more attention to the details rather than to dismiss them.

The detailed prescriptions in the Mosaic law regarding tithing become so important, especially when combined with the New

---

1. For an argument against this based on the etymology of the Hebrew word, see D. G. Barker, "The Old Testament Hebrew Tithe" (ThM thesis, Grace Theological Seminary, 1979), 4–6.

Testament's silence on details, because of the application of the tithe to Gentile churches. Tithing advocates are sometimes quick to point out that tithing was a widespread practice, but they typically neglect to mention the differences between the specific commands, for example, on what was to be tithed and when it was to be tithed (or even if it was 10 percent or 20 percent). These differences become important when trying to apply the Mosaic law of tithing to Gentile churches. No religion or culture has been found that had a tithe—that is, 10 percent of income—built into its practices. So, how were the Gentiles supposed to know that all the laws in the Mosaic code were supposed to result in a mandate for giving 10 percent of one's income? The more clearly the tithe is defined in the Mosaic law, the harder the application to Christians the tithe becomes.

Comments Needing a Response

Kidd made some comments that require a response. He hones in on the passage that I believe has the most potential for advocating the tithe for Christians (1 Cor 9:13–14). He says,

> It is in this regard that we should consider Paul's likening of financial support for gospel ministers to the financial support the Mosaic law had required for temple workers. . . . Paul likened gospel ministers to Levites and priests of the old covenant who "perform the temple services" and thus "eat the food from the temple" (vv. 13–14). Implicitly, Paul applied the typological significance of temple tithes in support of Jesus' directing that "those who preach the gospel should earn their living by the gospel" (v. 14).

Kidd is correct that Paul related the financing of the temple workers to the financing of gospel ministers. Two points should be observed here. First, Paul also likened supporting ministers of the gospel to soldiers, farmers, shepherds (1 Cor 9:7), and oxen (v. 9). To skip over these illustrations and focus on the fifth can cause one to miss the immediate point of the passage. Second, 1 Corinthians 9 is a great example of when chapter breaks in the Bible can cause the context to be missed. This entire passage is an illustration of what Paul was teaching in 1 Corinthians 8: while a Christian might have freedom in a certain area, sometimes he should not exercise that freedom for the sake of love for fellow Christians. Therefore, in 1 Corinthians 9,

Paul meant that as a minister of the gospel he had the right to be supported for doing ministry. But he decided to forego that right for the sake of the Corinthians. If 1 Cor 9:13–14 is advocating tithing, then a major reworking of teaching on tithing is necessary. This is because Paul meant that Christians must tithe *only if* the minister wants to receive support, which robs any universal mandate to tithe and leaves it up to individual ministers to decide if believers in local congregations must tithe. I have never heard an advocate of tithing teach this. Therefore, using 1 Corinthians 9 to advocate tithing is either entirely inappropriate or calls for a radical reworking of pro-tithe teaching.[2] It is consistent in this context to utilize this text to advocate the support of ministers of the gospel—as Kidd does.

In discussing Matt 23:23, Kidd concludes, "These are sobering words. I don't see how we can dismiss them." I'm not sure what definition Kidd has in mind for "dismiss," but in contexts like this one it usually means "to reject, to discard, to remove from consideration." Matthew 23:23 is not "dismissed," in that sense, by nearly anyone in this debate. However, the literal application to Christians is problematic. Giving the reasons that something does not directly apply is not the same as "dismissing" something. Kidd continues,

> It is inadequate to observe that Jesus was addressing scribes and Pharisees rather than post-Easter Christians. Even though he addressed His "woes" in the second person, Jesus considered the scribes and Pharisees to be beyond instruction. The disciples are the true audience—in fact, the audiences for the Sermon on the Mount and the denunciations of the scribes and Pharisees are one and the same: "His disciples" and "the crowds" (5:1; 7:28; 23:1).

Kidd argues that Jesus was addressing the crowds and disciples, and he appeals to Matt. 23:1. Regardless of the specific audience, let's suppose for a minute that Jesus' "true audience" was the disciples and crowds. What would the implications be? The fact remains that He was addressing Jews who were still under the Mosaic law of tithing. What was Jesus' alternative? Was He supposed to say, "These things should have been done, without neglecting the tithe, but only continue tithing until you begin to function under the new covenant"?

---

2. See D. Croteau, *You Mean I Don't Have to Tithe? A Deconstruction of Tithing and a Reconstruction of Post-Tithe Giving*, McMaster Theological Studies (Eugene, OR: Pickwick, 2010), 140–46, for reasons this passage is not advocating tithing whatsoever.

Of course not! Jesus was simply telling Jews under the old covenant (that is, the Mosaic law) to keep the laws of that covenant. These laws, as a reminder, commanded the giving of about 23 percent of the produce of the ground, not 10 percent of someone's income. So, even if the disciples and crowds were the "true audience," direct applicability, without seriously considering *when* this statement was made in salvation history, is still problematic.

Here is another of Kidd's claims:

> It is inadequate to observe that the original tithe was addressed only to original landowners in the Promised Land and that it only covered agricultural produce. Even the Mosaic law provided a "cash for cabbage" program so agricultural assets could be liquidated and presented in the temple (Lev 27:31–33; Deut 14:24–25). In the typological advancement of redemption past an agricultural economy and past a people defined by the geography of Palestine, Christians cannot figure out the implications of concepts like "firstfruits" and "tithe" in the post-Easter situation and in economies of manufacturing and services? Really?

It is inaccurate to say that Christians "cannot figure out" the implications; the problem is that we disagree on the implications. The implication of the tithe is not that Christians must give 10 percent, but that with all our possessions we must consider what we should give to God for use and distribution. The underlying concept relates to stewardship, not a precise percentage.[3]

Kidd actually says, "In a host of ways, Matthew expected his readers—including us, I submit—to make appropriate adjustments." I completely agree with this. The way obedience looks has changed. So why the necessity of 10 percent? Couldn't that be one of the adjustments?

Kidd recognizes that bridging the mandate of 10 percent to Christians today is problematic: "As clear as Jesus was that we are not to neglect 'the others' (Matt 23:23), a reference to the tithe, He did not say much about how to do that. He did not say whether and how to bridge the gap between Israel's agricultural tithe to other economies; that is, He did not say what artisans or bankers are obligated to do with the tithe principle." He continues by stating that we are neither explicitly told to tithe off our net or gross, nor explicitly told to give

---

3. See Croteau, *You Mean I Don't Have to Tithe?* 234–36, for implications of the tithe for today.

only to churches or para-church ministries. Some of the questions he raises here are fairly easy to answer. We do know that the tithe was at least 20 percent from ancient sources (see Tobit, Josephus, and the Mishnah). We also know that in Jesus' day artisans did not tithe off their increase.[4]

So, How Much Exactly?

The subtitle to Kidd's chapter says a lot: "'Yes' as Principle, 'No' as Casuistry." In the end, disciples of Jesus want to know if they are mandated to begin their giving at 10 percent. So, what's Kidd's answer to this question? He says we are to "exercise wisdom in dependence on the Holy Spirit." Kidd declares earlier in his chapter that "the tithing principle stands. . . . We offer a proportion of our wealth as the Lord's rightful due in view of His claim on all that we are and all that He has entrusted to us." I agree that the underlying principle to the tithe stands, as do the underlying principles of all the Mosaic laws. However, does that principle carry a numerical value? Is 10 percent tied to the principle? Proportionate giving may continue, but does a specific percentage carry over? If so, why 10 percent and not 23 percent? Simply calling it a principle but sticking with the details of the law doesn't really make it a principle. Kidd is unclear as to what he prefers. We need to get to the underlying principle of all the tithe laws and recognize that all of the laws have continuing significance. It's only when you neglect the underlying principles that you can try to keep just the percentage. However, the number is not the underlying principle.

Concluding Thoughts

Kidd's concluding thoughts are well written. Western Christians generally have enormous wealth, especially when compared with the human race through history. Too many of us *are* owned by our material possessions. Kidd provides a good anti-materialistic message for middle- and upper-class America. As I said in the concluding thoughts to my chapter, I agree with Piper that for those in the situation Kidd describes, giving only a tenth is robbing God. However, I would also say that for the impoverished, a tithe is unduly harsh and is not the foundation or minimum for Christian giving.

---

4. F. C. Grant, *The Economic Background of the Gospels* (London: Oxford, 1926), 95, n.1.

PART IV

CHAPTER 14

The Covenantal Tithe
Gary North

I wrote this chapter on the following assumptions:

1. You do not want to rob God.
2. You fear God, which David and Solomon said is the beginning of wisdom (Ps 111:10; Prov 9:10).
3. You want the blessings of God in this life (Deut 28:1–14).
4. You want to avoid the cursings of God in this life (Deut 28:15–68).
5. You want to see the kingdom of God prosper (Matt 6:33).
6. God's kingdom includes the institutional church, which possesses a lawful monopoly over the administration of the sacraments.
7. You want to pay your God-required share of the church's cost.
8. You do not want to be burdened with biblically needless guilt.
9. If the Bible says it, you believe it.
10. If the Bible commands it, you will obey it.
11. On the day of judgment, you will not be able to say, "But nobody warned me." I am warning you.

This article is a summary of my book, *The Covenantal Tithe*, which is scheduled to be published in the near future. It is a support volume for my series, *An Economic Commentary on the Bible*, an exegetical exposition of every passage in the Bible related to economics. I have written 21 books so far. Two of the books, commentaries on Leviticus and Deuteronomy, are in four volumes. The total set is around 11,000 pages. I began the project in 1973. I hope to complete the final volume, the book of Job, soon. Having said this, I now present my case for the covenantal tithe. My title raises two questions: What is a covenant? What is a tithe?

⟿ retinue

What Is a Covenant?

A covenant is a binding legal relationship between a self-asserted sovereign and his subordinates. It is established by a mutually binding oath, by which the subordinates promise to obey the sovereign, and he agrees to protect and benefit his subordinates. Should they break the covenant by disobeying its stipulations, the sovereign reserves the right to impose negative sanctions.

Covenant is an inescapable concept. It is never a question of covenant versus no covenant. It is always a question of *whose* covenant. Biblical covenants establish four governments: individual government, ecclesiastical government, family government, and civil government. The biblical covenant model has five aspects, in the following order: (1) transcendent God who is universally present; (2) hierarchical rule based on delegated representation; (3) ethics as the basis of God's kingdom; (4) oath-bound sanctions, both positive and negative; (5) succession based on covenant renewal: inheritance. The acronym THEOS makes this easy to remember.

To understand how a covenant works in practice, the answers to these five organizational questions are needed: (1) Who's in charge here? (2) To whom do I report? (3) What are the rules? (4) What do I get if I obey or disobey? (5) Does this outfit have a future?

An early discussion of this covenantal structure was provided in the 1950s by George Mendenhall.[1] Meredith G. Kline of Westminster Seminary developed Mendenhall's insights in his commentary on Deuteronomy, *Treaty of the Great King* (1963).[2] The thesis was

---

1. G. E. Mendenhall, "Law and Covenant in the Ancient Near East," *BA* (May 1954): 49–76.
2. Reprinted in M. G. Kline, *The Structure of Biblical Authority* (Eugene, OR: Wipf & Stock, [1972] 1997).

developed far more comprehensively in Ray Sutton's book, *That You May Prosper: Dominion By Covenant* (1987).[3]

The Covenantal Structure as Revealed in Scripture

The five-point biblical structure is found throughout the Bible, Old and New Testaments. Here are examples.

The Pentateuch

The sequence of the five books of Moses reveals the covenantal structure.[4]

Genesis. This is the book of God's sovereignty, which begins with an account of God's creation of the world out of nothing in six days, with a seventh day of rest. God owns the world because He created it. He is absolutely transcendent. He is in no way a part of the creation metaphysically. He sustains the world through His providence and presence. He established His covenant with Adam (Gen 1:26–28)[5] and again with Noah and his sons (Gen 9:1–3).[6]

Exodus. This is the book of the covenant (Exod 24:7). God established His civil and ecclesiastical covenants through His representatives, Moses and Aaron. They challenged a false divinity, Pharaoh.[7] God then broke the power of this false divinity by delivering His people from servitude, an oppressive covenant based on kidnaping. Moses set up a hierarchy of civil government (Exod 18). Hierarchy is basic to point two of the biblical covenant model. The nation then covenanted with God through Moses as its representative (Exod 19). Representation is basic to point two.

Leviticus. This is the initial book of the law. It established four legally binding forms of covenant law: seed laws (family/tribal), land laws (original inheritance: conquest), priestly laws (Levitical), and cross-boundary laws. The first three were tied exclusively to God's national covenant with Israel. The fourth category is universal.[8]

---

3. R. Sutton, *That You May Prosper: Dominion by Covenant*, 2nd ed. (Tyler, TX: Institute for Christian Economics, 1992).

4. G. North, *The Dominion Covenant: Genesis*, 2nd ed. (Tyler, TX: Institute for Christian Economics, 1987), x–xiii.

5. Ibid., chap. 3.

6. Ibid., chap. 14.

7. G. North, *Moses and Pharaoh: Dominion Religion vs. Power Religion* (Tyler, TX: Institute for Christian Economics, 1985).

8. G. North, *Leviticus: An Economic Commentary* (Tyler, TX: Institute for Christian Economics, 1994); cf. G. North, *Boundaries and Dominion: The Economics of Leviti-*

Numbers. This is the book of sanctions. The sanctions here are military. The book begins with Moses' numbering of God's holy army, in preparation for battle (Num 1). He numbers them again almost four decades later (Num 26). This book covers the years of wilderness wandering in which the exodus generation died off, because they feared imposing military sanctions on Canaan (Num 14). God imposed the negative sanction of death in the wilderness on all but Caleb and Joshua.[9]

Deuteronomy. This is the book of inheritance.[10] Moses read the law to the inheriting generation, because the exodus generation had died off. This was the first phase of national covenant renewal. The next phase was sealed by mass circumcision after they crossed the Jordan into Canaan (Josh 5:12).

The Ten Commandments

The Decalogue is structured in terms of two parallel sets of five points each. The first five are priestly (ecclesiastical). The second five are kingly (civil).[11] As we will see, this structure confirms the Protestant Reformers' numbering, as opposed to the Roman Catholic and Lutheran numbering.

First Commandment: No other gods. This declares God's sovereignty. He alone is God. All other claimants are false.

Second Commandment: No graven images. This denies the legitimacy of all physical representations of God as a means of worship. The idols represent divinities.

Third Commandment: No misuse of God's name. This establishes God's property right in His name. It may not be used except to honor God. It must not be invoked liturgically in an unauthorized manner.

Fourth Commandment: No work on the sabbath. The gift of one day of rest a week is a blessing. It must not be dismissed as being without value.

---

cus, 2nd electronic edition (Harrisonburg, VA: Dominion Educational Ministries [1994] 2003), 4 vols.

9. G. North, *Sanctions and Dominion: An Economic Commentary on Numbers* (Tyler, TX: Institute for Christian Economics, 1997).

10. G. North, *Inheritance and Dominion: An Economic Commentary on Deuteronomy*, 2nd electronic edition (Harrisonburg, VA: Dominion Educational Ministries, Inc., [1999] 2003), 4 vols.

11. G. North, *The Sinai Strategy: Economics and the Ten Commandments*, 2nd ed. (Harrisonburg, VA: Dominion Educational Ministries, Inc. [1986] 2006), Preface.

Fifth Commandment: Honor parents. This is the first commandment with a promise (Eph 6:2)—longer life in the land. This is an aspect of inter-generational protection: inheritance.

Sixth Commandment: No murder. Man is made in God's image. Murder is an attack on God's image (Gen 9:6) and therefore also on His sovereignty.

Seventh Commandment: No adultery. God loved Israel as a bride. Christ loves His church as a bride. Marriage is hierarchical. A broken marriage covenant represents the legal right to break with God: false representation.

Eighth Commandment: No theft. Property rights are legal ownership boundaries around property that have been assigned by God to His agents. Theft is an attack on God's property.

Ninth Commandment: No false witness. This has to do with a court of law, which imposes sanctions. False testimony is perjury and bears an appropriate negative sanction (Deut 19:19).

Tenth Commandment: No coveting. The neighbor possesses property and a wife. These are aspects of family capital accumulation: an inheritance. They are inviolable, in thought (#10) and deed (#7 and #8).

What Is a Tithe?

A tithe is a payment of 10 percent of net income, after deductions for capital expenditures. It is paid in the new covenant era to the judicial equivalent of an old covenant priest: the local congregation. This payment is made exclusively on the basis of participation in the ecclesiastical covenant.[12]

The collection of the tithe is uniquely priestly. In the old covenant, the tithe was paid to a higher priest by a lower priest. The first recorded instance of a tithe is in Genesis 14. Abram made a tithe payment to Melchizedek, the priest of the Most High God. This is also the first reference in Scripture to the office of priest.[13] First, Melchizedek

---

12. A sacrament has always been associated with an oath. It derives from the practice of early Roman law, where rivals took an oath verifying that they were telling the truth; see G. C. Lee, *Historical Jurisprudence: An Introduction to the Systematic Study of the Development of Law* (New York: Macmillan, 1922), 207–8. Later, it was a Roman military oath. A soldier swore allegiance to his superiors. There was even a gladiatorial oath called sacramentum; see D. G. Kyle, *Spectacles of Death in Ancient Rome* (New York: Routledge, 1988), 87.

13. Abel sacrificed an animal for God, a priestly act. Noah sacrificed animals after the flood. The practice was not yet institutionally ecclesiastical.

presented bread and wine to Abram (v. 18). This was clearly a sacramental meal, since he presented it as a priest. The meal had to do with covenantal sanctions: point four of the biblical covenant model.[14] Second, he blessed Abram, identifying Abram as also being of the Most High God (v. 19). This blessing had to do with covenantal sanctions. Third, he blessed God, who had delivered Abram's enemies into his hand (v. 20). Again, this was point four: sanctions. In response, Abram paid Melchizedek a tithe of the spoils that he had taken as a result of his defeat of Chedorlaomer's army (v. 20): sanctions.[15]

The tithe is an aspect of point two: ecclesiastical hierarchy. Abram's tithe to Melchizedek began a series of covenantal events that established Israel as a kingdom of priests (Exod 19:6).

Priesthood and Inheritance

Beginning with Abram's tithe to Melchizedek, the priestly office has been associated with inheritance. In the chapter following the introduction of the tithe, Abram asked for an heir. Inheritance is point five of the biblical covenant model, as it applies to family government. God promised Abram that his heirs would be numerous and would inherit the land. To seal this promise, God required Abram to sacrifice animals, which is a priestly act (Gen 15:9–10). This covenant had to do with family inheritance in the land of Canaan.

> "In the fourth generation they will return here, for the iniquity of the Amorites has not yet reached its full measure."
> When the sun had set and it was dark, a smoking fire pot and a flaming torch appeared and passed between the divided animals. On that day the LORD made a covenant with Abram, saying, "I give this land to your offspring, from the brook of Egypt to the Euphrates River" (Gen 15:16–18).

In Genesis 17 God renewed this covenant with Abram (meaning "high father"), changing his name to Abram (meaning "father of nations"). This renewed covenant reasserted the inheritance established by the first covenant: God's covenantal vow to Abram.

> "I will keep my covenant between Me and you, and your future offspring throughout their generations, as an everlasting

---

14. Sutton, *That You May Prosper*, chap. 4.
15. G. North, *The Covenantal Tithe* (Powder Springs, GA: American Vision, 2009), chap. 3.

covenant to be your God and the God of your offspring after you. And to you and your future offspring I will give the land where you are residing—all the land of Canaan—as an eternal possession, and I will be their God" (Gen 17:7–8).

To mark this covenant, God required Abram to perform circumcisions on every male in his household, including servants. "This is My covenant, which you are to keep, between Me and you and your offspring after you: Every one of your males must be circumcised" (Gen 17:10). Circumcision was a priestly task: administering a sacrament. Abram became a household priest. "And all the men of his household, both slaves born in his house, and those purchased with money from a foreigner, were circumcised with him" (v. 27). This priestly act would continue for as long as the old covenant did. Circumcision was a formal act of covenant renewal on Abram's part. It inaugurated the covenant representatively on behalf of the circumcised male.

Tithing and Inheritance

The next reference to the payment of a tenth came when Jacob was fleeing from Esau, which occurred after their father gave the inheritance to Jacob through his blessing. This blessing was comprehensive. Isaac said,

"May God give to you—from the dew of the sky and from the richness of the land—an abundance of grain and new wine. May peoples serve you and nations bow down to you. Be master over your brothers; may your mother's sons bow down to you. Those who curse you will be cursed, and those who bless you will be blessed (Gen 27:28–29).

Jacob was on the run. He was no longer under his father's jurisdiction as the household priest who had circumcised him. He was no longer set apart (holy) either familistically or ecclesiastically. He dreamed a supernatural dream in which he had been elevated to heaven. There, God reconfirmed His covenant with Jacob: *covenant renewal*. It was marked by God's vow: *inheritance*.

And he dreamed: A stairway was set on the ground with its top reaching heaven, and God's angels were going up and down on it. The Lord was standing there beside him, saying, "I am the Lord, the God of your father Abraham and the God of Isaac. I will give you and your offspring the land that you are now sleeping on. Your offspring will be like the dust of the earth, and you will spread out toward the west, the east, the north, and the south. All the peoples on earth will be blessèd through you and your offspring. Look, I am with you and will watch over you wherever you go. I will bring you back to this land, for I will not leave you until I have done what I have promised you" (Gen 28:12–15).

Jacob recognized that he was on holy (set apart) ground. "He was afraid and said, 'What an awesome place this is! This is none other than the house of God. This is the gate of heaven'" (see v. 17). He therefore took action as a priest. God had established terms for Himself in His renewed covenant with the seed of Abram. "Look, I am with you and will watch over you wherever you go. I will bring you back to this land, for I will not leave you until I have done what I have promised you" (v. 15). Jacob then confirmed this oath as God's vassal by stating his understanding of its terms. He also added a stipulation, which was a tithe:

> Then Jacob made a vow: "If God will be with me and watch over me on this journey, if He provides me with food to eat and clothing to wear, and if I return safely to my father's house, then the LORD will be my God. This stone that I have set up as a marker will be God's house, and I will give to You a tenth of all that You give me" (Gen 28:20–22).

Jacob's vow was not this sort of a conditional vow: "If you will not deliver the goods, then I am not bound by my oath." Rather, he was restating his understanding of what God had just promised. If God did as He promised, then He was surely who He said He was—the God of Abram and Isaac, the God who had promised land to Abram. God had just reconfirmed these stipulations on Himself. Jacob was verbally verifying them and thereby accepting them. Then he added his own promise of a tithe.

This vow—a covenantal oath—was not a conditional vow in the sense of "If you won't, then I won't." It was conditional only in the sense of "If you won't, then I can't." He was not calling God's promise into question by threatening to abandon faith in God if He refused to deliver the goods. Such a lack of faith would have undermined the Abrahamic covenant and its inheritance. Jacob knew exactly who he was dealing with: "When Jacob awoke from his sleep, he said, 'Surely the LORD is in this place, and I did not know it.' He was afraid and said, 'What an awesome place this is! This is none other than the house of God. This is the gate of heaven'" (Gen 28:16–17). God had just renewed the family covenant with him. Jacob was reminding God of his own inability to perform his end of the bargain—the tithe—if God failed to perform His. It was a way of confessing his need for grace—God's positive sanctions—so that he could adhere to his vow, which was a tithe.

Jacob promised to pay a tithe: "I will give to You a tenth of all that You give me" (28:22). Why did he make this promise? Because he was no longer under the jurisdiction of his father, the priest of his family, who was the agent of circumcision. He had not owed a tithe to Isaac while he was under Isaac's jurisdiction. Why not? Because Isaac was the family priest. Isaac in turn paid no tithe, because there was no priest above him. Jacob was now out from under his father's jurisdiction. He would owe a tithe on the net increase of anything he earned outside this jurisdiction. But to whom would he pay it? Not to some priest outside the covenant line of Abram. Then to whom? To Isaac, upon Jacob's return to the family's land. As a household priest, which he had not been before, he owed his tithe to a higher priest. Isaac was that priest.[16]

A Kingdom of Priests

The Israelites were outside the Promised Land when they were in Egypt. Exodus reveals nothing about any tithe in Egypt. To whom would they have paid? There was no hierarchy of Hebrew priests above the household priests. There was not yet a priestly tribe.

The old covenant tithe was always geographical. Abram paid a tithe to a higher priest while he was operating in that priest's jurisdiction. The Israelites did not tithe to Egyptian priests. Why not? Because they were not priests of the Most High God.

At Sinai, God made a new covenant with them. God initiated this, just as he had with Abram and Jacob. This was covenant renewal:

> Moses went up the mountain to God, and the Lord called to him from the mountain: "This is what you must say to the house of Jacob, and explain to the Israelites: You have seen what I did to the Egyptians and how I carried you on eagles' wings and

16. North, *Covenantal Tithe*, chap. 4.

brought you to Me. Now if you will listen to Me and carefully keep my covenant, you will be My own possession out of all the peoples, although all the earth is Mine, and you will be My kingdom of priests and My holy nation. These are the words that you are to say to the Israelites" (Exod 19:3–6).

The issue of the tithe resurfaced in the wilderness period. There was no longer a common household priest, as there had been in Jacob's day, when they came down to Egypt. Then who would serve as the higher priests for the lower priests when they reentered the Promised Land? The answer came after the tribe of Levi sided with Moses in bringing capital sanctions against 3,000 willing participants in the false covenant ceremony of the golden calf (Exod 32:26–28). God then separated the Levites to serve Him throughout the land. The other tribes would be tied to specific regions. Their inheritance in rural land could not be sold on a permanent basis (Lev 25:10). If daughters of a man without sons inherited, they could not marry outside their tribe and keep their inheritance in rural land (Numbers 36). This system of tribal land ownership decentralized political and economic power inside the boundaries of Israel.

It was not so with the Levites since they had no inheritance in rural land. Their covenantal inheritance was the tithe of the net output of rural land: "Speak to the Levites and tell them: When you receive from the Israelites the tenth that I have given you as your inheritance, you must present part of it as an offering to the Lord—a tenth of the tenth" (Num 18:26). The Levitical priests also ate the food offerings brought to the tabernacle: "The Levitical priests, the whole tribe of Levi, will have no portion or inheritance with Israel. They will eat the Lord's fire offerings; that is their inheritance. Although Levi has no inheritance among his brothers, the Lord is his inheritance, as He promised them" (Deut 18:1–2). The Levites received a tenth of the net output of rural land as the tribe's inheritance. This was an enforceable legal claim in the same way that a plot of rural land was an enforceable legal claim for families in the other tribes. It was a property right.

As lower priests (Exod 19:6), non-Levites paid agricultural tithes to the Levites who resided in their tribal districts. As middle priests, the Levites paid a tenth of this income from rural land to the tabernacle priests, who came from their tribe. The tabernacle priests paid no tithe on their income. There was no higher priest to tithe to.[17]

---

17. North, *Covenantal Tithe*, ch. 5.

The priests had no inheritance in rural land; hence, the tithe was limited to the output of rural land. Everyone had the right to buy and inherit real estate inside walled cities (Lev 25:29–30). Everyone had the right to start a business, so there was no tithe mandated on this net income. The Levites were not disinherited in these areas of the economy.

The Mosaic system of tithing applied inside the Promised Land. It was an aspect of hierarchy—lower priests to higher priests. It was an aspect of ecclesiastical sanctions: sacramental meals, which were associated with the tabernacle. It was an aspect of political decentralization: tribal control over specific regions. It was an aspect of common instruction: a priestly tribe separated from the others through geographical dispersion.

Tithes of Celebration

There were two other tithes in the Mosaic law. They were tithes of celebration.[18] The second tithe funded a family's participation at an annual festival, which was held at the nation's central ecclesiastical city where the tabernacle was located. The third tithe funded a family's participation at a local festival, held two years in seven.

These tithes have long been referred to as "poor tithes" (*maaser ani*), and rabbinic tradition is the source of this designation. This categorization is erroneous. These tithes were not charity tithes. They were covenantal tithes. They had to do with lawful access to communal holy meals—meals set apart by God. They had to do with inheritance, as the tithe always does.

Both of the celebration tithes required Israelite families to invite members of four groups: widows, orphans, strangers, and Levites. Not all of these people were poor. Levites could own real estate in any walled city. So could a stranger. So could anyone. This real estate was not governed by the jubilee law of redemption of rural land in year 50 (Lev 25:10). A person could leave it to his heirs (vv. 29–30). The Levites had 48 cities of their own (Num 35:7). Finally, they received a tithe on rural land. What distinguished the Levite was his non-membership in the other tribes. He was not part of their inheritance. The tithes in the Mosaic law were tied to inheritance.

A stranger could also be rich. A law of the jubilee year governed the repurchase of an Israelite who had been bought by a rich stranger

---

18. Ibid., chap. 6.

(Lev 25:47–52).[19] The tithe-funded meals were not a matter of charity. They were a matter of law. They were symbolic of God's single standard of equity in the law (Exod 12:49).[20] Strangers had lawful access to these meals. The third tithe was a third-year tithe mandating a local tribal festival. Non-members had to be invited.

> "At the end of every three years, bring a tenth of all your produce for that year and store it within your gates. Then the Levite, who has no portion or inheritance among you, the foreigner, the fatherless, and the widow within your gates may come, eat, and be satisfied. And the LORD your God will bless you in all the work of your hands that you do" (Deut 14:28–29).[21]

Strangers, widows, and orphans were judicially defenseless, yet they were entitled to the protection provided by God's law: "Cursed is the one who denies justice to a foreign resident, a fatherless child, or a widow" (Deut 27:19). The laws governing the tithes of celebration had to do with the guests' status as judicially defenseless. In contrast, the charity law governing their economic treatment was the gleaning law (Deut 24:19–21).[22] It applied to rural land. This had nothing to do with the tithe.

It is a mistake both exegetically and conceptually to categorize the second and third tithes as poor laws or charity laws. They were inheritance laws. Resident aliens inside the Promised Land's urban walls had the right of inheritance in the earthly kingdom of God. Their right to participate in a pair of family meals—one national, one tribal—testified to their access to an inheritance through God's common grace: real estate ownership and access to the courts on an equal basis with Israelites. This made Israel unique in the ancient world, both Near Eastern and Classical. As law professor Jeremy Rabkin observed, "Cicero notes that the ancient Romans had the same word for 'stranger' as for 'enemy.' In the ancient world, people didn't interact with foreigners enough to think about their relationship to them except insofar as it meant war."[23]

---

19. North, *Boundaries and Dominion*, chap. 32.
20. North, *Moses and Pharaoh*, chap. 14.
21. North, *Inheritance and Dominion*, chap. 34.
22. Ibid., chap. 61.
23. J. Rabkin, "The Constitution and American Sovereignty," *Imprimis* (July/August 2009): 1.

These tithe-funded celebrations were held inside a city's gates. The second tithe was held in the city where the tabernacle was. The third tithe was held locally, "within your gates." The presence of walls in a non-Levitical city made real estate ownership available to all. This was a matter of inheritance.

In contrast, gleaning took place in rural fields, where the jubilee law of original family inheritance prevailed. This was a charity law. It had nothing to do with the tithe.

The Second Tithe

While the first tithe was owed to the Levites as their inheritance since they were allowed to own or inherit rural land, the rules governing the second tithe required it to be consumed annually as follows:

> "Each year you are to set aside a tenth of all the produce grown in your fields. You are to eat a tenth of your grain, new wine, and oil, and the firstborn of your herd and flock, in the presence of Yahweh your God at the place where He chooses to have His name dwell, so that you will always learn to fear the LORD your God" (Deut 14:22–23).

This tithe required walking to the central city. It could not be consumed locally:

> "Within your gates you may not eat: the tenth of your grain, new wine, or oil; the firstborn of your herd or flock; any of your vow offerings that you pledge; your freewill offerings; or your personal contributions. You must eat them in the presence of the LORD your God at the place the LORD your God chooses—you, your son and daughter, your male and female slaves, and the Levite who is within your gates. Rejoice before the LORD your God in everything you do" (Deut 12:17–18).

The two tithe-supported national holy meals were Tabernacles (Booths), the Feast of Weeks, and Firstfruits (Deut 16:10–22; 26:10–11). The laws mandating the tithes of celebration were both land laws (inheritance) and seed laws (tribal). They had to do with joint participation in urban festivals. The Passover meal was closed to strangers who were not circumcised. It was a sacrament. To access that meal, a man had to be circumcised (Exod 12:48). A woman had to be under the covenantal authority of a circumcised male.

The Third Tithe

This tithe was different from the national festival tithe. It was less frequent, occurring every third year (i.e., the third and sixth years), with the seventh (sabbatical) year ending the cycle (Lev 25:1–7). As with the second tithe, it was a land law and a seed law.

"At the end of every three years, bring a tenth of all your produce for that year and store it within your gates. Then the Levite, who has no portion or inheritance among you, the foreigner, the fatherless, and the widow within your gates may come, eat, and be satisfied. And the Lord your God will bless you in all the work of your hands that you do" (Deut 14:28–29).

This tithe celebrated the gifts of God to the local community. It was a family celebration that was attended by members of the same tribe, plus the local Levites, plus local resident aliens. It affirmed the legitimacy of a family's tribal covenant. This covenant governed the inheritance of rural land. This tithe funded tribal covenant renewal.

There is no textual evidence that these two tithes were to be enforced by the civil government. They were to be enforced by the ecclesiastical government. The penalty could have been excommunication, such as the denial of access to the tabernacle as well as the revocation of citizenship, which was based on the confession of faith in the God of Israel. "Listen, Israel: Yahweh is our God, Yahweh is One" (Deut 6:4). In contrast, the first tithe was enforceable in both civil and ecclesiastical courts. The first tithe was a matter of lawful inheritance by the tribe of Levi. It was as enforceable as the property right of rural land.

The Post-Exilic Tithe

The tithe before the exile of Israel and Judah was based on the tribal system of inheritance of rural land. Families that were heirs of the conquest generation inherited rural land. Levites had no inheritance in rural land. They inherited the tithe of the net output of rural land.

There is no evidence that the tribes reclaimed their original land after the exile. Samaritans—foreigners brought in by Assyria and Babylon—now occupied these lands. They were not evicted by the kings who ruled the succeeding empires: Medo-Persian, Greek, and Roman.

Only 341 non-priestly Levites returned with Zerubbabel (Ezra 2:40–54). In contrast, 4,289 priests returned (vv. 36–39). The priests received income as Levites from the general population. The language of Malachi refers only to the fruit of the ground (Mal 3:8–12). The tithe was still agricultural, as far as the post-exilic texts indicate. Operationally speaking, this tithe came directly to the priests as Levites because there were so few non-Levitical priests. The nation still tithed to the Levites as Levites. The people vowed:

> We will bring a loaf from our first batch of dough to the priests at the storerooms of the house of our God. We will also bring the firstfruits of our grain offerings, of every fruit tree, and of the new wine and oil. A tenth of our land's produce belongs to the Levites, for the Levites are to collect the one-tenth offering in all our agricultural towns (Neh 10:37).

The Levites still lived in villages and cities. Their inheritance was still a tenth of the nation's agricultural net output. The non-priestly Levites still tithed to the temple priests (vv. 38–39). So did priests (Levites) who were not serving at the temple. The tithes went to the local priests and Levites, and from there, a tithe of the tithe went to the temple, which was the nation's common storehouse. "Bring the full 10 percent into the storehouse so that there may be food in My house" (Mal 3:10). This was the same as in pre-exilic times.

The Rabbinical Tithe

Was the tithe still limited to rural agricultural output, or did it also apply to urban gardens? To answer this, we must look at the rabbinical tithe in Jesus' day. Jesus did not mince words when He dealt with the scribes and Pharisees. This was surely the case in His accusation against them with respect to their commitment to tithing: "Woe to you, scribes and Pharisees, hypocrites! You pay a tenth of mint, dill, and cumin, yet you have neglected the more important matters of the law—justice, mercy, and faith. These things should have been done without neglecting the others. Blind guides! You strain out a gnat, yet gulp down a camel" (Matt 23:23–24). The key words for the purposes of this exposition are: "These things should have been done without neglecting the others." What did Jesus mean by "these things"? He was referring to "the more important matters of the law—justice, mercy, and faith." Then what did Jesus mean by "the others"? He was referring to the tithe of "mint, dill, and cumin," which were spices.

Pharisees and scribes tithed. They were not necessarily Levites. They were masters of the Mosaic law and the rabbinical oral tradition. Yet most of these leaders to whom Jesus spoke were urban dwellers. This was obvious in the case of leaders in Jerusalem. Then why did they owe a tithe on urban agricultural output? Because in postexilic Israel, the old tribal boundaries no longer existed. The pagan emperors and rulers did not reestablish the preexilic tribal and family boundaries. Jesus' words indicate that a tithe on the agricultural produce of all of the land went to the Levites and from them to the temple priests.

The leaders of Israel still tithed on whatever they grew agriculturally. They were careful to tithe on herbs and spices. They did not try to shortchange the Levites or the priests. The New Testament does not mention this, but the Sadducees were the temple priests in Jesus' era.[24] The Pharisees were the Sadducees' main rival sect.[25] They were not priests. The Pharisees were careful to pay their tithes to the Levitical priests, despite the fact that they were rivals. The Pharisees adhered to the letter of the law. Jesus recognized this and did not fault them. He challenged them to adhere to "the more important matters of the law—justice, mercy, and faith."[26]

The Christian Tithe

The central theme of the book of Hebrews is the ascension of Jesus Christ to the right hand of God as the high priest. Jesus Christ was the true high priest in history:

> Therefore, He had to be like his brothers in every way, so that He could become a merciful and faithful high priest in service to God, to make propitiation for the sins of the people. For since He himself was tested and has suffered, He is able to help those who are tested. Therefore, holy brothers and companions in a heavenly calling, consider Jesus, the apostle and high priest of our confession (Heb 2:17–3:1).

---

24. K. Kohler, "Sadducees," *JE* (New York: Funk & Wagnalls, 1906).
25. K. Kohler, "Pharisees," *JE* (New York: Funk & Wagnalls, 1906).
26. North, *Covenantal Tithe*, chap. 9.

Jesus is the high priest in heaven (Heb 4:14). He is not a Levitical priest. He is a Melchizedekan high priest: "He was declared by God a high priest in the order of Melchizedek" (Heb 5:10). This doctrine lays the foundation of the Christian covenantal tithe: "For this Melchizedek—King of Salem, priest of the Most High God, who met Abram and blessed him as he returned from defeating the kings, and Abram gave him a tenth of everything; first, his name means king of righteousness, then also, king of Salem, meaning king of peace (Heb 7:1–2). The principle of the tithe was established by Melchizedek. He possessed ecclesiastical authority over Abram. Only when Abram acknowledged this by paying a tithe of his gains that he had made under Melchizedek's jurisdiction (Gen 14:17–20) did God make Abram a household priest by covenant (Genesis 15; 17). The future lower priest tithed to the high priest.

Christians are the heirs of the Israelites as the kingdom of priests. Peter declared: "But you are a chosen race, a royal priesthood, a holy nation, a people for His possession, so that you may proclaim the praises of the One who called you out of darkness into His marvelous light" (1 Pet 2:9). This is John's meaning also: "[He] made us a kingdom, priests to His God and Father" (Rev 1:6).

The kingdom of priests under the Mosaic law was confessional and sacramental: citizens of Israel by profession of faith and by the sacraments. Here was the profession of faith: "Listen, Israel: Yahweh is our God, Yahweh is One. Love the LORD your God with all your heart, with all your soul, and with all your strength" (Deut 6:4–5). The sacraments were circumcision and Passover.

The kingdom of priests under the new covenant is also confessional and sacramental: citizens of "the Israel of God" (Gal 6:16), the church, by profession of faith and by the sacraments. Here is the confession: "If you confess with your mouth, 'Jesus is Lord,' and believe in your heart that God raised Him from the dead, you will be saved. One believes with the heart, resulting in righteousness, and one confesses with the mouth, resulting in salvation" (Rom 10:9–10). The sacraments are baptism and the Lord's Supper.

A kingdom of priests is marked by tithing—from lower priests to higher priests. To whom should Christians tithe as members of this kingdom? There are no Levites, a tribe set aside to defend the temple from trespassing and to sacrifice animals to placate God's wrath. There is only the functional-judicial equivalent of the tabernacle-temple, where the high priest Jesus Christ resides judicially: the institutional church, which administers the sacraments of bread and wine to members of God's royal priesthood, just as Melchizedek did. Covenantally, by family representation, Levi paid his tithe through Abram to Melchizedek, a superior priest (Heb 7:6–11). The new law of the tithe is that Christians must pay their tithes to the local church, as the ecclesiastical representative (point two) of the high priest. They are under a hierarchy of authority (point two). There is a new law of tithing, for there has been a change in the priesthood from Levi to Melchizedek: "For when there is a change of the priesthood, there must be a change of law as well" (Heb 7:12).

Christians are priests through Jesus by adoption: "When the time came to completion, God sent His Son, born of a woman, born under the law, to redeem those under the law, so that we might receive adoption as sons" (Gal 4:4–5). We are priests through adoption into the family of the high priest. The transfer of the priestly line from Levi to Melchizedek marked the transition from the old covenant to the new covenant: "So Jesus has also become the guarantee of a better covenant. Now many have become Levitical priests, since they are prevented by death from remaining in office. But because He remains forever, He holds His priesthood permanently" (Heb 7:22–24). The lower priest pays a tithe to the higher priest. This is the covenantal structure of the tithe. The Melchizedekan priesthood is the biblical model of the high priest.

The tithe is no longer exclusively agricultural. There is no Holy Land in Palestine. There are no family farms based on an original inheritance established by the military genocide of Canaan. Holy land now encompasses whatever is made holy—set apart—through ownership by Christians. That which we redeem—buy back—from the kingdom of mammon is made holy: it is set aside because it is under our lawful jurisdiction. This is our inheritance from God, and it is the inheritance that we leave behind to our heirs. Therefore, God's high priest deserves His tithe on the net output of this inheritance. This is a matter of godly inheritance.[27]

Implications

First, you owe God a payment of 10 percent of your net earnings and profits, as surely as the owners of tribal rural land in Mosaic Israel owed the Levites 10 percent.

---

27. North, *Covenantal Tithe*, chap. 10.

Second, the civil government has nothing to do with tithing. The church is not Levitical. It did not gain an inheritance that is enforceable by civil law. The Levites did gain such an inheritance, which was enforceable by civil law just as ownership of a crop in Mosaic Israel was enforceable by civil law.

Third, if you pay your tithe, you have met your obligation to God. You need not worry about not having paid enough. You can abandon all guilt for not having paid enough.

Fourth, if you do not pay your tithe, you are guilty before God. Start paying your tithe.

Fifth, you owe all of your tithe to your local congregation.

Sixth, if you choose to support other charities, these donations constitute your offerings above your tithe.

Tithe on Gross Income or Net?

Net income. Here is why: locusts.

When there is famine on the earth, when there is pestilence, when there is blight, mildew, locust, or grasshopper, when their enemies besiege them in the region of their fortified cities, when there is any plague or illness, whatever prayer or petition anyone from your people Israel might have—each man knowing his own affliction and suffering, and spreading out his hands toward this temple—may you hear in heaven (2 Chron 6:28–29).

Locusts are a curse from God. When they come, the fields are stripped of their crops and the result is devastation.

A man owes a tithe on his increase. He does not owe it for that which the locusts consumed in the day of the locust.

The payment is owed on the increase when you convert the asset into money. It is not owed on the income before you deduct your original capital investment. If you paid a tithe on an ounce of gold you earned, then invested it, and you get back two ounces of gold, you owe a tithe on only one ounce. God does not tax the same income twice. We know this because of the Mosaic law of the tithe that governed animals. The owner paid the Levite the tenth animal that passed under the bar. If nine passed through, he owed nothing. If one animal in nine died during the year, but another animal was born, still totaling nine, he owed nothing.

"Every tenth animal from the herd or flock, which passes under the shepherd's rod, will be holy to the Lord. He is not to inspect whether it is good or bad, and he is not to make a substitution for it. But if he does make a substitution, both the animal and its substitute will be holy; they cannot be redeemed." These are the commands the Lord gave Moses for the Israelites on Mount Sinai (Lev 27:32–34).[28]

Tithing and Taxation

Should a Christian pay his tithe first or his income tax? The answer depends on the tax code.

In the United States, taxpayers are allowed to deduct charity payments from their gross income. They pay income tax on their net income after charitable donations.

Here is a hypothetical case. A man earns $50,000.[29] Let us make this calculation easy. Let us say that the United States government is merely as tyrannical as the prophesied Hebrew king (10 percent, as in 1 Sam 8:14,17). Let us say that he must pay 10 percent on his income to the federal government. He can do this in one of two ways. Pre-tax: $50,000 minus $5,000 tax = $45,000 after taxes. Tithe owed: $4,500. Total retained after tax and tithe = $40,500. After-tax: $50,000 minus $5,000 tithe = $45,000 after tithe. Tax owed = $4,500. Total retained after tax and tithe = $40,500. For a Christian, this decision is a no-brainer. Pay the tithe on gross income. The church gets $5,000. The federal government gets $4,500. No prayer required

If a tax is imposed before charity, as the Social Security (FICA) tax is, pay the tithe on whatever is left over.

Legitimate Negative Sanctions

The tithe is paid by recipients of the sacraments to ministers of the sacraments. What if they refuse to pay tithes? The civil government imposes negative sanctions for a refusal to pay a tax. The government requires residents to fill out a form providing information on what they earned. Residents think nothing of this. They would howl in protest if the church required this. "We're under grace, not

---

28. North, *Boundaries and Dominion*, chap. 38.
29. About 50 ounces of gold.

law!" In fact, we are under Christ-denying secular civil rulers. To them we bow the knee.

The tithe is not a tax. It is a payment from church members to the church for their membership in the kingdom of priests.

Should non-tithers be excommunicated? No. Why not? Because that would constitute a sale of the sacraments. They are not for sale. Then what should be the penalty? Removal of the right to vote in church elections. Non-tithers should be treated as children. They refuse to come under the law governing the tithe, yet they want full benefits. They want to avoid negative sanctions for not paying, yet they vote for officers who allocate positive ecclesiastical sanctions, such as charity.

In theory, a scheming group of non-tithers could join the church and then vote away the property and transfer it to a different church, which they would run. What could stop this? A requirement to tithe in order to vote would reduce the risk.

There are no negative sanctions imposed for not tithing today. It is no surprise that no denominations tithe. Churches must beg. Representatively, Jesus Christ, the high priest, is reduced to begging. As a representative symbol of Christians' assessment of Christ's authority, this speaks loud and clear. "Shape up, Jesus, and I may decide to pay what the Pharisees dutifully paid to their rivals, the priests. Don't call me. I'll call you."

If your local church is not worthy of your tithe, transfer your membership. Until then, pay your tithe to it.

Conclusion

The biblical tithe is based on the biblical covenant model.

1. **Transcendence/presence:** A sovereign Creator God establishes a covenant with His people.
2. **Hierarchy/representation:** God's high priest, Jesus Christ, is represented by the institutional church.
3. **Ethics/kingdom:** The law of the tithe is an aspect of church membership, which identifies a person's membership in the kingdom of God.
4. **Oath/sanctions:** Access to God's oath-bound sacraments is free to all church members as a right. Access to judicial authority (imposing sanctions) is not.

5. **Succession/inheritance:** Those who are covenantally meek before God will inherit the earth.

Abram's payment to Melchizedek is the model for the New Testament, because Christians are part of a kingdom of priests. Jesus Christ is the high priest after the order of Melchizedek. His representative agency in history is the institutional church, which alone supplies the sacraments. So, church members owe their tithes to their local congregations.

A tithe is a payment of 10 percent of income after the deduction of capital expenses, i.e., the previous year's seed corn and animals. The payment is made by lower priests to higher priests. It is made by church members to the New Testament's equivalent of the Old Testament priesthood, the institutional church.

Offerings are voluntary contributions above the tithe. These can go to any charitable organization or directly to the poor.

CHAPTER 15

Response to Gary North
Reggie Kidd

I appreciate Gary North's attention to the inheritance—and sacrament—dimension of tithing. I do not think, however, we can be as certain as he is of the priestly structure of life during the patriarchal age, especially as regards the shape of tithing in the wake of the Melchizedek-Abram encounter in Genesis 14.

I do not think it is possible to sustain North's claim that Abram's tithe established an institutional priestly tithe. Scripture says nothing about Jacob giving his tithe to Isaac, nor about Isaac's being excused from a tithe by virtue of living under his father-priest's roof; nothing about Joseph; nothing about any of the judges. North's view is not impossible, certainly not implausible, but I do not think it is demonstrable, given the limits of revelation.

For all of Jacob's craftiness, I do not think that his cynical craftiness was in play in his vow of a tithe in Genesis 28. In this I agree with North over Croteau (if I read Croteau correctly). What is on display is not the ambivalence of Jacob's character, but, as North nicely puts it, his need for grace. Now, when North proceeds to assert that Isaac had not had to pay a tithe because there was no priest above him, nor had Jacob heretofore had to pay a tithe to Isaac his father-priest while living under his jurisdiction but now will have to do so because he has renewed the covenant independent of Isaac's jurisdiction, thus making Isaac "a higher priest," I think North thinks he knows more than he actually does know.

Moreover, I think (with Croteau and others, and against North) the third-year tithe is in fact a poor tithe. The tithe in Deut 14:28–29 does not specify that the "eating" and "being satisfied" have to do with "lawful access to communal holy meals—meals set apart by God."

The storing up of this tithe appears, rather, to ensure a longer-lasting, more predictable source of poor relief than the gleaning law of Deut 24:19–21, which forbids collecting anything to be eaten later.

When it comes to the tithe in the new covenant, I think North has a partial grasp of the typological significance of the tithe in Hebrews 7. The lesser Aaronic priests tithed to the higher Melchizedekan priest. With a change of priesthood there is indeed a change of law (Heb 7:12); now believers as lesser priests give to their unique and singular high priest. I agree that they do so in a sacramental context, and that means that believers are called preeminently to support the church.

Beyond that, however, I wish North worked the typology out with a subtlety that was more congruent with that of the New Testament authors themselves. What I would wish for in a line of analysis like North's is more of an appreciation of what happens when that grace that Jacob had sought has taken the field, as the writer to the Hebrews maintains he has. The New Testament does not support the notion that "if you pay your tithe, you have met your obligation to God" or that "if you do not pay your tithe, you are guilty before God." The new covenant is one in which all of us must confess that the most we are able to give is entirely incommensurate with the inexpressibly lavish and undeserved gift that we have received (see Luke 17:10). Conversely, by virtue of Christ's final and complete sacrifice, under the new covenant there simply is no guilt for the believer, no "consciousness of sins" (Heb 10:2).

It so happens that the one congregation Paul told to keep "God's commandments" (1 Cor 7:19) is also the one congregation he exhorted to give more generously (see 1 Cor 16:1–4; 2 Cor 8–9). What is striking, though, is that Paul did not appeal to the commandments to make the Corinthians feel guilty or to accuse them of robbing God. He invoked the commandments to take the Corinthians more deeply into the story of redemption ("you were bought at a price," 1 Cor 6:19; 7:23, and "although He was rich, for your sake He became poor," 2 Cor 8:9), to the end that they may think more deeply about the implications of being the recipients of God's indescribable gift ("do not become slaves of men," 1 Cor 7:23, and "excel also in this grace," 2 Cor 8:7).

CHAPTER 16

Response to Gary North
David A. Croteau

Gary North does a great job of defending the requirement of tithing for Christians in the context of his specific understanding of the covenants. However, try as he may to make the passages that mention the tithe directly applicable today, his exegesis of specific texts is lacking.

It's in the Details

I critiqued North previously and concluded that "he never gives any detailed analysis of tithing in the Mosaic law or in the New Testament. Since nearly all of North's statements are declarative, with some minor proof-texting, he fails to answer clearly whether 10 percent or 23 1/3 percent is required."[1] North has still not engaged deeply with the texts of Leviticus 27, Numbers 18, or Deuteronomy 14. His analysis of the patriarchs is also puzzling.

In his analysis of Jacob's vow, he makes some fascinating statements. However, one interpretive clue that he did not discuss was Jacob being "afraid." This was a key indicator of the whole context of Jacob's understanding of the dream. His response was not of faith, but of fear. Once this is seen, then the narrative makes more sense. North tries to solve the dilemma over to whom Jacob was going to pay his tithe, and he suggests Isaac. While he makes a fairly logical argument, he still does not explain to whom Jacob would pay the tithe

---

1. D. Croteau, *You Mean I Don't Have to Tithe? A Deconstruction of Tithing and a Reconstruction of Post-Tithe Giving*, McMaster Theological Studies (Eugene, OR: Pickwick, 2010), 194.

after more than 20 years *outside* Isaac's jurisdiction and his return to the land.

Interestingly, North says that "Isaac in turn paid no tithe, because there was no priest above him." So, if the head of a family pays no tithe because he functions as the family priest, then why did Abram pay his tithe to Melchizedek? North answers that it is because Abram was working within the jurisdiction of Melchizedek. But does that mean Abram never tithed outside of that event? Also, does that mean that Jacob no longer had to pay his tithe when he returned because Isaac had died? Why does Abram have to pay a tithe to Melchizedek when he has gains after *entering* Melchizedek's jurisdiction, but Jacob has to pay a tithe to Isaac because he *leaves* Isaac's jurisdiction?[2]

Finally, while North insists that Jacob's vow was not conditional, does he really prove this? He says that Jacob was not questioning that God would fulfill His promise, but just restating it. What makes the reader think that Jacob would have trusted God at this point? He is not someone who appears without spot or wrinkle in the narrative of Genesis. In fact, he appears to be converted in Genesis 32 when he wrestles with God. The context of Jacob's life seems to go against North's reading of the Jacob narrative.

Here is North's declaration regarding the second and third tithes: "These tithes were not charity tithes. They were covenantal tithes. They had to do with lawful access to communal holy meals—meals set apart by God. They had to do with inheritance, as the tithe always does." The typical discussion in scholarly research regarding the tithes is that the second one is not considered a charity tithe but the festival tithe; the third tithe is called the charity or poor tithe. Also, the closest we have to understanding the purpose of the third tithe is either in the description of the recipients or the closing statement: "the LORD your God will bless you in all the work of your hands that you do" (Deut 14:29). It seems that the result is blessing, but what is the purpose? That is probably found in the description of the recipients of the tithe. North says, "Both of the celebration tithes required Israelite families to invite members of four groups: widows, orphans, strangers, and Levites. Not all of these people were poor." North is correct that the Levites were not necessarily poor, but widows and orphans were (which he ignores), and strangers (foreigners) were usually poor. But more problematic is that Deut 14:22–27 says *nothing*

---

2. North says Jacob was "no longer under the jurisdiction of his father," but he would give the tithe to "Isaac, upon Jacob's return to the family's land."

about the foreigner, widow, or orphan being invited; it just says for the Israelites not to forget the Levite. The same idea is present in Deut 12:17–19, which is about the festival tithe. While Deut 26:11, probably the festival tithe also, does mention the foreigner, the references to the Levite, foreigner, orphan, and widow in Deut 26:12–13 are referring to the charity tithe. Missing some of these details has caused North to misunderstand the purpose of the third tithe.

Finally, North never seems to interact with the real purpose of each of the tithes in the Mosaic law. The purpose of the festival tithe was to teach the fear of the Lord (Deut 14:23). The Leviticus tithe functioned to replace the Promised Land as the inheritance of the Levites. And it is in this last area, in the issue of inheritance, that another problem arises.

Exactly! Therefore . . .

A few times North makes some observations that are very important for understanding the applicability of the tithe for Christians. However, he doesn't seem to grasp the implications of these statements. He was correct in focusing on the concept of inheritance; he was amiss in not tracing that motif into the new covenant. The Israelites were given the land of Canaan as an inheritance (with certain obligations) and the Levites were given tithes as an inheritance (with certain obligations). This is why the Old Testament consistently says that the Levites did not receive an inheritance "among their brethren" (Deut 10:9; 14:27; 18:1; Josh 13:32–33). When the theme of inheritance is traced into the New Testament, something fascinating occurs: every believer—whether male and female, clergy and laity, slave or free—receives the same inheritance (Acts 20:32; 26:18; Gal 3:18; Eph 1:11–12,14; 5:5; Col 1:12; 3:24; Heb 9:15; 1 Pet 1:4). Acts 20:32 is particularly important since here Paul addressed the elders in Ephesus. Paul told the elders that they would receive an inheritance, the same inheritance as "all who are sanctified." "Sanctified" in this verse is a reference to those who have been "set apart" at salvation; it is not a reference to progressive sanctification.[3] Therefore, all who are saved now receive the same inheritance, and it is not the Promised Land or tithes.

---

3. See D. G. Peterson, *Acts of the Apostles*, Pillar New Testament Commentary (Grand Rapids: Eerdmans, 2009), 572, especially n.77. For clarification, see his *Possessed by God: A New Testament Theology of Sanctification and Holiness* (Grand Rapids: Eerdmans, 1995), 55–58.

In another example, North says, "The old covenant tithe was always geographical." Exactly, it was always connected to the land after it was incorporated into the Mosaic law. This connection to the land is an issue that impacts applicability for Christians. He also concludes that "the Mosaic system of tithing applied inside the Promised Land." The Mosaic covenant is in no way geographically neutral; therefore, it is not uncritically universal. God manifested His eternal character for a certain people, during a certain time period, *in a certain place*, during a certain agreement. For the Israelites to prosper, they needed to follow the directions God provided for life in the Promised Land. Verse upon verse could be shown that demonstrates the tight connection between the land and the Mosaic covenant. For example, "Now, Israel, listen to the statutes and ordinances I am teaching you to follow, so that you may live, enter, and take possession of the land Yahweh, the God of your fathers, is giving you" (Deut 4:1).[4]

Cognitive Dissonance

Regarding the festival and charity tithes, North says, "There is no textual evidence that these two tithes were to be enforced by the civil government. . . . In contrast, the first tithe was enforceable in both civil and ecclesiastical courts. The first tithe was a matter of lawful inheritance by the tribe of Levi. It was as enforceable as the property right of rural land." North said previously that all tithes were an issue of inheritance,[5] and now he says that some are not, since he is contrasting the first tithe with the second and third tithes.

North states that "The Levites still lived in villages and cities. Their inheritance was still a tenth of the nation's agricultural net output," and that "The Levites received a tenth of the net output of rural land as the tribe's inheritance." How can North declare their income to be "a tenth" of the agricultural output when they obviously received more than a tenth? They were partial recipients of mandated tithes, both the festival and charity tithes. Thus, their income from tithes exceeded a tenth.

---

4. See Deut 4:5,14,40; 5:16; 6:1,18,20–25; 8:1; 11:8; 12:1; 15:4–6; 26:1–2; 27:1–3; 30:5,17–18; 31:13; cf. J. D. Hays, "Applying the Old Testament Law Today," *BSac* 158 (January-March 2001): 21–35, especially 27.

5. See above.

Prove it, Don't Just Say it

The biggest problem with North's presentation is his declaration of his view without any attempt to prove it. Here are several examples.

He cites Hebrews 7, then says: "The new law of the tithe is that Christians must pay their tithes to the local church, as the ecclesiastical representative (point two) of the high priest. They are under a hierarchy of authority (point two). There is a new law of tithing, for there has been a change in the priesthood from Levi to Melchizedek." These points need to be proved, not just stated. He needs to make the connections explicit.

North says that Abram was made a household priest because he tithed to Melchizedek. Where is that in Genesis 14? Simply referencing Genesis 14 does not prove the statement. Is there a particular verse that says this? Is there some background information to help demonstrate this interpretation? He says that Jacob would not have tithed while living under Isaac because Isaac would have functioned as the family priest. Where is an example of a family member who was a priest or where tithes were paid in a family setting? He says that Isaac paid no tithe because there was no priest above him. Was Melchizedek gone? Was there no priest of God in the area like Melchizedek? How does he know that Isaac did not pay tithes? He says that when Jacob left the jurisdiction of Isaac, any income he made would then have to be tithed to Isaac, the family priest. What is the biblical reasoning for this? What is the ancient Near Eastern parallel to justify this?

North opens his chapter with eleven assumptions. Some of these assumptions should be directly challenged and others are manipulative.[6] In nearly all of them, he is assuming the (direct) applicability of the Mosaic law. This becomes apparent on close examination. The Mosaic law was not given to Gentiles, so why does he assume they apply? Psalm 147:19–20 says, "He declares His word to Jacob, His statutes and judgments to Israel. He has not done this for any nation; they do not know His judgments. Hallelujah!" North is guilty of flattening the testaments by treating everyone as though they are under the same covenant.

---

6. For example, the first assumption is taken from Malachi 3 and is manipulative. In the second assumption, he never mentions that the book of Proverbs mainly contains meditations on the Mosaic law, which means that the individual proverbs were stated in the context of that covenant. He cites Deuteronomy 28 for assumptions three and four. The word "land" is mentioned eight times in that chapter alone!

In his most important paragraph, North again states but never proves the following:

> The tithe is no longer exclusively agricultural. There is no Holy Land in Palestine. There are no family farms based on an original inheritance established by the military genocide of Canaan. Holy Land now encompasses whatever is made holy—set apart—through ownership by Christians. That which we redeem—buy back—from the kingdom of mammon is made holy: it is set aside because it is under our lawful jurisdiction. This is our inheritance from God, and it is the inheritance that we leave behind to our heirs. Therefore, God's high priest deserves His tithe on the net output of this inheritance. This is a matter of godly inheritance.

How did we go from "Holy Land" to "ownership by Christians"? Whatever we own is holy? Why? He declares that what we redeem, or "buy back" from the world, is "our inheritance from God." That is not what the New Testament says. Gary North spilled a lot of verbiage, but he did not make arguments because he just assumed they are true with his *a priori* statements. Then he simply explained his position. This is more of a position paper than an argument. He fails to make arguments from the text of Scripture; instead, he simply states his views.

CHAPTER 17

Response to North
Ken Hemphill and Bobby Eklund

Comments on the Covenantal Tithe

In commenting on this chapter, we focus on six areas of discussion followed by more general comments on Gary North's system of thought or formulaic approach to the matter of the tithe.

In his analysis of the Ten Commandments, North states that God's Name may not be "invoked liturgically in an unauthorized manner." While we fully support his other comments on this commandment, the phrase in question is not clear and he offer no references for this position. Further, regarding the commandment against adultery, he comments that "a broken marriage covenant represents the legal right to break with God: false representation." Again, the idea is neither defined nor referenced and he does not speak to the larger issues of broken fellowship, exclusivity, and intimacy—the ideals in marriage and in one's relationship with God. We use but two examples that illustrate the theme throughout the discussion: a formulaic, legalistic approach that lists God's right and intent to punish infractions but entirely omits His merciful desire and gracious plan to bless those in real and concrete ways who keep His commandments. We agree with Mark Rooker's assessment:

> Leviticus focuses on how God is to be worshipped—by the offering of sacrifices. In a word, Leviticus contains the laws that outlined what it meant for Israel to serve the Lord. These sacrifices were essential for Israel's existence as the covenant people of God because the existence of sin and impurity constantly threatened

their relationship with God. Therefore, the tabernacle and its sacrificial services were gracious gifts from God enabling the people of God to serve Him in purity and holiness.[1]

We understand the tithe to be 10 percent, an act of obedience, to be paid on one's income, regardless of how one's income is derived (i.e., cattle, produce, money, etc.). But we find North's definition of tithe as "ten percent of net income, after deductions for capital expenditures" to be unsupported.

We can heartily concur that North has correctly identified Jacob's pledge to tithe as affirming God's promises (Gen 28:20–22) and not an attempt to bargain. Further, the practical aspects of Jacob's inability to tithe if God did not provide is not a conditional vow as some suppose, but as North points out "it was a way of confessing his need for grace." Kenneth A. Matthews seems to support this conclusion in the New American Commentary.[2] North steps away from his purely formulaic approach here and goes to the heart of the matter.

We would expect to have seen supporting references regarding the author's understanding of guidelines for enforcement of the tithe, but God is never ambivalent about the consequences of a lifestyle characterized by disobedience. Malachi offers abundant testimony of the results of unfaithfulness in marriage as well as the people's failure to bring His tithes into the storehouse.

We found the discussion of three tithes most interesting, and North seems to indicate (we cannot be sure of this) that the result would be a 23.5 percent sum total of tithes. There is no mention of the commonly held view that the tithe of 10 percent was used for three purposes, including the tithe of income to be given to the Levites (Deut 12:19; 14:27).[3] If the entire tithe of the nation had been given to the Levites every year they most certainly would have been wealthier than anyone else living at that time. The same tithe, we believe, funded the annual congregational celebration that taught the redemption of God; and every third year, the tithe was set aside for the poor, for widows, and for those who were unable to produce income (Deut 14:28–29). We do confess that there is much disagreement and speculation about the uses of the tithes, and that many scholars depend on extra-biblical sources to support their positions on the number and use. The definition of "tithe," however is 10

---

1. M. F. Rooker, *Leviticus*, NAC (Nashville: B&H, 2000), 39.
2. K. A. Matthews, *Genesis 11:27—50:26*, NAC (Nashville: B&H, 2005), 455.
3. E. H. Merrill, *Deuteronomy*, NAC (Nashville: B&H, 1994), 226.

percent and nowhere in Scripture is a tithe interpreted as anything but 10 percent.

In his discussion of the post-exilic tithe, North's emphasis again is on who pays what to whom, "The nation still tithed to the Levites as Levites." Since they were God's designated representatives, this is not to be disputed, but lost in the discussion is the thematic idea that the tithe "belongs to the Lord; it is holy to the Lord" (Lev 27:30).

North's arguments of tithing on gross or net income based on the locust passage are mysterious, seemingly constructed to move toward legalism, and, in our opinion, completely unsupported. Likewise, North's contention that "the law of the tithe is an aspect of church membership, which identifies a person's membership in the kingdom of God" is broad, overreaching, and cannot be supported theologically. We do not dispute that the tithe is a mandate, nor that every church member should tithe, but sanctions for not doing so, we believe, are in the purview of God since, once again, the tithe is His. Would that every believer were as firm in his belief as that of North when he states, "If your local church is not worthy of your tithe, transfer your membership. Until then, pay your tithe to it."

Perhaps one of the most serious aspects lacking in the entire discussion of the payment of the tithe—how it is defined, to whom it is paid, under what hierarchy, and for what use—is the concept of returning to God a portion of one's income in grateful acknowledgment of the Giver's provision and in recognition of His ownership of all (cf. Ps 24:1). Clearly, the matters discussed are essential in understanding the tithe, but as we see in virtually all God's requirements of His people, He is deeply interested—we could safely say more interested—in one's heart, attitude, and motive rather than the amount or percentage above the tithe.

We see no elements of joyful worship in any of the discussions, but rather ideas of having "met one's obligation" and an achievement of the "absence of guilt." True, several verses are printed in the text (Deut 16:10–11; 26:10–11), but the conclusions and supporting text single out only the laws relating to such celebrations and the mechanics thereof. Absent entirely is any discussion of grace giving, the desire of an individual to please or praise God, or to show gratitude through giving lavishly and beyond the requirements of law as described in Paul's teachings and Jesus' recorded words. Nor do we see any real discussion of the blessings of obedience in rendering the tithe; it still opens the windows of heaven for us and pours out God's blessings (physically, spiritually, and evangelistically). Giving beyond the tithe adds to those blessings. Most disappointing are the absence of references to other scholarly works and the presence of a heavy—one could say disproportionate—reliance on North's own writings as supporting documentation.

CHAPTER 18

Excursus

WHAT'S HAPPENED TO GIVING—OR STEWARDSHIP FOR THAT MATTER? AND HOW CAN WE SAVE IT IN OUR TIME?

Scott Preissler

Introduction

In his editorial for *Christianity Today*, David Klinghoffer made the case to recognize today's secularism as having now grown into a full-fledged religion unto itself. We've watched biblical stewardship—which for over 100 years started with worshipful, generous giving—largely diminish into philanthropy for fundraising's sake for the purpose of keeping nonprofit organizations operating. Even Christian organizations can be observed to be acting this way, and without the Evangelical Council for Financial Accountability (ECFA),[1] whose mission it is to stand in the gap in this dilemma, who knows how much farther down the road we might have seen this trend increase by now?

I agree with Klinghoffer. For the past 24 years I have been prescriptively writing, teaching, and speaking nationally and internationally in national steward leadership roles that evangelicals need to counteract these progressive, incrementally building, encroaching phenomena that have invaded the American church as well as many nationally recognized parachurch ministries. Klinghoffer stated that "it's time to start identifying the secular faithful as such. The word

---

1. See www.ecfa.org.

'Secular' should be capitalized, indicating a distinctive philosophical orientation."[2]

This leaderless national movement, aided and abetted with the context and effects of our materialistic culture, is picking up steam and speed now. Josh McDowell is not the only leader now proclaiming that we may be in the last Christian generation.[3] Those in stewardship education circles of influence know too well that we have no time to waste in making a way out and back to our biblical stewardship roots while we can still influence our emerging leaders.

And what of this pertains to stewardship and the practice of giving?[4] A quick survey of new literature publications easily shows that more books are written each year now suggesting a diversion away from tithing than there are books written supporting the practice of tithing. As we enter this new century, we find writers largely rejecting tithing. Many of them have a disdain for the practice of tithing, and almost all of them seem to neglect replacing the tithe with any substantial grace-giving paradigm. Consider the titles of some books published in recent years:

- *Tithing Promotes Big Lies*
- *Should the Church Teach Tithing?*
- *Tithing and Still Broke!*
- *This Bu_ _ Cr_ _ Called Tithing*
- *Tithes and Offerings: Where Pastors Err*
- *Tithing: Low Realm, Obsolete & Defunct*
- *The Tithe: Allowing Confusion to Stand in the Way of Truth*
- *Tithing, Nailed to the Cross*
- *Why Tithing Is not for the Church*

Owning the largest library in the world on the subject of biblical stewardship, I would venture to say that I have never witnessed a time in my life's last 40 years where there has existed such an attack on Christian giving.

---

2. D. Klinghoffer, "That Other Church," *Christianity Today*, <http://tinyurl.com/Klinghoffer> (accessed August 4, 2010).

3. J. McDowell, *The Last Christian Generation* (Holiday, FL: Green Key Books, 2006).

4. For the purposes of this chapter, I refer to "giving" rather than tithing, offering, or contributions. This is simply an attempt to promote giving from any perspective one may have on the relationship between the tithe and Christians.

How Did We Get to This Point?

There is a compelling case today to teach Christian giving as an outgrowth of maturity in one's spiritual, discipled life. This may simply be to recognize how far we have drifted. We have drifted in three primary areas. First, there is an almost complete lack of teaching on giving and stewardship in American Christian higher education today. Second, there is a perceived amnesia in seeing any connection between teaching stewardship and meeting or exceeding the local church budget. Third, believers are ignorant of the opportunities and threats in the coming wealth transfer regarding emerging Christian leaders.

The Lack of Education

Though steward leadership is a part of God's high calling for every leader, unless things change, few will ever learn about it in their formative Christian education. This is surprising because every leader eventually experienced the life, growth, or death of a ministry based on the stewardship of others to it. The sheer benefits of educating future givers to sustaining ministry would seem reason enough to teach it, if only for the immediate benefit of Christian higher education institutions themselves. By Christian higher education, I imply every type of Bible college, Christian liberal arts universities, seminaries, and so on. Christian higher education seems content to leave stewardship education they so desperately depend on to the development office and their fundraisers—which do little if anything about educating, nor are they poised to undertake such a task.

In 1998 Kenneth Kantzer, founder and dean of Trinity Evangelical Divinity School, made a shocking statement regarding this issue. He said:

> Christian higher education institutions intend to teach students about the world and prepare emerging Christian leaders for leadership and service. Today there is a prime opportunity to mentor emerging student leaders and enhance their education if one Christian educational institution will rise to teach about stewardship studies influence on the American and international nonprofit sectors. Last year in America, over 1.5 million 501(c) 3 organizations collectively received and spent over $150 billion dollars. Students are not being taught about tithing and stewardship issues in evangelical leadership. If they don't

understand, they won't effectively lead in the very sector their ministries are headquartered within and which makes America the most unique among all the nations.

The reality of Christian higher education teaching stewardship is the following. Today, fewer than ten of 375 Christian higher education institutions offer a single course on stewardship studies based on a review of their curriculum content. In contrast, more than 275 secular state colleges and universities offer undergraduate courses and full graduate programs on philanthropic studies and voluntarism in the nonprofit sector of the United States. Interestingly, it is within America's nonprofit sector that virtually all Christian ministries root themselves as 501(c) 3 or any type of 1–18 category operating organizations for IRS purposes.

The Connection between Teaching Stewardship and Meeting a Church Budget

Among a seeming epidemic of "affluenza" or affluence in our materialistic culture, there seems also to exist amnesia by pastors that teaching about giving and stewardship are related to church survival, growth, and spreading the gospel locally, nationally, and internationally. Stewardship remains the once-a-year sermon for most pastors, who seem afraid to deliver this biblical teaching to their local church members. In this last decade, grant-funded research by the Christian Stewardship Association provided some chilling factoids that may explain this dilemma in our churches today:

- The old rule in churches was that 20 percent give 80 percent, but that has changed to less than 10 percent giving 75 percent of any church's funds. The implications are that, for any church to continue operating, let alone be responsive to God's leading, it will need to depend on a very small group of aging members. Stewardship is an invitation for every discipled member to participate in and advance God's gift of salvation and life to people on earth. Sadly, we are not doing a very good job of inviting God's people to share in His work in our time on earth.
- 90 percent of churches today have no active plan for stewardship or tithing education. This fact exists though Crown Financial Ministries and Compass Ministries and a host of

others have shown marked success every time a tithing education program is introduced in a church of any size.

- 85 percent of pastors reported they feel unequipped and uncomfortable teaching on tithing, finances, or other aspects of stewardship.
- We are living in the thirty-ninth year of decline in the percentage of income Christians give. Christians gave more as a percentage of income during the Great Depression than today.
- 97 percent of pastors feel people's income has increased but tithing 10 percent has remained unchanged.
- 30–50 percent of church giving records are blank at year end.
- The result is that 93 percent or more of Christians are not giving 10 percent, much less generously giving more.

The Coming Wealth Transfer and Emerging Christian Leaders

A very frequent topic in the world of Christian financial professionals is what effect the coming wealth transfer will have on young leaders, based on how they are acting as stewards today. So how are they doing, given that churches and Christian educational institutions are not teaching about stewardship?

- 90 percent of Christian college students today have one or more credit cards before the second semester of their freshman year of college.
- 28 percent of those 18–22 years old report they do not know how much they accumulate or about the positive or negative effects of compound interest.
- Gambling via the internet is growing faster among 18–22-year-olds than any other segment of the population.
- The average family today is only three to four weeks away from a financial crisis should unemployment happen.

Clearly, not learning about good stewardship and disciplines of the practice of giving could cost an emerging student leader his entire financial future and rob him of the calling to use his education to serve the Lord where He calls him. How can we defeat this culturally secular dragon in our churches?

Inspirational Teaching for Congregational Transformation in Giving

We need to get creative and inspire God's people if we want to see them transform into generous givers. What would happen if emerging leaders went to churches that taught biblical truths of giving and encouraged maturity in giving practices? What would happen if our Christian educational institutions systematically taught the benefits of biblical giving with goals of maturing and discipling young leaders? In a short time, these emerging leaders could lead a national reversal of negative trends in giving. Their stewardship modeling and commitment would become a mooring for a generation financially adrift in the sea of materialism.

Teaching biblical giving again would unlock each student's return on investment, so each could develop his own opportunity to build a Christ-centered family legacy. And we have no time to waste.

If you gave away one million dollars a day it would take more than 27,000 years to give away just 10 trillion dollars. Yet that is not even close to the amount that will pass from older generous generations to younger materialistically minded youth in the next 20 years. This transfer will happen, either responsibly or irresponsibly. The bottom line is that wealth planners reliably predict that 40 trillion dollars in family estate transfers will pass from those giving 10 percent to non-tithers, who are mostly non-givers, as quickly as within the next 20 years!

Will this current generation pass it forward into ministry and the advancement of the gospel like the last generation has?

A Short History of Tithing in the Christian Church

David A. Croteau

Historical Overview

The purpose of this section is to give a brief overview on the history of perspectives on tithing. Some pro-tithing advocates have said that Christians have always practiced tithing and that only recently has this practice fallen to the wayside. Several books have been written to support this argument, but they are very selective in their evidence and, at times, are self-refuting. This is by no means an extensive discussion on tithing in church history, but simply an attempt to demonstrate that various views have been expressed by Christian leaders throughout the past two millennia, with some accepting and some rejecting tithing as a practice for Christians.

Early Church History: 100–604

While many of the church fathers discussed below appear to be against the tithe as binding for Christians, this is not to paint the picture that no one advocated tithing. Several early church fathers did advocate tithing and three are discussed now: Clement of Alexandria, Augustine, and Jerome.

Clement of Alexandria (150–215) advocated tithing for Christians. However, that statement *by itself* is misleading. Clement's comments, as well as the whole issue of tithing, need to be understood in the context of how the Mosaic law relates to Christians. For Clement, in the same paragraph that he advocated tithing, he also concluded that the sabbatical year and the year of jubilee laws are also applicable for Christians. Clement truly had a misunderstanding of how the Mosaic law applied to Christians. It would be borderline deceitful to proof-text his view and not put it into the proper context.[1]

Augustine (354–430) is one of the most beloved church fathers. He noted that Christians paid tithes before him, but at his time they were not giving adequately. He did not believe that the New Testament command was for Christians to tithe. Instead, he believed that Jesus commanded all Christians to sell their possessions and give all the proceeds to the poor. He realized that this would be problematic as most Christians would not be willing to obey this command of Jesus. So, since Christians would be unwilling to obey this command, they should *at least* imitate the Jews and tithe. While Augustine supported tithing, he did so through concession based on an unusual interpretation of Matt 19:21.[2]

Jerome (347–420) believed that, since the clergy were in the line of the tribe of Levi and the Jewish priesthood, they should be given tithes. He said, like Augustine, that Jesus commanded Christians to sell everything and give all the proceeds to the poor. But, since they were unwilling to do that, they should at least imitate the Jews by giving tithes to the poor and clergy. Jerome, like Augustine, advocated tithing through an unusual interpretation of Matt 19:21.[3]

While there were other early advocates for tithing, like Hilary of Poitiers (300–368),[4] Basil of Caesarea (330–379),[5] and Ambrose (340–397),[6] several early church fathers described the collection in

---

1. See Clement of Alexandria, *Stromata* 2.18 (*ANF* 2:366).

2. See Augustine, *On the Psalms: Psalm 147* 13 (*NPNF*1 8:668); Augustine, *Sermon 35* (*NPNF*1 6:367–68); *Sermon 56* (*NPNF*1 6:435–36); J. Bingham, *The Works of Joseph Bingham*, ed. R. Bingham (Oxford: University Press, 1855), 2:180; H. Lansdell, *Sacred Tenth or Studies in Tithe-Giving Ancient and Modern* (Grand Rapids: Baker, 1955), 187; J. González, *Faith and Wealth* (San Francisco: Harper, 1990), 219.

3. Jerome, *Letter to Nepotian* (NPNF2 1:91); Jerome, *Commentary on Matthew* 2.22 (cited by S. Murray, *Beyond Tithing* [Carlisle: Paternoster, 2002]), 117; J. Sharp, "Tithes," in *Dictionary of Christian Antiquities*, ed. W. Smith and S. Cheetham (London: John Murray, 1893), 2:1964.

4. Hilary, *Commentary on Matthew* 23 (cited by T. J. Powers, "An Historical Study of the Tithe in the Christian Church to 1648" [PhD diss., Southern Baptist Theological Seminary, 1948], 42; Lansdell, *Sacred Tenth*, 192–93).

5. L. Coleman, *Ancient Christianity Exemplified in the Private, Domestic, Social, and Civil Life of the Primitive Christians, and in the Original Institutions, Offices, Ordinances, and Rites of the Church* (Philadelphia: Lippincott, Grambo & Company, 1852), 229.

6. Sharp, "Tithes," 2:1964.

a manner inconsistent with tithing. Clement of Rome (c. 100) urged Christians to give according to God's laws. While this might sound like a reference to tithing, he made no *direct* reference to it. While he does use the word "laws," his discussion on Christian contributions seem more likely based on the Pauline Epistles, especially 1 Corinthians 16.[7]

Justin Martyr's (100–65) description of an early church service is very valuable for this discussion. After providing details about the order of service, he said that the offering took place at the end of the service to help the poor, widows, and others in need. The offering contained two parts. The first part consisted of food. The congregation would eat part of this offering during the love feast and the rest of the offering was taken to absent Christians. Anything left over was given to the poor. After the Lord's Supper, they took a second offering which included both money and food. The second offering was for the clergy and the poor. Not only did this description not mention tithing, but Justin's emphasis on personal responsibility in giving and that the contributions were largely dependent on the rich argues against his advocacy of tithing. Only those able to give (the rich) took part in this offering.[8]

Tertullian (160–230) said that Christians contributed to the church treasury every month. The way that he described the offering is intriguing: the offering appeared to be completely voluntary and Christians only took part in the collection if they so desired.[9]

While a document from about 225 argued against all the laws in the Pentateuch after the Ten Commandments being applicable (specifically mentioning tithes),[10] Origen (186–255) provided a more subtle rebuke of the applicability of the tithe. He said that Christians should give far more than the scribes and Pharisees, but he explicitly said that he did not participate in giving tithes and firstfruits. He also exhorted Christians not to regulate their lives like the Jews.[11]

---

7. Clement of Rome, *The First Epistle of Clement to the Corinthians* 40 (*ANF* 1:16).

8. Justin Martyr, *First Apology of Justin* 67 (*ANF* 1:185–86); Justin Martyr, *Dialogue with Trypho, a Jew* 17, 19, 33, 112 (*ANF* 1:202, 204, 211, 255).

9. Here is the quote: "on the monthly day, if he likes, each puts in a small donation; but only if it be his pleasure, and only if he be able: for there is no compulsion; all is voluntary" (Tertullian, *Apology* 39 [*ANF* 3:46]).

10. H. R. Connolly, *Didascalia Apostolorum: The Syriac Version Translated and Accompanied by the Verona Latin Fragments* (Oxford: Clarendon Press, 1929), 2:34–35.

11. Origen, *Origen Against Celsus* 2.4 (*ANF* 4:431); 8.34 (*ANF* 4:652); 5.60 (*ANF* 4:569); Origen, *Homilies on Numbers* 11.2 (cited by Sharp, "Tithes," 2:1963); Origen, *Commentary of the Gospel of John* 1 (cited by Murray, *Beyond Tithing*, 97). Another early church father, Epiphanius (315–403) rejected tithing. He said that tithes are like

Middle Ages: 604–1517

Thomas Aquinas (1225–75) said that oblations and firstfruits were part of the ceremonial aspects of the old law and therefore not required for Christians. He declared that tithes were no longer an applicable command since they were given in the old law. Furthermore, he concluded that tithing was not a moral precept because nothing in natural reason could dictate that Christians should give a tenth rather than a ninth or an eleventh. He discussed the three main tithes in the Pentateuch and said that Christians do not need to pay any of them.

John Wycliff (1328–84) and John Huss (1373–1415) held very similar views on tithing, with Huss being dependent on Wycliff. Both likened tithes to freewill offerings. While Wycliff said that tithes were not commanded in the New Testament but were a practical way for the priesthood to be supported, Huss (and his followers) concluded that the Old Testament law was not binding for Christians.

There were many in support of the tithe. Though their individual contributions to the debate were not overly insightful, it seems that Egbert (750),[12] Pipin (750),[13] Charlemagne (779),[14] William the Conqueror (1066),[15] and Bernard of Clairvaux (1139)[16] advocated tithing.

Reformation Period: 1517–1648

Martin Luther (1483–1546) made his views clear, even though scholars have disagreed on what he believed. While his comments on tithing during the German Peasants' revolt were ambiguous, he made his thoughts lucid in a sermon in 1525 titled "How Christians Should Regard Moses." In this sermon, he said that since all of the Mosaic laws were given to Israel, they were not binding on Christians. The Mosaic law was only mandated for Christians when it was in accordance with both natural law and the New Testament. Luther

circumcision and thus are not binding on Christians (see Epiphanius, *Against Heresies*; cited by Powers, "Historical Study of the Tithe," 43; Lansdell, *Sacred Tenth*, 218).

12. Sharp, "Tithes," 2:1965.
13. Ibid.
14. L. Buck, "Opposition to Tithes in the Peasants' Revolt: A Case Study of Nuremberg in 1524," *Sixteenth Century Journal* 4 (1973), 2:13; Sharp, "Tithes," 2:1965; J. C. Robertson, "Sketches of Church History, from AD 33 to the Reformation," *Bible Truth Library: Bible and Church History Collection*, 108 (available from: www.bibletruthforum.com. CD-ROM).
15. Lansdell, *Sacred Tenth*, 267.
16. Ibid., 233.

declared that he very much liked the law of tithing and he argued for its usefulness. However, just like other fine rules in the Mosaic law, tithes are not binding on Christians. He specifically declared that the tithe did not pertain to Gentiles.[17] Anabaptists (c. 1525) in general, and the Swiss Anabaptists more specifically, reacted radically against the use and abuse of tithing and called for its abolition. Leaders of these groups included Felix Mantz, Conrad Grebel, Simon Stumpf, and Wilhelm Reublin. Hubmaier, the Hutterites, and Thomas Müntzer also opposed the exacting of tithes. The Anabaptists maintained that the New Testament taught nothing about tithing. Ministers of the gospel should be supported through voluntary contributions by the congregations they serve.[18]

John Smyth (1609), a Separatist whom many credit with being the first Baptist, said that Christ abolished tithes. He said that since there was a change in the priesthood, there was a change in the law

---

17. P. P. Kuenning, "Luther and Müntzer: Contrasting Theologies in regard to Secular Authority within the Context of the German Peasant Revolt," *Journal of Church and State* 29 (1987): 308–14; M. Luther, *Works of Martin Luther* (Philadelphia: A. J. Holman, 1931), 4:68, 4:239–40; E. Sehling, "Tithes," in *The New Schaff-Herzog Encyclopedia of Religious Knowledge*, ed. S. M. Jackson (Grand Rapids: Baker, 1950), 11:455; Murray, *Beyond Tithing*, 160; H. F. Mackensen, "Luther's Role in the Peasant Revolt," *CTM* 35 (1964): 197–98, 207–9; T. Scott, review of *Die Antwort der Reformatoren auf die Zehntenfrage. Eine Analyse des Zusammenhangs von Reformation und Bauernkrieg*, by G. Zimmermann, *CHR* 69 (1983), 4:610; M. Luther, "How Christians Should Regard Moses," in *Luther's Works* 35, ed. and trans. E. T. Bachman (Philadelphia: A. J. Holman, 1931), 164–68; R. Kolb, "The Theologians and the Peasants: Conservative Evangelical Reactions to the German Peasants Revolt," *ARG* 69 (1978): 117. J. T. Mueller (*Christian Dogmatics: A Handbook of Doctrinal Theology for Pastors, Teachers, and Laymen* [St. Louis: Concordia, 1934], 414–15) mentioned Luther's belief in the non-binding nature of tithes to Christians. This conclusion regarding Luther and tithing is rare. Cf. Sehling, "Tithes," 11:455; Powers, "Historical Study of the Tithe," 129–31.

18. E. B. Bax, *Rise and Fall of the Anabaptists* (Eugene, OR: Wipf & Stock, 2001; reprint of 1903 ed.), 12, 31, 37; J. F. G. Goeters, "Die Vorgeschichte des Taufertums in Zurich," in *Studien zur Geschichte und Theologie der Reformation: Festschrift fur Ernst Bizer*, ed. L. Abramowski and J. F. G. Goeters (Neukirchen-Vluyn: Neukirchener Verlag, 1969), 255–59; J. M. Stayer, *The German Peasants' War and Anabaptist Community of Goods* (London: McGill-Queen's University Press, 1991), 61–62, 95–106; T. N. Finger, *A Contemporary Anabaptist Theology: Biblical, Historical, Constructive* (Downers Grove: InterVarsity, 2004), 19–20, 236; M. Pearse, *The Great Restoration: The Religious Radicals of the 16th and 17th Centuries* (Carlisle, UK: Paternoster, 1998), 77; A. Friesen, *Thomas Muentzer, a Destroyer of the Godless: The Making of a Sixteenth-Century Religious Revolutionary* (Berkeley: University of California Press, 1990), 193–94; R. Heath, *Anabaptism* (London: Alexander and Shepheard, 1895), 29; R. J. Smithson, *The Anabaptists: Their Contributions to our Protestant Heritage* (London: Clarke, 1935), 122–23, 128–30, 148; L. Keller, *Geschichte der Wiedertaufer und ihres Reichs zu Munster* (Munster: Verlag der Coppenrathschen Buch und Kunsthandlung, 1880), 11.

(Heb. 7:12). Tithes were a part of this law of the Old Testament and Christ had set Christians free from that yoke.[19]

Post-Reformation: 1648–1873

There was division on the issue of tithing during the Post-Reformation period as well. Matthew Henry (1662–1714) advocated tithing for Christians. In his comments on Gen 14:20, he said that 10 percent was "a very fit proportion" and that "not only the tithe, but all we have, must be surrendered and given up to him." Thus, Christians "must" give tithes. He also said, commenting on Lev 27:30–33, that there is not a "fitter and more equal proportion" than 10 percent, the proportion that God appointed. He also referred to tithing as a commandment that must not be transgressed.[20]

Cotton Mather (1663–1728) said that a Christian should not give less than 10 percent. His argument was based on how ancient the practice of tithing was and from Abram's offering to Melchizedek.[21]

Charles Finney (1792–1875) also advocated that Christians must tithe. Commenting on Mal 3:10, Finney concluded, "Let Christians but bring in their tithes and make ready their vessels to receive, and then, having fulfilled the conditions, they may 'stand still and see the salvation of God.'"[22]

There were several people from this time period who rejected tithing as a requirement for Christians. Roger Williams (1603–83) has been credited with founding the first or second Baptist church in America.[23] In 1652 Williams concluded that ministers of the gospel are to serve freely and be supported freely—not in tithes, stipends,

---

19. J. Smyth, *Parallels, Censures, Observations* [Amsterdam]: n.p., 1609, text-fiche, 120–21.

20. See M. Henry, *Matthew Henry's Commentary on the Whole Bible* (Peabody: Hendrickson, 1991), 1:79, 440, 562–63, 612, 648; 4:1179; 5:273.

21. See A. L. Vail, *Stewardship among Baptists* (Philadelphia: American Baptist Publication Society, 1913), 49. But Increase Mather (1639–1723), Cotton Mather's father, concluded that tithes are not due to ministers, yet he also concluded that Christians must give at least 10 percent (I. Mather, *A Discourse Concerning the Maintenance Due to Those That Preach the Gospel: In Which, That Question Whether Tithes Are by the Divine Law the Ministers Due, Is Considered, and the Negative Proved* [Boston: B. Green, 1706], text-fiche).

22. C. G. Finney, *Prevailing Prayer: Sermons on Prayer* (Grand Rapids: Kregel, 1965), 34–35.

23. There have been debates for centuries as to whether Roger Williams or John Clarke founded their respective churches first. For a summary, see W. H. Brackney, *Baptists in North America: An Historical Perspective* (Malden, MA: Blackwell Publishing, 2006), 23.

or salaries. He saw a sharp contrast between the maintenance of the priests and Levites and ministers of the gospel.[24]

English (mainly Particular) Baptists (c. 1656) also denied the necessity of the tithe. Several Baptist churches rejected tithing as a biblical practice to support clergy since it was an Old Testament ordinance and inappropriate for the new covenant. One group claimed that tithing went against the priesthood of Christ because Heb 7:12 declares that when a priesthood is changed, the law changes as well. They believed that this specifically referred to tithing, but it also applied to other parts of the Mosaic law. In fact, some English Baptist churches concluded that if any minister accepted tithes then he should be dealt with according to Matt 18:15–17, that is, be subject to church discipline.[25] One English Baptist has gained prominence through his book, *The Pilgrim's Progress*: John Bunyan (1628–88). Commenting on Luke 18:10–13, he said, "This paying of tithes was *ceremonial*, such as came in and went out with the typical priesthood."[26]

In the late eighteenth century, the Quakers engaged in a debate with the English government. They argued vociferously that the tithes were not applicable because they were only for the Levites, were ceremonial and not moral, and that they were abolished. They were so certain of their views that some Quakers went to prison for refusing to tithe.[27] In fact, any Quaker who did tithe was to be expelled from the group.[28]

While John Calvin's view on tithing is ambiguous,[29] Francis Turretin (1623–87), pastor at the church in Geneva and professor of theology, declared that Christians are not bound by certain Old Testament

24. R. Williams, *The Complete Writings of Roger Williams* (New York: Russell & Russell, 1963), 7:164–65.

25. See B. R. White, *Association Records of the Particular Baptists of England, Wales and Ireland to 1660* (London: Baptist Historical Society, 1974), 1:44, 45, 48, 151; 3:153–57, 226; B. R. White, "The English Particular Baptists and the Great Rebellion, 1640–1660," *Baptist History and Heritage* 9 (1974): 23, 27–28; E. Terrill, *The Records of a Church of Christ in Bristol, 1640–1687*, ed. R. Hayden (Bristol: Bristol Record Society, 1974), 134–35.

26. J. Bunyan, *Bunyan's Searching Works: The Strait Gate, The Heavenly Footman, The Barren Fig-Tree, The Pharisee and Publican, and Divine Emblems* (Philadelphia: American Baptist Publication Society, 1851), 24.

27. H. W. Clarke, *History of English Nonconformity* (London: Chapman and Hall, 1911–13), 2:171.

28. So Murray, *Beyond Tithing*, 170.

29. See discussion in D. Croteau, *You Mean I Don't Have to Tithe? A Deconstruction of Tithing and a Reconstruction of Post-Tithe Giving*, McMaster Theological Studies (Eugene, OR: Pickwick, 2010), 31–33.

laws such as tithing and firstfruits. He concluded that the method chosen for supporting the pastor should emphasize voluntariness.[30]

A little-known figure in Baptist church history is John Newton Brown (1803–68). Brown wrote the draft of the New Hampshire Confession of Faith (1833), the precursor to the Baptist Faith and Message (the current statement used by the Southern Baptist Convention). He also edited an encyclopedia. The article on tithes in this encyclopedia explicitly said that tithes had ceased.[31]

The Tithing Renewal: 1873–Present

One of the interesting pieces of history discussed in books arguing for the continuation of tithing is that they recognize that tithing had been virtually nonexistent in the American church until 1873. Two enormously important books were published in that year, one by Alexander L. Hogshead[32] and the other by A. W. Miller.[33] This was followed by the ministry of Thomas Kane, who is credited as the popularizer of tithing in America. The mere fact that there was a *renewal* demonstrates that tithing was not always practiced by Christians throughout the centuries. Many men reacted against the tithing renewal, while others were ardent supporters of it.

G. Campbell Morgan (1863–1945), two-time pastor of Westminster Chapel in England, concluded that the basic New Testament principle of giving was that Christians ought to place all their resources at God's disposal, since God has manifested his grace by putting His resources at Christians' disposal. Campbell's comments on 1 Corinthians 16 further clarified his view on tithing:

> I hear a great deal about the tithing of incomes. I have no sympathy with the movement at all. A tenth in the case of one man is meanness, and in the case of another man is dishonesty. I know men today who are Christian men in city churches and village chapels, who have no business to give a tenth of their income to the work of God. They cannot afford it. I know other men

---

30. F. Turretin, *Institutes of Elenctic Theology*, ed. J. T. Dennison, Jr., trans. G. M. Giger (Phillipsburg, NJ: P&R, 1997), 3: 270, 272. He is also known as François Turrettini.

31. J. N. Brown, ed., "Tithes," in *Encyclopedia of Religious Knowledge* (Brattleboro: Fessenden, 1836), 2:1124.

32. A. L. Hogshead, *The Gospel Self-Supporting* (Wytheville, VA: D. A. St. Clair, 1873).

33. A. W. Miller, *The Law of the Tithe, and of the Free-Will Offering* (Columbia, SC: Presbyterian Publishing House, 1873).

who are giving one-tenth, and the nine-tenths they keep is doing harm to their souls.[34]

Morgan said that rather than 10 percent belonging to God, 100 percent did. He urged Christians to consider giving in the context of the stewardship of all money and possessions.[35] Several men who belong to the dispensationalist theological system shunned tithing, like Lewis Sperry Chafer,[36] Ray Stedman,[37] J. Vernon McGee,[38] and Charles C. Ryrie. Ryrie, editor of the popular *Ryrie Study Bible*, encouraged Christians not to give 10 percent. He said that people can get stuck in the "10 percent rut"[39] and give only that amount out of habit. John MacArthur, editor of the popular *MacArthur Study Bible*, is a resolute opponent of tithing. In a question-and-answer session at his church, MacArthur stated plainly, "Tithing was a way of funding the national government. Jesus carries it into the New Testament by saying Give Caesar what Caesar asks. Paul adds, pay your taxes. So the equivalent now to the Old Testament tithe system is taxation. . . . Free-will giving has always been the same."[40] The giving paradigm for Christians is different from giving in the Old Testament; the New Testament "doesn't tell you how much [to give], just whatever you want."[41]

Craig Blomberg represents some of the finest of evangelical New Testament scholarship today. He referred to tithes and offerings as cultic laws, in the same category as sacrifices and dietary rules. In a discussion on applying Old Testament laws to Christians, he said that "Just as poor people could offer less costly sacrifices in those days (Lev 12:8; cf. Lk 2:24), so Christians should not require identical lev-

---

34. G. C. Morgan, *The Westminster Pulpit* (1906–1916; repr., Grand Rapids: Baker, 1995), 4:39.

35. Cf. ibid., 4:40–43, 44, 46–47; G. C. Morgan, *Wherein Have We Robbed God? Malachi's Message to the Men of To-day* (New York: Revell, 1898), text-fiche, 58–59, 77–78.

36. L. S. Chafer, *Systematic Theology* (Dallas: Dallas Seminary Press, 1948), 7:294, 304; Chafer, *Major Bible Themes: 52 Vital Doctrines of the Scripture Simplified and Explained*, rev. J. F. Walvoord (Grand Rapids: Academie, 1974), 253.

37. R. C. Stedman, "Giving Under Grace: Part 1," *BSac* 107 (1950): 317–34; Stedman, "Giving Under Grace: Part 2," *BSac* 107 (1950): 468–80; Stedman, "Giving Under Grace: Part 3," *BSac* 108 (1951): 68–73; Stedman, "Giving Under Grace: Part 4," *BSac* 108 (1951): 205–15.

38. J. V. McGee, *Malachi*, Thru the Bible (Nashville: Nelson, 1991), 81–86.

39. C. C. Ryrie, *Balancing the Christian Life: Biblical Principles for Wholesome Living* (Chicago: Moody, 1969), 89.

40. J. MacArthur, *Bible Questions and Answers, Part 53*, <www.gty.org/Resources/Sermons/70–25> (accessed June 12, 2009).

41. Ibid.

els of giving from all believers today. In fact, the NT does not promote a fixed percentage of giving."[42]

Many pastors and scholars (probably the majority) have come to the support of the Tithing Renewal. One early advocate wrote what has become the most groundbreaking work on tithing produced to date: Henry Lansdell.[43] Lansdell's book argued from almost every conceivable angle that tithing is mandated for Christians. His original two-volume work is required reading for anyone wanting to be informed on this subject.

Several Baptists have come to the support of tithing: Monroe E. Dodd,[44] A. T. Robertson,[45] Billy Graham,[46] Herschel H. Hobbs,[47] and John R. Rice.[48] Robertson said that "grace should do as well as law" and that the tithe should be the minimum. Hobbs concluded that tithing began before Abram and was a widespread practice. He believed that Jesus both tithed and taught tithing (by implication) and that Christians should not give less than 10 percent. Rice stated that tithing was not part of the ceremonial law and therefore Scripture mandates it. However, he did say that the "storehouse" concept was ceremonial and not applicable to Christians.

George A. E. Salstrand wrote a very important book on tithing in 1952.[49] He argued that tithing was the time-tested practice of the Christian church, that it was practiced before the Mosaic law, and that it was both commanded in the Old Testament and recommended in the New Testament. He concluded that tithing is required for all Christians.

---

42. W. W. Klein, C. L. Blomberg, and R. L. Hubbard, Jr., *Introduction to Biblical Interpretation* (Nashville: Nelson, 1993), 415; cf. comments on p. 279; C. L. Blomberg, *1 Corinthians*, NIVAC (Grand Rapids: Zondervan, 1994), 326; C. L. Blomberg, *Heart, Soul, and Money: A Christian View of Possessions* (Joplin, MO: College Press, 2000), 31, 85–87.

43. Lansdell, *Sacred Tenth.*

44. M. E. Dodd, *Concerning the Collection: A Manual for Christian Stewardship* (New York: Revell, 1929), 134.

45. A. T. Robertson, "Paul's Plans for Raising Money," in *Classic Sermons on Stewardship*, compiled by W. W. Wiersbe, Kregel Classic Sermons (Grand Rapids: Kregel, 1999), 110–11.

46. B. Graham, *Rules for Christian Living* (Minneapolis: Billy Graham Evangelistic Association, 1953), 40–43.

47. H. H. Hobbs, *The Gospel of Giving* (Nashville: Broadman, 1954), 13, 15, 17–18, 42–43.

48. J. R. Rice, *All About Christian Giving* (Wheaton: Sword of the Lord, 1954), 23, 39.

49. Salstrand, *Tithe*, 19–21, 39–43, 52.

Several other popular authors have advocated tithing recently, including Arthur W. Pink,[50] Elmer Towns,[51] John Stott,[52] W. A. Criswell,[53] John Piper,[54] Randy Alcorn,[55] Rousas John Rushdoony,[56] and R. T. Kendall.[57]

Conclusion from Church History

Christians have not been unified on their view of tithing. Many fine theologians can be found on both sides of this debate. Since the debate cannot be settled through a study of church history, more emphasis should be placed on the biblical text.

---

50 A. W. Pink, *Tithing* (Swengel: Reiner Publications, 1967), 4–26.

51. E. Towns, *Tithing Is Christian* (Ivyland: Neibauer Press, 1975).

52. John Stott chaired the committee that composed The Nottingham Statement of the second National Evangelical Anglican Congress in April 1977. It is supposed that he agreed with the contents of the statement. See "The Nottingham Statement," <http://www.spurgeon.org/~phil/creeds/nott.htm> (accessed June 10, 2009).

53. W. A. Criswell, *Criswell's Guidebook for Pastors* (Nashville: Broadman, 1980), 154–57. For another source for Criswell, see W. A. Criswell, ed., *The Believer's Study Bible: New King James Version* (Nashville: Nelson, 1991), 1309.

54. J. Piper, "Total Abstinence and Church Membership," sermon delivered on October 4, 1981, <http://tinyurl.com/piper-membership > (accessed June 12, 2009); Piper, "I Seek Not What Is Yours but You: A Sermon on Tithing," sermon delivered on January 31, 1982, <http://tinyurl.com/ydg528g> (accessed March 5, 2010); Piper, "These You Ought to Have Done Without Neglecting the Others," sermon delivered on January 13, 1991, <http://tinyurl.com/piper-tithing> (accessed June 12, 2009); Piper, "Toward the Tithe and Beyond," sermon delivered on September 10, 1995, <http://tinyurl.com/piper-towardthetithe> (accessed June 12, 2009).

55. R. Alcorn, *Money, Possessions, and Eternity* (Carol Stream, IL: Tyndale House, 2003).

56. E. A. Powell and R. J. Rushdoony, *Tithing and Dominion* (Vallecito, CA: Ross House, 1979); R. J. Rushdoony, *Systematic Theology* (Vallecito, CA: Ross House, 1994), 2:974, 994; Rushdoony, *The Institutes of Biblical Law* (Vallecito, CA: Ross House, 1986, 1999), 1:29, 31, 118, 127, 261, 264.

57. R. T. Kendall, *Tithing* (Grand Rapids: Zondervan, 1983), 4.

Name Index

Scripture Index

BOOKS IN THIS SERIES

Perspectives on Children's Spiritual Formation: Four Views, ed. Michael Anthony; contributors: Greg Carlson, Tim Ellis, Trisha Graves, Scottie May

Perspectives on Christian Worship: Five Views, ed. J. Matthew Pinson; contributors: Ligon Duncan, Dan Kimball, Michael Lawrence and Mark Dever, Timothy Quill, Dan Wilt

Perspectives on Church Government: Five Views, ed. R. Stanton Norman and Chad Brand; contributors: Daniel Akin, James Garrett, Robert Reymond, James White, Paul Zahl

Perspectives on the Doctrine of God: Four Views, ed. Bruce A. Ware; contributors: Paul Helm, Robert E. Olson, John Sanders, Bruce A. Ware

Perspectives on Family Ministry: Three Views, ed. Timothy Paul Jones; contributors: Timothy Paul Jones, Paul Renfro, Brandon Shields, Randy Stinson, Jay Strother

Perspectives on Election: Five Views, ed. Chad Brand; contributors: Jack W. Cottrell, Clark Pinnock, Robert L. Reymond, Thomas B. Talbott, Bruce A. Ware

Perspectives on Your Child's Education: Four Views, ed. Timothy Paul Jones; contributors: Mark Eckel, G. Tyler Fischer, Timothy Paul Jones, Troy Temple, Michael S. Wilder

Perspectives on the Ending of Mark: Four Views, ed. David Alan Black; contributors: Darrell Bock, Keith Elliott, Maurice Robinson, Daniel Wallace

Perspectives on Spirit Baptism: Five Views, ed. Chad Brand; contributors: Ralph Del Colle, H. Ray Dunning, Larry Hart, Stanley Horton, Walter Kaiser Jr.

Perspectives on the Sabbath: Four Views, ed. Christopher John Donato; contributors: Charles P. Arand, Craig L. Blomberg, Skip McCarty, Joseph A. Pipa